CW00548626

GEORGE MOORE AND FRIENDS

Letters from a Manx Merchant (1750-1760)

Other books by the same author also published by Wyre Forest Press

The Isle of Man in Smuggling History
Scottish Customs & Excise Records, with particular reference to
Strathclyde
Strathclyde's Smuggling Story
Dumfries & Galloway's Smuggling Story
Family Histories in Scottish Customs Records
The Smuggling Story of Two Firths (Montrose to Dunbar)
The Smuggling Story of the Northern Shores (in preparation)

GEORGE MOORE AND FRIENDS

THE LETTERS FROM A MANX MERCHANT (1750-1760)

Frances Wilkins BA

Computer Sketch Maps by Phil Link

Wyre Forest Press

© Frances Wilkins 1994

Published by Wyre Forest Press
8 Mill Close, Blakedown, Kidderminster
Worcestershire DY10 3NQ

Printed by The Bath Press
Lower Bristol Road
Bath BA2 3BL

ISBN 1 897725 07 8

Contents

Illustrations

Notes on Illustrations: Sources and Acknowledgments

Sources
1 Sir George Moore of Ballamoore, Patrick, Speaker of the House of Keys (1769-1787). Manx National Heritage
2 Plan of Cherbourg. Gentleman's Magazine August 1758
3 & 4. Extracts from maps of Europe and South America in Charles Vyse *A New Geographical Grammar* 1779
5 From John Davidson & Alexander Gray *The Scottish Staple at Veere. A Study in the Economic History of Scotland*. Longmans, Green & Co 1909
6 From Fry and Jefferson *Map of Virginia* 1775
7 George Murdoch by David Martin
9 From H Moll *Map of North America* 1715
11 From Seale *A Correct Chart of St George's Channel and the Irish Sea* 1744
12 From Nicholas Visscher *Anglica Regnum* 1690
16, 18 and 20 From Peter Fannin *A Correct Plan of the Isle of Man* 1789
17 S Hooper *Peel Castle, Isle of Man* April 1775
19 Photographed by D A Wilkins 1994
21 W C Leach *Castle Rushen with Ships* c 1830 Printer H Caddell
p 107 Sample Ship Bank Bill from *Banking in Glasgow During the Olden Times*
p 258 George Moore's handwriting from Manx Ingates

Acknowledgments
Figure 1 and page 258 reproduced by courtesy of Manx National Heritage

Figure 7 reproduced by courtesy of Glasgow Museums: Art Gallery & Museum, Kelvingrove

Figures 11, 12, 16, 17, 18, 20 and 21 reproduced by courtesy of Martin Moore

Cover: From Murdoch Mackenzie (the elder) *The Isle of Man* 1775 reproduced by courtesy of Martin Moore

Inserts and Tailpieces

INTRODUCTION

There is something remarkably satisfying about coming full circle. Two years ago *The Isle of Man in Smuggling History* was published. Its theme was an attempt to prove whether or not the Isle of Man really was the warehouse of high duty and uncustomed goods that all the Customs reports suggested. Now this book is based on the letters of George Moore, Manx merchant extraordinaire, who dedicated his life to keeping his customers on the Scottish coast supplied with these goods - mainly brandy, wine and rum - that were of as good a quality and price as they could obtain from any other Manx merchant. Therefore instead of being forced to concentrate on the official correspondence - the letters from the collectors at the outports to the Board of Customs in Edinburgh or London - this work looks at the situation from the other side, giving the viewpoint of one of those who specialised in 'frauds against the revenue'.

Although it should be emphasised that, as far as Moore was concerned, he did nothing illegal. There were no (Manx) laws against the import of his goods into the Island. It was only once they reached the Scottish mainland that they were 'smuggled'. And Moore made sure that as soon as they left the quayside at Peel these cargoes were the responsibility of the customer. An outstanding debt for such goods was treated by Moore as a civil debt, liable to utmost diligence and he employed writers in Scotland to ensure that he received as many of his due payments as possible. In this context his relationship with Captain Crawford of the king's boat at Cumbrae is particularly interesting. Crawford promised, verbally, to ensure that one of his boatmen, James Fisher, would make regular payments to Moore until the debt for 'goods delivered' was extinguished (see Chapter Eleven). When a wherry, which was transporting goods to Ayrshire was seized, and when on this occasion Moore's son, Philip, was involved, Crawford advised Moore about the best method for recovering the wherry at the Exchequer Court in Edinburgh. Whether or not the master, Lawrence Rigg, followed Crawford's advice, the wherry was reclaimed (see Chapter Thirteen).

How is it possible to gain an insight into what a Manx merchant was doing over a ten year period in the mid-eighteenth century? The book into which copies of George Moore's outgoing correspondence were transcribed has survived. This includes nearly one thousand six hundred and fifty letters written to some three hundred and twenty individuals and companies between 8 October 1750 and 22 September 1760. The letters are not continuous. There is a gap between January 1756 and May 1757 when, as Moore notes, the letters were transcribed into another book. Also he tended to write letters when on one of his annual trips to Scotland or Ireland and these were not recorded in the same letter-book. Sometimes there are references to 'my former letter' of such and such a date and this is not present, although it is surrounded by other letters of the same date.

Despite this the letters are of particular significance because of the wide range of people with whom Moore corresponded: from merchants in Europe, Boston and the West Indies to his ship masters to his bankers in Glasgow to other Irish/Scottish merchants who might be interested in joint ventures to customers and agents on the west coast of Scotland from Maryburgh near Fort William to Kirkcudbright to suppliers of hoops and glass bottles for his coopers to his brother-in-law in Dublin, who also conducted much of his Irish based business, to his own brothers to his sons' headmasters to his daughter, Sally, As a result the letter-book provides valuable source material for an economic/social history study and for an insight into the smuggling trade, from the other side.

All the letters have been transcribed, chronologically. The computerised version printed off at over 800 pages of A4, compared with 500 pages of the letter-book on microfilm. This put an end to the original idea, which had been to publish the letters in toto, with notes. The size and cost of such a work would have been prohibitive. At the same time anyone wanting to make a proper study of the letters would have had to start from scratch, making their own analysis. Add to this the fact that while Moore was an excellent business man he was not a man of letters in the literary sense so that the letters are not a joy to read - in places some slight amendments have been made to the quotations used to illustrate this book in an attempt to make the meaning more obvious.

As the letters had been computerised it was possible to analyse them in terms of destination - Europe, subdivided into Spain, France and Holland; the West Indies; Ireland; London, where many of Moore's payments were made, so that he had to ensure that sufficient funds were available at the right time, and where insurance on vessels and goods would be taken out; Glasgow, the headquarters of his Scottish bankers plus the source of the manufactory goods which he sent to Boston as the first stage of the journey which then took fish to the Mediterranean and brought home brandy and wine and Ayrshire, where he wrote over three hundred and forty letters to customers and agents from Old Kirk to Ballantrae etc etc. This formed the basis of the chapters for the book. These chapters have been grouped into three parts: The Merchants, The Smugglers and the Family and Friends.

The Merchants deals with the legal side of Moore's trade - his activities as a merchant, the sources of his brandy, wine, rum and tea, the tobacco manufactory which he set up on the Island for the benefit of his son, Philip, his banking arrangements in Glasgow and London and his two vessels, the *Peggy* and the *Lilly*. The Smugglers considers the market for the goods described in the first part. The smuggling business is explained. There are comments about the smuggling agents, customers and their debts and a chapter on the smuggling wherries, which transported the goods from the Isle of Man to the Scottish mainland. Finally The Family and Friends section describes Moore's intimate family, his garden at Ballamoore, his other acquaintances and his gradual but sure drift towards a more politically-based life-style. Two Appendices list the Letters and the Friends.

It soon became apparent that any particular 'story' came not only from the obvious letters but also from odd comments in letters to quite unexpected people. When the *Grizzy* hit a 'rock or fish' off the west coast of Ireland, her crew escaped with their lives by abandoning ship, leaving the vessel to float, unexpectedly, to the shore by herself The best description of what happened is in a letter to George Ainslie in Bordeaux, who had nothing to do with the vessel or her cargo. The remainder of the letters describing the problems for the owners over claiming part of the vessel's cargo were sent to Ireland, London, Glasgow, Fairlie, Douglas, Dublin and Cork. There was a second problem relating to this incident - the vessel was uninsured. As a result there was a long-running dispute with William Snell & Co in London, who should have looked after the insurance for Moore, in the standard way. Again information about this dispute comes from a wide range of sources and is summarised in one of the few long letters to Moore's brother Phil in Douglas. A problem between George Moore and both his brothers, Philip and James, over an inheritance is best described in a letter to James Crosbie, who was Moore's 'postman' in Liverpool. Another important point is the time factor. Any dispute might rumble on for several years, surfacing time and time again in unexpected places.

Throughout the letter-book Moore refers to his 'friends'. This produced the second part of the project - an attempt to see if it were possible to identify these friends from other contemporary sources and so put flesh on the bones of his correspondents. The most obvious source of this information was the custom house letter-books for the west coast of Scotland during the period covered by the letter-book and beyond. If the Moore letters were not pure fiction then the friends should appear as both honest men and smugglers in their local letter-books. The result was impressive. There was even one reference to George Moore himself and his son Philip. Several of these stories have been selected and included in appropriate chapters. No excuse is made for a slight repetition of some of the stories already used in *Strathclyde's Smuggling Story* - they were too good not to be used in this different context.

Apart from comments about individuals, there is also information in the letter-books about the arrivals and departures of vessels - some of these can be definitely identified as 'Moore' vessels. At the same time there is information about his masters, and particularly Pat and Robert Montgomerie, when they were not in charge of Moore's vessels the *Peggy* and the *Lilly*.

From the beginning there was a major question: where did Moore's customers come from? How did he manage to develop such an intricate network of contacts over such a wide area? Were they each recommended to him by word of mouth or was there some strong link which Moore simply tapped into and used for his own means? The first possible solution was that all Moore's customers might be Jacobites. However, apart from the odd individual in one place or another, this does not seem to have been so - and there is a suggestion that, based on his personal feelings, Moore would not have been involved with these people anyway. So the question remains unanswered. But along the way a considerable amount of information was collected about some of these people. This has not been included in the main text as it did not seem appropriate. However the following comments are appropriate here.

A correspondent produced the following information about one of Moore's customers. 'The Laird of Largie is chief of the MacDonalds of Largie, known as Clan Ranald Bane, an offshoot of the Lords of the Isles. They were always supporters of the Stewarts and held their lands from at least 1505 but had them forfeited for a short time for supporting the king in Scotland's Civil Wars. The young laird and his tutor were killed at Killicrankie. In 1745 the Laird of Largie was active but was prevented from joining the Prince by a kind friend inviting him to drink some punch as a stirrup cup and accidentally on purpose spilling the boiling kettle over his foot'. (Personal communication). Moore's problems with the Laird are mentioned in Chapter Twelve.

Another source of information comes from the physical remains from the Isle of Man to Scotland. It takes less than a day to drive round the Cowal peninsula, visiting the extant locations where Moore's friends lived (see Chapter Eleven). It takes longer to drive round Kintyre or along the Ayrshire coast.

The first gravestone located was that of James Orr at Inverkip. Kilfinan churchyard is filled with appropriate names. An interesting comment was made to the author while listing these names in May 1993. 'It isn't just the excitement of finding the name on a stone. Do you realise that all the people who are mentioned in the letters to John Munn probably stood were we're standing now when they attended the funeral?'

Other positive sightings have been sent to the author. On 25 September 1752 Moore referred to Mr McAlister's death. The following inscription has been supplied from Tarbert old burial ground. 'Archibald McAlister, merchant, Tarbert died July 9 1752 aged 32 years also here lies the corps of Anna McDougall, spouse to Archibald McAlister, merchant, Tarbert'. Moore referred to McAlister's relict in the context of hoping that she would pay off what was owed by her late husband.

One of Moore's commonest phrases is that a situation grudges him or that he is greatly grudged by someone's behavoiur (usually in the context of the non-payment of a debt). It is this approach to life which makes the letter-book so valuable. Had he been of a placid, easy-going nature then he would not have put pen to paper so frequently to outline, often to more than one correspondent, the full reasons for his current grudge. The author hopes that the present study, which is in essence a tribute, would have met with his approval.

ACKNOWLEDGEMENTS

First and foremost very many thanks are due to Chris Pickard, Manx maritime historian, who introduced the author to the George Moore letter-book in 1992. Many thanks are due to the Manx National Heritage Library for help with the original Manx material; to Strathclyde Regional Archives and to the West Search Room of the Scottish Record Office for providing copies of the custom house letter-books from Dumfries to Campbeltown covering the period 1750 to 1760.

Having transcribed the letter-book there were two main aims. First was to identify any incidents in alternative contemporary sources and second to find out as much as possible about the 'Friends', and in particular the smugglers, in an attempt to discover how Moore's address list developed and to provide more 'sightings' for the book. For this the author was dependent on the help of people on the ground from local libraries and museums to societies and individuals. Particular thanks are due to June Anderson, The Archive, Blair Castle; Rosemary Bigwood, Edinburgh; Piet Boon, West Friesian Archives, Hoorn; Dr Maureen Callow, Birmingham; Frank Cowin, Douglas; Ewart Library, Dumfries; the Hibernian Research Co, Dublin; Harry Kelly, Glasgow; Dr Bill Laing, Fairlie; Jean McColm, Kirkmaiden Information Centre; Ian MacDonald, Tarbert. Isa MacIntyre, Dunoon; Sue Mowat, Dunfermline; Canon Peter Raban, Northants; Drs F A M Schoone, Municipal Archives Rotterdam; Ian Stewart, Campbeltown; Stewartry Museum, Kirkcudbright; Mrs Steele, Curator, Raby Castle; District Museum, Stranraer and Joyce Valentine of the Tay Valley Family History Society research service. Also to Eric Graham who made contact towards the end of the research but who produced some invaluable information on the ships and their masters. And to my husband, son and Iain Shute for their painstaking work in Douglas, checking that my transcript of the letter-book was complete.

Finally sincerest thanks are due to John Gibson-Forty (MRO), practitioner of cranial osteopathy in Ross-on-Wye, whose patient treatment made it possible for the book to be completed, despite the author's apparent determination to undo his work all too regularly.

This is dedicated to Martin Moore, whose interest in research into the eighteenth century Manx merchants stimulated a book on George Moore.

THE MERCHANTS

Figure 1: Sir George Moore

CHAPTER ONE: THE MERCHANT

'My profession has from my youth up all along been that of a merchant'. [Sir John Stewart, 12 March 1760]

George Moore was, first and foremost, a merchant. His two vessels, the *Peggy* and the *Lilly*, crossed and recrossed the Atlantic, carrying goods to well-calculated markets. Other goods were imported into the Isle of Man as joint ventures with Manx or Scottish merchants. Sometimes Moore acted as an agent, selling a cargo for someone else to the highest bidder.

The trade was highly organised. Once a need had been identified, Moore would write several letters until a source had been located - rum in one or other of the West Indian Islands, brandy in France or Spain. He would then search for an outward cargo, the proceeds of which would go a considerable way towards covering the costs of his homeward goods - butter and beef to the West Indies, Scots manufactory goods to Boston, fish to the Straights. A vessel would be engaged and arrangements made for the outward cargo to be purchased on credit, which had been established with bankers in Glasgow or London. Insurance would be arranged, usually in London, on the vessel and goods, or at least Moore's share of each. Further negotiations were needed to check that the price of a second cargo (for example, fish from New England to the Straights) was such that it would meet a 'good market' and assurance given that any balance would be paid, again on credit. Further insurances had to be made, on Moore's forewarning, either by the overseas merchants or the masters of the vessels. Once the goods arrived at the Isle of Man, preferably discharged directly at Peel, the local duties would be paid. The goods were then disposed of as quickly as possible, as cellarage costs were an unnecessary additional charge and inconvenience, particularly as the goods would probably deteriorate on keeping. Now payments were needed from his customers to cover the costs incurred during the voyage.

As there were problems at every stage in the process, Moore's letters provide intimate details of all the frustrations that he had to overcome.

The *Peggy* & the *Lilly*

Moore's two vessels, both built in Boston during 1750, were the *Peggy* & the *Lilly*. He held a five-eighths interest in the *Peggy*, John Kelly and John Callin, also of Peel, holding the other three-eighths, and he sold a quarter of the *Lilly* to her master, Robert Montgomerie, in 1752, although he maintained a 100% interest in her cargo, apart from one voyage in partnership with Thomas Finlay and Robert Patrick of Dublin. One of the more significant points about the letter-book is that it covers the early voyages of these two vessels, with more detailed instructions to both their masters and the merchants with whom they would be dealing than at a later stage, when Moore felt more secure. These letters are the basis for Chapters Two, Three, Seven and Eight.

'The estimate of the value of the goods to be taken on board for the cargo outwards is £1,200 of manufactories of Glasgow, Irvine or of what ever other place you esteem necessary to make a collection of goods to the above-mentioned value'. [Pat Montgomerie, 11 December 1750]. 'At Boston I desire you will dispose of the goods outward in the best manner you can and invest the proceeds in the purchase of dried fish, fitting for the Mediterranean market ... On your coming to the Straights, if it be not inconvenient, you may touch at Gibraltar, where probably you may meet a letter from me, and thence proceed to Benicarlo, where you will receive a letter from me in the care of Mr Pat White, merchant, in which letter I shall let you know the place or places I design your proceeding to to take on board a cargo of brandy'. [Open letter to the new master of the *Lilly*, 21 January 1751]

Although clearly he had been a merchant for several years before the letter-book begins, Moore collected many of his overseas contacts between 1750 and 1760. There were three ways of locating these people. They would be introduced to Moore through a third party, they would contact him direct, offering their services, or he would ask advice from several contacts about whom could be trusted in a particular port. Moore would send an initial letter, describing the voyage that he planned and his requirements. Copies of this would be sent by various routes to ensure that at least one version arrived safely.

'You will receive herewith a letter from my friend **Mr William Snell** in London, relating to two vessels with fish from New Foundland or New England on my account I have directed to touch at your port. The one is named the *Lilly*, a snow burthen about 120 tons, Robert Montgomerie master, the other is named the *Peggy*, a snow about 180 tons, Pat Montgomerie master, for whom are letters enclosed. On their arrival should the market with you prove inviting I have desired that said captains submit the sale to your direction'. [John Blundell, Alicante, 1 July 1751]

A further letter would be handed to the master to be delivered as and when required. It was at this stage that final details would be given about payment arrangements. 'This will be handed to you by **Mr Robert Montgomerie**, master of the snow *Lilly*, intended to the Leeward Islands, with provisions and to load rum. Should Mr Montgomerie apply to you, please favour the interest of the concerned ... I desire you will draw on Messrs Abraham James Hillhouse, merchants in London, one quarter account for said Thomas Finlay and Robert Patrick. For my account, which shall be duly honoured, write Mr Hillhouse to assure my three-quarters of the value of the rum and £600 on the snow *Lilly*'. [Robert Colhoun, St Christophers, 20 September 1752]

Despite all the intimate arrangements, often there were problems with the merchants. The story of Walter Logan of Boston is told in the tailpiece to this chapter.

Insurance
One of the more worrying parts of the whole process was ensuring that both a vessel and her goods were covered by sufficient insurance. Before a voyage started, this was comparatively simple. Moore would write to his agent in London explaining the amount to be insured on the

vessel and estimating the value of the outward cargo, instructing the master to send the agent the exact figures as soon as she was fully laden.

'On the 14th August I gave Pat Montgomerie ... who was then here, directions to ship goods for me in Scotland to the value of £600 sterling. I've not since received a letter from Pat Montgomerie and suppose it mislaid or miscarried for he has proceeded some time ago, having left Ayr in September. You have underneath a copy of my directions to him. What goods he took on my account I can only make appear by the account of the persons from whom he had them ... this is necessary to mention with respect to the insurance I desire you will make for me on the *Peggy* to Boston equal to the value I directed, £600, which I desire you will accordingly cause be insured'. [Richard Oswald & Co, 26 October 1754]

There was less certainty about the next stage. The master would not know the exact value of the cargo until on board. If he were going, say, from Boston to the Straights, then any vessel Liverpool or Scotland bound would be able to deliver letters to the agent. But if he were coming directly home, either from the West Indies or the Straights, then the chances were that he would arrive before or at the same time as the insurance instructions.

'The *Peggy* ... is probably now at Boston to load fish for the Mediterranean. If no fish is to be had, New England rum is to be shipped for this town. Not hearing of her arrival at Boston and the uncertainty of her proceeding I must respite giving directions about insurance of her thence ... assure what you judge will be the value of the cargo'. [William Snell & Co, 16 October 1752]. 'I am favoured with yours of the 9th ult in reference to the assurance to be done on the *Peggy* ... I have not received any advice from Pat Montgomerie nor have I yet any account of his arrival at Boston'. [William Snell & Co, 14 January 1753]. 'I have received advice of the *Peggy* ... loading fish in Boston for the Straights ... not to be completed I expect till towards the end of January. My interest in the cargo will I compute be about £1,000, which sum I desire you will cause be assured'. [William Snell & Co, 8 March 1753]

If instructions misfired and Moore were subsequently left incompletely insured when the vessel was wrecked, then he would put pen to paper to justify his case for full cover regardless. This will be seen in the wrecks of the *Grizzy* (Chapter Three) and the *Lilly* (Chapter Eight). If, however, the ship arrived early, as in the case of the *Lilly*, which reached Ramsey from Boston on 17 December 1753, then he would be only too quick to write a letter hoping that insurance instructions could be cancelled. 'Should this advise come in time it will take off the assurance on the cargo I directed you formerly to make for me'. [Abraham James Hillhouse, 18 December 1753]. And 'Mr Montgomerie's letter to Messrs Johnson I see has prevented further insurance be done on the cargo, as the *Peggy* returned with convoy. There will arise a deduction on the further insurance you'll please acquaint me to settle with the person who is a small part concerned thereon'. [Richard Oswald & Co, 16 August 1757]

The insurance would cover sea risk and while the vessel was lying in port waiting for a cargo. There were two ways of doing this, through underwriters or through a formal company.

'One of my underwriters in this adventure (the *Peggy* to Barbados, where she was taken by a privateer) John David Ziegel, I hear is broke, which is an unlucky circumstance'. [Richard Oswald & Co, 1 June 1757]. 'Ziegel's bankruptcy is a great deduction. The extent of what can be got must be wanted. This instance of loss revises my inclination of dealing with the Royal Insurance Company on any future occasions. Please therefore acquaint what difference is made in premium given to them and to underwriters'. [Richard Oswald & Co, 6 October 1757]. 'If this insurance can be done at 1 or ½ per cent more with the Royal than with the underwriters, to me it seems eligible to deal with so secure a company than with the underwriters, whom by experience are found precarious. Therefore I recommend in this instance that the insurance be made with the company'. [Richard Oswald & Co, 29 March 1758]

Moore was always looking for a cheaper insurance system. 'Mr Robert Finlay in Glasgow has been telling me of a gentleman in London who transacts the business of insurance for him without charging the ordinary commission at ½ per cent. It seemed new to me that business could be thus done and I asked him what benefit could the gentleman propose answerable to his trouble. He told me that the gentleman's accounts with the assurers were regularly settled once in the year and at that time the gentleman paid the entire premiums of the sums insured in the preceding year and that for the payments being thus regularly paid the assurers allowed to the gentleman a discount of 5% on the sum he thus annually paid. At the same time Mr Finlay told me that the gentleman transacted in this manner in a few instances for merchants not resident in London but if I pleased he would introduce my correspondence with him. This circumstance seems inviting to have my business of assurance transacted in this channel from the saving obvious therein comparative with the ordinary way of commissioning assurance. Now whether this be corresponding with your method or it be inconvenient to you to manage in this way I shall wait your answer for my government'. [Abraham James Hillhouse, 20 November 1752]. 'I hear that the insurances are done at Glasgow for the Leeward Islands 7 or 8 per cent cheaper than at London. If so, such difference inclines me to insure there. I submit to you to cause insurance for me at London or at Glasgow'. [Richard Oswald & Co, 1 June 1757]

Credit

Most of Moore's trade was conducted on a credit basis. This credit had to be established with his 'bankers' in Glasgow and/or London. The system of in- and out-payments was intimately regulated. When money was required in Glasgow, Moore would write to his agents/customers in Scotland (see Chapter Six). There would be an inevitable time-lag before the funds reached Glasgow (see Chapter Twelve). They would then be sent to London, where credit was needed both for insurance and payment for the goods. Moore would arrange for the merchants or masters to draw bills directly in London. Any over-drawing by these people, and the acceptance of such an overdraft by the 'bankers' would cause inevitable friction.

When the outward cargo was sold, the proceeds were applied directly towards the purchase of the next cargo. Again, despite his accurate calculations, problems were inevitable. In 1750 goods from Glasgow and Liverpool were sent to Boston to fund the building of the *Lilly* and her homeward cargo of rum. Part of these funds were mis-applied to another, non-Moore, voyage (see tailpiece) and the homeward cargo was worthless timber and a little 'extravagant' priced rum. The situation was so disastrous that Moore seriously contemplated selling the *Lilly* (see Chapter Eight). Having been forewarned, on subsequent occasions Moore would make sure that no funds were left behind in the wrong place at the wrong time.

When the cargoes of fish were sold in the Straights, if the brandy were not to be purchased at the same port, then Moore would instruct the master on the method of payment. 'The proceeds thereof be given you in specie or, as I rather prefer, in bills in Paris. The first of these bills let be enclosed to Mr P Berail, merchant in Cette, and forwarded by post. The second of these bills or the specie you may take with you to be given to Mr Berail on your arrival at Cette.' [Robert Montgomerie, 1 July 1751]

Despite his frequent worries, Moore was rarely disastrously caught out. Examples of such failures were all around. 'I've received a letter from my friends in Cork advising that Mr Joseph Popham has failed. They desire me to acquaint you least he owes you money and you suffer by delay'. [Phil Moore & Sons, 14 August 1753]. 'I'm sorry to hear of the failures of Messrs Willocks & Dawson and of Messrs Lennox & French as public credit will be affected and private losses considerable'. [Thomas Finlay & Robert Patrick, 22 March 1755]

In 1759 Moore succeeded in a double order of a cargo of brandy from Bordeaux and from Lisbon. The story is told in Chapter Two. This is one of the few occasions on which tension and near despair is apparent in the letters.

The Vessel and Crew
Before each voyage, Moore's own vessels would need a refit and 'necessaries' for the crew. The cost of the refit was often more than Moore had estimated but it was something over which he had little or no control, as it was usually undertaken either in Scotland or Ireland.

'Mr Callin has this day shown me the account of the outfits furnished by Captain Pat Montgomerie of the *Peggy* for 1752 and 1753, which I've looked over. I'm much surprised how they come to exceed the sum he told me or computed but a balance is owing him £44 2s 8½d on outfits 1752, £38 18s 6d on outfits 1753 ... Mr Montgomerie has directed me to order payment of to you'. [Pat Ewing, 8 November 1753]. Moore wrote to Robert Montgomerie on 27 September 1755: 'I've received your letter of the 14th this month advising me that two sums are owing for sail cloth and rigging in Irvine for the *Lilly* 1754, namely £5 2s 6d and £1 8s 3d. I imagined that these like sums had been accounted for. As you say they are due it is necessary they be paid which I desire you will do for me'.

Moore's problems over finding a new master for the *Lilly* are discussed in Chapter Eight. Having taken charge of the vessel, the master was to 'direct she be caulked and in every respect properly furnished for the voyage to be done in the frugalest way ... towards victualling for the voyage I've now shipped ten barrels beef, a cask of butter and eleven cheeses. What also you think proper to add let be provided occasionally during the voyage'. [Open letter to the new master dated 21 January 1751]. On this occasion 'a hogshead or two of bottled wine that is twenty or forty dozen more or less', were added to the cargo at Peel. as you think convenient and have time here. Leave in Peeltown your account of disbursements.'

The master and crew were, in theory, contracted for each voyage, although Moore frequently refers to the Montgomeries as being in his 'employ'. An insight into the master's responsibilities is seen in his letter to Joseph Scott when searching for a new master for the *Lilly* (see Chapter Eight). 'The present master, John Laing, has not in my mind capacity or address to transact a voyage ... so that I must have a new master. For this I apply to you and to the assistance of your brother, Mr Robert Scott, who I hope will give his best advice in having the snow a proper commander. The qualifications of one I would choose is the person whom Mr Scott would entrust on the like voyage. The terms, namely his wages, cabin stores and consideration for his trouble in the sales and purchase, let this be agreed on and I'm hopeful the captain's behaviour will so prove that I may have reason to keep him in my employ, which will give me great pleasure ... Six hands and a mate with the commander will I think be a crew sufficient.' [Joseph Scott, 21 January 1751]

In 1755 Robert Montgomerie's wages were £4 10s per month. On top of this the master would be paid a freight for the journey. 'It remains that I mention to you the condition of freight. It is the ordinary custom with us here in our freighting vessels this way to give 4d English per gallon for each gallon landed here, if the vessel sails out in ballast, and 4½d English per gallon if the vessel takes in goods outwards, which condition in this instance will I hope be not disagreeable to you'. [Thomas Finlay & Robert Patrick, 20 September 1752]

The *Lilly* carried six apprentices on board. Arrangements were made for these. 'The *Peggy* sailed with two apprentices (James Cowle and Mathew Quirk) for the *Lilly* I expect will soon be delivered you. These same Manx apprentices have great dependence I find on your care of them. They expect too that I will give a helping hand ... For the uses of the apprentices belonging to the *Lilly* be a few books purchased to ten shillings worth at Cork so that any of them that are disposed may read. For any of them disposed to write and to figure a little let a little paper be provided and on the voyage, as there will be leisure, let the mate instruct them, which I shall acknowledge when I see him to provide'. [Robert Montgomerie, 18 April 1752]

'It gives me pleasure to hear the crew is well, by which I conclude all the apprentices prove to your liking'. [Robert Montgomerie, 23 May 1753].

A complete list of the *Lilly*'s apprentices was sent to Richard Oswald & Co in August 1755.

Name	Date Indented	Wages per month
James Cowle	19 January 1751	21 shillings
Mathew Quirk	29 January 1751	21 shillings
Sil Revel	17 April 1752	20 shillings
Pat Kelley	19 April 1752	20 shillings
Mathew Crelling	19 April 1752	15 shillings
Dan Mollechrist	25 September 1752	15 shillings
John Kelly	July 1753	10 shillings

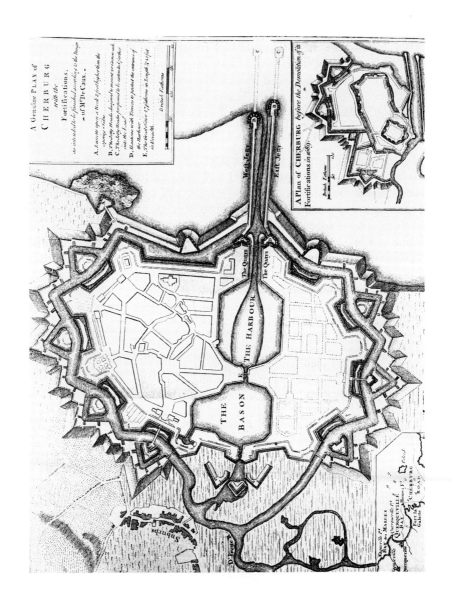

A Genuine PLAN of
CHERBURG
with the
Fortifications.
as intended to be finished according to the Design
of Mr The Caux.

A. Intended upon a Rock of a higher than the spring tides.
B. The Jetty Heads designed to mount 20 canon each.
C. The Jetty Heads proposed to be canted further into the sea.
D. Bastions with Towers to protect the entrance of the Harbour.
E. The Strait Line of fathoms in Length 3 or 400 in breadth.

British Fathoms

A Plan of CHERBURG before the Demolition of its Fortifications in 1689.

British Fathoms

West Jetty
East Jetty

The Quays
The Quays

THE HARBOUR

THE BASON

Suburbs

Figure 2: The Impact of War

This plan of Cherbourg comes from the Gentleman's Magazine dated August 1758. According to their report: 'While these things were doing on the continent, advices were received at Whitehall from Lt Gen Bligh and Com Howe, dated the 7th and 8th inst, giving an account that his majesty's troops had affected a landing, under cover of the frigates and bomb ketches, in the bay des Marees, two leagues westward of Cherbourg, in the face of a large body of the enemy, prepared to receive them; and that on the 8th in the evening Cherbourg surrendered at discretion, the enemy having marched out and abandoned the place on the approach of his majesty's troops'.

'We are rejoiced at the success of the British arms at Cape Briton and have hopes for Crown Point. May these with our success at Cherbourg prove happy omens'. [Haliday & Dunbar, 29 August 1758]

The possibility of war with France was a great concern to Moore. 'The apprehensions of a French war are daily increasing, which I have communicated with respect to the *Lilly* and *Peggy* and have desired to get French passes for them, if it can be done by soliciting this at Paris. If a French war does break out or you apprehend so, it will be alike necessary to have English passes for them, which if you can compass please act accordingly'. [Richard Oswald & Co, 25 March 1755]. 'I see that no passes are given at Paris until the circumstances require it ... the circumstance of war are here so alarming that by every vessel from England we expect a declaration'. [Peter Berail, 15 August 1755]

'Current public affairs at present render it very difficult (to know) how best to determine on private means whereby to be supplied with brandy'. [Peter Berail, 8 November 1755]

'Notwithstanding all reports the French have not yet made a declaration of war ... at this distance it looks as if the French and the underwriters are in concert and so under the notion of insurance are authorised to make reprisals in that way wherein they have been so successful that I'm persuaded they are prepared for a storm'. [Claud Johnson & Son, 24 December 1755]

Papers and Passes

Moore was so well-pleased with Robert Montgomerie's management of his first voyage that he sold him a quarter share in the *Lilly*. 'You are therefore to take out a new register in your name and my name, the present owners'. [Robert Montgomerie, 11 April 1752]. 'In the seemingly most unfavourable event that you cannot get your register at Irvine or Cork you must proceed on the original one. On your arrival in Barbados before you make a report consult the gentlemen there you are consigned ... If any hazard there it will be less at the Leeward Islands or St Eustatius ... act accordingly. But I expect you have succeeded in getting a register and all doubts about it thereby removed'. [Robert Montgomerie, 18 April 1752]

A Mediterranean Pass was also needed. 'Should you have to meet any difficulty or apprehend it about the Mediterranean Pass write a letter to Messrs William Snell & Co to provide you with a new (one) ... which they may forward you immediately in a letter to the care of Messrs James & George Piersy, merchants in Cork'. For some reason this arrangement did not work. 'How Robert Montgomerie has blundered about his writing to you for the Mediterranean pass I do not understand for the certificate he refers to could not be in a proper channel than under your direction and I cautioned him thereof in his sailing instructions. Rather than to wait at Cork till this matter be cleared up perhaps he may proceed without a pass, as the chance of meeting a Barbary corsair on his voyage is inconsiderable ... The assurances I hope will be equally done with little difference for want of said pass or have you found means to send him a pass. Conform to the expected certificate or without it are the insurance terms not so explicit?' [William Snell, 18 May 1752]. 'I'm pleased the Mediterranean pass came in time to Mr Montgomerie. The old one he returned I shall send up to London'. [James & George Piersy, 20 July 1752]

The Coopers

Once the goods were landed on the Isle of Man they had to be transferred into smaller, handier casks for transport to the Scottish coast. Moore employed his own coopers, and these had to be trained. He sent John Addi to Hamilton & Kissack in Dublin. 'I'm very much obliged to your Mr McKissack's interesting himself to get my young cooper ... instructed in the wine business'. [Hamilton & Kissack, 25 May 1753]

These coopers needed a constant supply of barrel staves and hoops.

Hoops from Newry

'Mr Radcliff has been telling me that he was several days with you in the Lodge and that you hinted something about my not taking the quantity of hoops I used to do. I do not now incline to deal in more than what the coopers who immediately work for me want, owing to their complaints of the quality. But this proves of no inconvenience to you as the sale here is not lessened though in other hands ... (I) am encouraged to this (future orders) by hearing that the person you employ to make them is become more diligent to have good hoops to content the coopers'. [Robert Ross, 6 September 1753]. As a result he ordered 20,000 hoops for ten gallon casks. The following month he extended the order to 120,000. Whether these were received or not by February 1754 Moore was corresponding with Roger Hall. His hoops cost 10s Irish per thousand, 1s Irish per thousand freight plus the duty payable at the custom house.

A long gap in the correspondence is partly explained in a letter to John Callin. 'The hoops I want for my coopers I depend on your getting for me, about 100,000 to be sent me so soon as possible. I wrote to Mr Hall long ago for them and have been all this winter expecting them. Why he has delayed and thus long disappointed my expecting them I know not'. [John Callin, 17 January 1755]. The first hoops from this source arrived on 29 September 1757. 'Our coopers have no objection to the quality of the hoops, for they are better than what Mr Ross used to send them. Yet I observed several of the bundles that were not sufficient hoops. I mention this for I incline to deal with you and would wish that the coopers have right good hoops'. [Roger Hall, 6 October 1757]

Glass bottles from Bristol

In August 1751 Moore ordered glass bottles from Bristol, by way of James Crosbie in Liverpool. There was a long delay because the company in Bristol had difficulty in getting a boat to freight them. 'This long suspense proves of very great inconveniency to me'. [James Crosbie, 27 January 1752]. In the meantime Moore had spoken to John Moore 'master of a small sloop that has been on a trip to Scotland and is now wind bound here in his way to Liverpool. Moore says he will readily go to Bristol immediately on his arrival at Liverpool and promises I may depend on his carriage of the bottles'. [James Crosbie, 27 January 1752]

The detailed order transcribed in the letter-book is also dated January 1752: 100 or 120 gross long necked quart bottles 13 to the dozen; 6 dozen rough cider; 6 dozen sweet cider - and for domestic use: a crate of window glass; 4 dozen wine drinking glasses of one sort; 2 dozen 'whip silly bub' glasses; 2 dozen jelly glasses and 2 quart & 2 pint glass decanters.

'I am well-pleased with the quality of the goods by Captain Moore ... to whom I observe your having forwarded the certificate of the bottles being landed in this Isle. It is a particular pleasure to me you think my claim of debenture is reasonably founded'. [James Crosbie, 20 May 1752]. Yet, 'I'm very glad you have succeeded in getting a debenture on empty bottles from Liverpool. Surely I shall benefit at Bristol by the precedent you have established and I'm hopeful Messrs Tyndall & Co will not be wanting to favour me'. [James Crosbie, 15 January 1753]. 'I have wrote to Bristol with respect to the drawback of the bottles thence by Moore, to which I have received no answer. One of the gentlemen concerned in that works I hear is dead but this circumstance surely cannot withhold their answering my letter, namely by some of the company'. [James Crosbie, 6 September 1753]

'James Moore is with me, talking about bottles. I'm reminded that I can have them from your bottle works in as easy a way as I can from Bristol'. [James Crosbie, 4 June 1753]. As a result Moore ordered 100 gross 'champain' bottles. But 'I'm extremely sorry to tell you that the bottles by Moore are by no means fitting for my purpose. They are not wine bottles or those kind of bottles wherein wine is usually designed. My cooper tells me that he's sure a wine hogshead will not fill above seventeen dozen and the common sort of champain bottles will run to about twenty-two dozen per hogshead. On seeing the bottles I told Captain Moore that I would not agree to discharge but to return them directly back to Liverpool. He told me this he could not possibly do for that he had entered into bonds to return a certificate of their being landed here and that they must be landed here. I'm giving Captain Moore half a dozen of the bottles to show you that they are above quarts. They may be used for ale but for wine, which is my purpose, they are utterly unfit and therefore neither for my use, profit or account. Moore has the certificate of their being landed to entitle your obtaining the debenture'. [James Crosbie, 18 October 1753]. Moore modified his viewpoint 'The first view of the bottles by Moore happened to be a parcel of the make of those I returned, too large and not a handsome bottle. But on a stricter examining I find less cause to complain ... you'll please let me know the debenture of the bottles that I may account accordingly'. [James Crosbie, 4 December 1753]

The bottles also required corks and these came from Ireland. 'Calvin I find has forgot my corks and he should not. He says he did not receive them. No opportunity has offered since'. [Thomas Finlay & Robert Patrick, 20 September 1752]. On this occasion Moore did not have to wait long 'The corks are safe for me in Douglas'. [Thomas Finlay & Robert Patrick, 13 October 1752]

Correspondence

Moore sent letters, in duplicate at the very least, via any available, and sure, method from the Island. He used various 'post offices' on the mainland. Letters could be forwarded to him by way of Glasgow, London, Liverpool or John McCulloch, merchant in Kirkcudbright. The Liverpool connection also supplied Moore with newspapers and periodicals. 'I received your letter of the 22nd last month covering letters, evening posts and magazines (see insert). I desire you will please forward the enclosed three letters for London'. [James Crosbie 20 February 1754]

By 1754 James Crosbie was in partnership with his son, John. On 18 April 1755 they wrote to Moore with the information that James Crosbie had joined 'with four gentlemen to open a bank in Liverpool and offering that any remittance I may have to make to London in sending cash to the bank it will be remitted without charge or if I choose the remittance in the same manner by your means it be alike done. I thank him for this favour, which occasionally I shall use but I have now seldom to remit by way of Liverpool. My payments are mostly made in Scotland and thence the remittances (see Chapter Six)'. [James & John Crosbie, 2 June 1755]. The new bank was clearly hoping to attract the Duke of

Correspondence: Current Affairs

'The calamity at Lisbon is dreadfully alarming and what following accounts we have are attended with fatal circumstances'. [Richard Oswald & Co, 24 December 1755]

Letter from Abraham Castres Esq, Envoy Extraordinary to the King of Prussia. Lisbon, November 6 1755

'You will, in all likelihood, have heard before this of the inexpressible calamity befallen the whole maritime coast, and in particular this opulent city, now reduced to a heap of rubbish and ruins, by a most tremendous earthquake on the first of this month, followed by a conflagration, which has done ten times more mischief than the earthquake itself ... God be praised, my house stood out the shocks, though greatly damaged; and that happening to be out of the reach of the flames, several of my friends, burnt out of their houses, had taken refuge with me, where I have accommodated them, as well as I could, under tents in my large garden; nobody but Lord Charles Douglas ... besides our chaplain and myself, having dared hitherto to sleep in my house since the day of our disaster ... This, with the anguish I have been in for these five days past, occasioned by the dismal accounts brought to us every instant of the accidents befallen one or other of our acquaintances among the nobility, who, for the most part, are quite undone, has greatly affected me; but in particular the miserable objects among the lower sort of his majesty's subjects, who all fly to me for bread and lie scattered up and down my garden, with their wives and children. I have helped them all hitherto, and shall continue to do so as long as provisions do not fail us ...

'As I have large sums deposited in my house, belonging to such of my countrymen as have been happy enough to save some of their cash, and as my house was surrounded all last night with ruffians, I have this morning written ... to desire a guard which I hope will not be refused'.

From: The Gentleman's Magazine, December 1755

Moore's main contact in Lisbon was Cunningham & Gordon. They seem to have survived the earthquake as he corresponded with them from March 1753 to November 1758. Further details of this correspondence are found in Chapter Two.

Atholl as a customer. 'I should sooner have answered Mr Crosbie's letter but I waited to see our governor with respect to his proposal about remitting the Duke's money ... it seems to me as if the remittance of his Grace's money from Liverpool has been usually done at par for the governor did not eye the proposal as if attended with any advantage to his Grace and only said that whatever his Grace would direct should be observed. How for me to manage evenly in this affair I know not for the last summer at the instance of the Old Bank in Glasgow I made a parallel proposal to the Duke in their favour and to this day I have not had his answer ... there is one way whereby you may probably create a circulation of this money in your bank, if you like it, by allowing me to receive the money and on such receipt to draw on your friends in London for the like value at a month or two, as may be agreeable, and as I receive the specie I shall forward it to you in Liverpool. In this scheme the inconvenience is the risk. You are best to judge in respect to your interests whether or not to dispense with. I wish the new company all imaginable success.' [James & John Crosbie, 2 June 1755]

Whatever may have come of this suggestion, James Crosbie died later that year. 'I was extremely sorry to hear of the death ... being a loss in general to his friends and family, with whom I heartily sympathise.' [John Crosbie, 24 December 1755]. This letter was also the final contact. George Moore complained about John debiting an old bill to his account, which his father had discounted. 'As in a larger so in a smaller sum the arguments are the same, which disallow your debiting my account at this time with any part of the value'.

By 1757 George Moore was using Haliday & Dunbar in Liverpool. Again they forwarded the letters, newspapers and magazines, including on 22 August 1758 a copy of Lloyd's Chronicle 'and the terms whereon it is to be supplied. I think them dear but I suppose they are on equal terms with others. I am satisfied that you continue the favour of forwarding them to me by any opportunity for a year'. [Haliday & Dunbar 8 September 1758]. The main interest of these letters is in the information they provide about both Moore's daughter Sally (see Chapter Fourteen) and about developments at both Douglas and Peel harbours (see Chapter Sixteen).

Following this introduction to George Moore the merchant, Chapters Two to Five describe the brandy and wine, rum, tea and tobacco trades. His banking arrangements are detailed in Chapter Six while Chapters Seven and Eight concentrate on the *Peggy* and the *Lilly*, considering their respective voyages. Then it is time to turn to the less-legal side of his business in the next Part.

THE STORY OF WALTER LOGAN, MERCHANT IN BOSTON

'There was one Walter Logan, a young merchant in Boston, with whom I had dealings purely from the connection he had with my friends in Glasgow and hence I reposed a greater confidence than he deserved. However I suffered considerably by him, for he owes me several hundreds and I know not which way to turn to look for payment. Is he yet in Boston and what hopes may I have?' [John Rowe, 24 April 1753]

George Moore's dealings with Walter Logan in Boston not only caused him disappointment but also became one of the main factors behind the termination of his connection with P & J Murdoch in Glasgow (see Chapter Six). They also affected the *Lilly*'s maiden voyage (see Chapter Eight). The following letters tell the story:

'I observe what you mention of Mr Walter Logan, that he has absconded to wait the success of one Rowan's return of some voyages this Rowan had undertaken wherein Logan is concerned. How different is this shape of affairs had the Liverpool goods I sent him been as represented not portables for the summer season and therefore to wait a more favourable season of sale and thus unportable to wait a future market. It would appear plain that the proceeds or the value of these Liverpool goods are still in Mr Logan's hands, for Rowan's vessel parted from Boston long before my vessel the *Lilly* parted thence. My suspicions of Logan with respect to the cargo he sent by the *Lilly* and with respect to his detaining her were no way favourable to him and how I relished his proceedings for me. I gave you the most early intimation I could notwithstanding your manner of writing me was such as inspired me with confidence. It is very certain my correspondence with Mr Logan was begun of myself, by sending him the goods from Glasgow, and so certainly my correspondence would then have stopped until I had some experience of his manner of dealing had not the confidence you inspired me too much made me rely on his probity. And to this was owing that I sent him the goods from Liverpool some months thereafter'. [Peter & John Murdoch, 20 May 1752]

'In this month I received your letter of the 27th December (1754) with account sales of the goods you had from Liverpool on my account together with my account current. Your letter of the 24th June preceding said letter is not come to hand. However by means of another friend (John Rowe in Boston) I was enough made acquainted with the circumstances of your condition, which to him I urged was not a regular motive for your delaying so long to furnish me with said account sales and said account current, at least thereby to have the satisfaction of knowing to what extent I became a sufferer by your insolvency, as well as that thereby the sum might be ascertained due me for which you are so solicitous that I indulge with that clemency, deriving from a letter of licence. By the state of your account current the balance you allow due me arising therein is lawful money £1027 7s 3½d making sterling currency £770 10s 9½d, whereon I have to observe that if, as you wrote, my goods were sold on credit, the payment must have been made to you since your shipping the goods by the *Lilly* and since your friend Mr Rowan and left Boston so that the produce of my own effects might have been expected to have been applied to my own account or in some manner to have remained subject to my order. But if the produce of my goods was applied to the furnishing of a cargo for your friend Rowan in what light am I to esteem your drawing on my account on Messrs Murdochs in Glasgow in sundry bills of exchange sterling value £435 14s 6d and to your further charge of 2½ per cent commission on these your said drafts? ... If I have been deceived in the confidence I reposed in you, the misfortune is my family's and they the objects. For their sakes therefore it is that I have at any time listened to granting you a licence and hence it is that I now write to Mr John Rowe merchant in Boston to act herein for me'. [Walter Logan, 26 August 1755]

Referring to the account sales 'which whenever I think of I know not whether to blame him (Walter Logan) or myself most. I've herewith answered Logan's letter but could not conclude it without showing some resentment. However, I desire you may sign the letter of licence or, as I would have it, a letter of licence for seven years. For at the expiration thereof I may expect of his being an honest man, that he will make me some satisfaction and thereon it may be renewed. On your application it is that I make this concession'. [John Rowe, 26 August 1755]. There is no further reference to Walter Logan in the letter-book.

The very first letter in the letter-book is addressed to William Rowan, to the care of Mr Blair, Dublin. 'Last night I received a letter from our mutual friend Mr Walter Logan ... wherein he acquaints me that he is concerned with you in a snow, burthen about 115 tons, mostly loaded with New England rum for the Dublin market and desires my writing to you of the prices of this kind of rum in this Isle for your government. I'm sorry I cannot give any encouragement to you coming to this Isle, whereby if it was in my power to serve Mr Logan ...' [William Rowan, 8 October 1750] - see Chapter Three.

CHAPTER TWO: BRANDY AND WINE

'Brandy is the principal commodity I have traffic in'. [Peter Berail, Cette, 21 November 1752]. 'The consumption or demand in this Isle was the last year principally supplied by imports from Spain, where I can assure you they have greatly improved in the distilling way. The use of spirits is principally amongst the lower class of people, who are not very curious in the quality, so that spirits of the cheapest quality serve their occasions. For this reason it is that excepted to a very few no difference of quality is now made. If therefore Spanish brandy continues in proportion as lower than French I'm satisfied Spanish will prevail here'. [George Ainslie, 24 November 1752]

Although it is clear that George Moore personally preferred the French brandy, the price difference necessitated his dealing with Spain. The length of time involved in one of these voyages (see Chapters Seven and Eight) was often such that the situation changed completely between Moore giving instructions to his captain and the vessel actually arriving at the market. When the *Peggy* and the *Lilly* left Scotland in 1751, laden with manufactory goods for New England, where they were to purchase fish for the Mediterranean, Moore intended that one should load with Spanish brandy and that the other should have a French cargo. Further details of the subsequent events are given below. Following this somewhat traumatic experience, the *Peggy* continued to load brandy regularly at Barcelona under Green, Stanton & Ford (see Chapter Seven), while the *Lilly* was diverted to the West Indies for rum (see Chapters Three and Eight). The 'apprehensions of war' in 1755 changed this pattern and the remaining voyages described in this chapter belong to that period. Figure 3 shows eighteenth century Europe and gives some details of Moore's wine trade.

To Load a Cargo of Brandy 1751 Style

On 1 July 1751 Moore wrote to Green & Stanton, in Barcelona, Pat White in Benicarlo (see tailpiece), Peter Berail in Cette, John

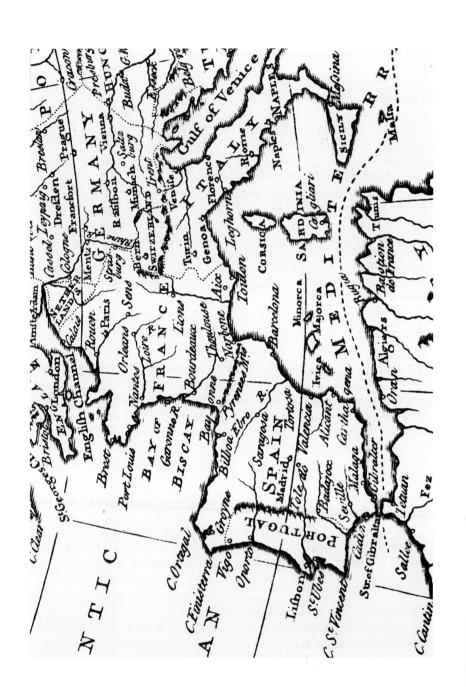

Figure 3: Europe in the Eighteenth Century: The Wine Trade

Moore tended to import his wine in small lots as part of another cargo. This wine mainly came from Bordeaux, Barcelona, Alicante and Lisbon. One of the Bordeaux orders, dated 7 March 1753, included:

one tun old claret at 800 livres per tun, one tun new claret at 800 livres, two tuns new claret at 150 livres, two tuns old claret at 400 livres, six tuns new claret at 400 livres, two tuns port wine at 100 to 120 livres, two tuns white wine at 200 to 300 livres for Moore's account and for his brother, Philip Moore & Sons in Douglas, one tun old claret at 800 livres per tun and one tun new claret also at 800 livres.

The small articles included in this order are also listed: 5 hundredweight Martinico coffee, 2 casks or bags of Catherine rum, 16 yards of yellow lute string, 3 gauze dressed caps, 2 silver tippets, 2 boxes of head & breast flowers, 6 bottles of orange flower water, 12 bottles of hungary water, 1 silver handkerchief, 3 pairs of ear rings, 3 necklaces, 4 fans. [George Ainslie, 7 March 1753]

As always, Moore had strong views about the wine. 'I find the quality rich coloured so that it is not very suitable for my design. Pray have you any sort of white wines not sweet, pale coloured and stronger?' [Harris Crisp & Co, Barcelona, 9 January 1753]. There were also transportation problems. 'Let vent holes be put nigh the bung of each cask to prevent leakage'. [John Blundell, Alicante, 30 October 1753]. There was also the problem of fretting 'which new wine of that kind is now apt to suffer by the rolling of the sea'. [Peter Berail, 20 November 1753].

Cunningham & Gordon were mentioned in Chapter One. In 1753 Moore imported from them ten pipes of white Lisbon wine and four pipes of red Lisbon wine on a vessel freighted by John Allan of Ballantrae (see Chapter Ten). The wine arrived in October on the Molly of Irvine, Thomas Boyd master. 'I have tasted the white Lisbon and find it very good. The Methuen (red) is a kind of wine we have no acquaintance of here but I think it will do and am pleased you sent it'. [30 October 1753]. Boyd was on the Isle of Man in February 1754 offering to freight more wine to Moore. In the meantime he had received Cunningham & Gordon's letter of 9 February 'advising that the last vintage did not produce so great a quantity as usual but that you had arranged some of the best to serve your friends whereof I am hopeful that I shall partake'. [4 May 1754].

Blundell in Alicante and James Reid at Gibraltar about the *Peggy* and the *Lilly* which were to load fish at Boston and exchange it for brandy in the Mediterranean.

Moore's original idea, based on what he understood to be the relative prices, was that both vessels should sell their fish at Alicante and then the *Peggy* should load brandy at Benicarlo and the *Lilly* at Cette.

His next letters were dated 15 August. 'I had some thoughts that brandy made at your place was not as good as that made at Benicarlo. However, as I had no experience of the quality of yours I was diffident or declined giving any directions about a cargo. From what character you give of its quality I leave it to the opinion and choice of Captain Pat Montgomerie'. [John Blundell]

'I hear the prospect of a vintage at Cette is very indifferent, which will enhance the price of brandy there, and that the prospect of a vintage with you is very promising and that brandy may be expected in a moderate way with you'. [Green, Stanton & Ford]

Then on 3 September 1751 'I can propose having no means of a profit by loading brandy at Cette'. [Peter Berail]. The next letter from Cette, dated 7 October 1751, changed Moore's mind. It was a copy of the one addressed to Robert Montgomerie 'advising him of the price of brandy with you and the expectance you had of its fall, when the price of new brandy would come to the time of its being fixed. I should be well pleased that Mr Montgomerie would find encouragement to proceed to Cette to load brandy as I have a firm persuasion you would do the utmost in your power to render his coming there in every respect serviceable to me and from this opinion it is that I have long ago wrote Montgomerie if he does not find a material difference in the price with you and in Spain that he proceed to Cette and apply to you. So indeterminate is the market here that little or no difference is made between the quality of Cette and Spanish brandy'. [22 November 1751]

Yet in the case of Pat Montgomerie, 'By your state of the prices of brandy with you and at Cette it is obvious that Montgomerie's choice will determine him to proceed to load brandy under your address, in which case let me rely on your having a particular regard to the quality. For I'm concerned in another vessel that is to load Valencia brandy at Benicarlo and I would not have this in point of quality superior to the cargo by the *Lilly*'. [Green & Stanton, 22 November 1751]

'You do not think it would be to my interest that the *Peggy* loaded brandy at Alicante as the vintage has proved so scarce that the wines for distilling are pushed up to a monstrous price ... By what Mr White writes me the prices in Valencia are considerably cheaper so that Pat Montgomerie will doubtless proceed there'. [John Blundell, 22 November 1751]

'Both these captains have a discretionary power to load brandy in Spain, arising from the low prices that were at first quoted. But the price is there unequally risen so that I should be very content the *Peggy*'s or *Lilly*'s cargo were shipped under your address'. [Peter Berail, 27 December 1751]

'The price of brandy is with you I observe very considerably advanced ... this greatly exceeds what I expected and as the quality with you proves much inferior to Cette brandy and as this difference is not equalled by the price with you it would give me great pleasure that the *Lilly*'s cargo of brandy was loaded at Cette under the direction of my friend Mr Berail merchant there, if the *Lilly*'s cargo is not already engaged in Spain, as it would prove to my benefit'. [Green & Stanton, 27 December 1751]

Both the Montgomeries loaded their brandy cargoes with Green & Stanton. 'The brandy I've had by the Montgomeries is a supply that will furnish my demand the approaching season of sale, which does not begin in any considerable degree till August, so that I have no immediate prospect of purchasing brandies'. [Green, Stanton & Ford, 21 April 1752]

War with France: Brandy and wine from France and Spain via Bordeaux

There is evidence that Moore had been trading with George Ainslie for some time. When offered the services of a new establishment in France, he wrote 'My occasions at Bordeaux are very small. They have been with a gentleman whose transactions I have reason to be satisfied with. In the cause of any change in my correspondence I shall apply to you'. [Messrs John Black, 7 March 1751]

In August 1755 Moore wrote to Ainslie 'The present appearances indicate a war and such are our advices that by every opportunity from Liverpool we are expecting the declaration of terms. In this event I would be glad to know if you can accommodate me with brandies, as my occasions require, on neutral bottoms to be shipped at Cette or Barcelona and be landed in this Isle, my payment to be ascertained on the delivery payable at London or remitted you thence, three or four months following such delivery, your demand to be ascertained by the value of the original cost and charges per invoice and an agreed on sum in gratification for such your trouble and all manner of relative risks, on which subject if your letters be such as appears suitable I shall close herewith and motively renew our correspondence'. [George Ainslie, 18 August 1755]

The next letter is quoted in detail as it established their manner of trading. 'Your favour of the 13th September I have received, communicating the terms whereon you will furnish me brandy in the event of a war with France. Namely for an allowance of 10 per cent on the original invoices from Cette or Barcelona and of 8 per cent on the original invoices from Bordeaux or Cognac, the accounts of the invoice with said allowance to be paid four months after delivery of the goods in this town or in any other port of this Isle. This allowance seems high on your adventure but as it corresponds with my agreement with you on similar transactions in the last war I agree herewith hereby understanding that from the agreement of purchasing the goods to the shipping of them and from that time until their delivery at the destined port in this Isle you stand or are in place of proprietor and that said allowance comprehends satisfaction to you for all manner of relative risks that may happen or arise. I also understand that the purchase of any other commodity or merchandises is comprehended or included in this agreement, namely wine or prize rum or what else my occasions may and are from time to time to write to you for. I also understand that I may receive the benefit of the four months credit in whatever manner may prove most suitable to me. Formerly I observe that the condition of payment was a moiety of the value to be paid in three months after delivery and the other moiety at five months after delivery, which is equal to the payment of the whole value in four months, corresponding wherewith if I remit you bills on Paris or Bordeaux I suppose it will be alike agreeable to you as paying said value at London to your order there.

'In consequence hereof and on the French declaration of war against Britain I desire you will immediately order to engage two neutral vessels on freight with brandy, one of which cargoes to be shipped at Cette I desire may consist of a quantity not exceeding two hundred large pieces or thereabouts, the other of said cargoes to be shipped at Bordeaux I desire may consist of a quantity not exceeding two hundred and fifty puncheons, both which cargoes let be purchased and all matters there to relative let be done in the frugalest way and, as a great deal of the success allowing these adventures in speculation depends on the speedy arrival, I desire you will cause all possible dispatch be given to answer my purpose. If either or both the vessels contain less than I have wrote for I would prefer that to their containing more. But I would by no means allow any other person's goods to be shipped on either of said vessels. I design that both cargoes be directed to Douglas to be discharged there. But if it should so happen that it would be more to my advantage to direct either of them thence to proceed here to discharge it would be agreeable to me that you ascertain this ... in your agreement with the shipmasters'. [George Ainslie, 24 December 1755]

There is no information in the letter-book about any subsequent voyages in 1755. However, on 31 May 1757 Moore wrote 'I have been communicating my manner of dealing with you for brandy etc to Messrs John Callin & Co ... Mr Callin and my son are the concerned in this company (see Chapter Fourteen). I showed them your letter of the 30th March 1756 ... my connection with this company introduces recommendation of them to you for experiment, which I am hopeful will lead to mutual advantage'.

According to this letter Ainslie's charges had reduced to 9 per cent from Cette or Barcelona and 7 per cent from Bordeaux or Cognac. 'Messrs Callin & Co propose that you freight and load a neutral vessel at Bordeaux of the burthen of about two hundred puncheons or 80 tons and

that you cause be freighted and loaded at Salloe, which is one of the
shipping ports of Barcelona for brandy, or at any other convenient port in
Catalonia, a neutral vessel of about the burthen of two hundred pipes or
100 tons ... It is proposed that on your receipt hereof you proceed
immediately to freight and load the vessel at Bordeaux and so soon as
that is loaded that you proceed to give directions to freight and purchase
the said cargo in Spain and that you agree for the delivery of both
cargoes in this town or harbour thereof. While you are providing the
Bordeaux cargo it will give room for your writing to Spain to be
informed of the prices of brandy and where best to load there'. [George
Ainslie, 31 May 1757]

The Bordeaux Cargoes

The arrangements for these went comparatively smoothly. Between
December 1757 and February 1759 there were some four deliveries of
brandy on the *Catherine Elizabeth*, Peter John Schutt master, on the
Young Henry, Marius Vanden Linden master and on the *Mary Elizabeth*,
Hoog master. The standard turn round was four months from first letter
about the order to delivery of the cargo on shore. In 1758 Moore was
able to report proudly that as there were no other brandies in town then
his latest cargo from Bordeaux was selling at 2/3 to 2/4 per gallon.

The Salloe Cargoes

Unfortunately the deliveries via Barcelona were not so successful,
possibly because Ainslie was dependent on others for all the
arrangements. The letters about these cargoes take on a repetitive theme.
'Several vessels are loading brandy at Salloe for this Isle for I hear that
upwards of one thousand pieces are engaged besides your commission.
The purchasing is favourable for the price is lowered. On Mr Callin's
return from Scotland, expected in a day or two, I shall communicate the
difficulty you have in procuring a vessel to freight and therefore that you
intend enlarging the quantity for their approbation'. [George Ainslie, 1
October 1757]. 'I observe you have not yet succeeded in freighting a
vessel for the Spanish brandy. I am hopeful your next letter will advise'.
[George Ainslie, 10 December 1757]. 'We are unlucky in your not finding a
vessel to load the brandy'. [2 January 1758]. 'It proves a great
disappointment the delay that has attended the Spanish cargo and is the
more disagreeable as we have accounts that large loads are bought and

shipping at Salloe for this Isle'. [George Ainslie, 11 March 1758]. By the end of the month Moore was informed that a Swedish vessel had been freighted.

As a result, he immediately ordered the next shipment. But the same delays occurred. 'With the two hundred butts of brandy already purchased in Spain I observe you have further directed Messrs Duran Duran to buy two hundred butts more to answer the lading and expedition in case the vessel should be 150 tuns. The delay which this brandy is subjected to my waiting a vessel to freight proves very inconvenient to me as the cargo under your direction was discretionary'. [George Ainslie, 8 September 1758]. And 'I am extremely surprised at the delay which has attended the shipping of the brandy in the Mediterranean. That neutral vessels are to be had to freight is a thing past doubt for three vessels with brandy thence are lately discharged in this Isle. Having no brandy thence is a circumstance attended with peculiar inconvenience to the importations which are made here from your parts as these must suffer from the cheapness of the other'. [George Ainslie, 23 November 1758]

The Peter Berail Affair: A Pretended Voyage

In the meantime Moore was writing to Peter Berail in Cette. 'Your wishes for my welfare are extremely acceptable and meet with a sincere and equal return for your prosperity. My inclination and the season invite me to address you and to desire that on your receipt hereof you proceed to freight a neutral vessel from 100 tuns to 150 tuns burthen or if a few tuns more are required to complete the cargo I admit thereof. So soon as the vessel is engaged and not before I desire you will proceed to purchase brandy sufficient for said cargo, which is to be landed in this town to me or my order. With this brandy I have to desire you will purchase and ship in secure places in the hold two tuns of frontiscet white wine (see Figure 3) and the sundry small articles mentioned underneath. For the value of said cargo and sundry small articles I desire you to draw on Messrs Richard Oswald & Co merchants in London, whom I shall direct to give due honour to your drafts and in due time it is necessary that you acquaint them so as that orders be forwarded them for insurance being made before the vessel sails from Cette, which please observe and write to said Richard Oswald & Co accordingly. The vessel I call neutral is a Dutch, a Danish or a Swedish one … the charter party and all papers relative to the ship and cargo, destination for this town, must not be forwarded by the vessel let them be sent by post. All papers by the vessel, by which I mean a letter from you, a bill of lading and clearances at your custom house and passports, let these be for Bergen in Norway, addressed to Mr Alexander Wallace, merchant there, as if the cargo was his property (see *The Smuggling Story of Two Firths*). I ask care is necessary to be observed concerning the colouring of the destination of the voyage, that it's necessary that the captain of the vessel keeps private from the crew that the cargo is intended to be discharged in this port. If the postage of letters be free from your place to London I desire you to forward your letter to me to the care of Messrs Richard Oswald & Co there. If the postage is indirect let your letters for me be recommended to the care of Messrs Livingston & Symson, merchants in Rotterdam. I rely on your management of this affair in the best and most circumspect manner'. [Peter Berail, 29 March 1758]

The problem was that Berail purchased some of the brandy, charging Moore for it, before he had obtained a vessel. 'I wrote to you from Scotland the 25th last month acknowledging two your drafts on Messrs Richard Oswald & Co London for £230 and am since advised by these gentlemen would you have further drawn on them two drafts for £330. As these bills are on account of the cargo of brandy which I addressed you to purchase and load on a neutral vessel I am waiting your advise of the relative transaction and hope by this time that the lading thereof is anticipated. This I am rather persuaded of as I directed the freighting of the neutral vessel as a circumstance necessarily previous to your purchasing any brandy for the cargo and I expect with your next drafts on said gentlemen that the invoice and bill of lading will be forwarded to them or to me under cover of their letter'. [Peter Berail, 12 August 1758]

'This year has proved unfavourable to my design of brandies. To this design I wrote Mr Peter Berail in Cette and directed his purchasing a cargo and freighting a vessel. On the purchase he made he had drawn about £550 on my friends in London, who write me that he advised them the 8th June that he was hourly in expectation of the vessel he had hired to carry my brandies but Mr Berail has been silent to me and to this day I have no other account'. [George Ainslie, 8 September 1758]

'I am now favoured with your letter of the 3rd August mentioning that you had been disappointed in your expectance of freighting a vessel for the brandy I commissioned you eventually to purchase, which therefore you have withdrawn and have sold fifteen pieces ... From what Messrs Richard Oswald & Co wrote me in consequence of your letter to them advising of your drafts I have been expecting that you were proceeding in the dispatch of the cargo and relying hereon I suspended giving any directions to replace the cargo I had wrote to you for, so that your not being able to succeed herein for me happens to prove a great inconvenience to me. The freight which you mention the Dutch captain demanded was by much too dear to give.

'How to manage to replace this cargo, which my occasions very pressingly require, remains that I gave directions about and have resolved on a cargo of Bordeaux or Cognac brandy and have wrote to Mr George Ainslie, merchant in Bordeaux, on this subject. On this account the money I intended to discharge the value of said cargo must now be applied to reimburse Mr Ainslie the value of the brandy I have wrote to him about and therefore I have to desire that you will remit to Mr Ainslie's order or honour his drafts to the amounts of the drafts which you made on Messrs Richard Oswald & Co ... In your letter to me you mention that your drafts in whole on them were for £340 sterling. In their advice to me they mention a greater sum but I have desired them to write to Mr Ainslie the specific value so that the same may be invested in the cargo which he is to receive as reimbursement from me.

'I observe what you say of your present vintage the prospect is promising and it is to be hoped that the new brandy is to be purchased cheap. The getting of a neutral vessel with you to freight I find is very uncertain and therefore not to be depended on. It hence occurs to me that the buying up any quantity of brandy to wait the freighting whereof is attended with uncertainty is a circumstance that should be avoided, as the lying of the brandy is attended with great charges. Therefore it is that I prefer that the vessel be freighted previous to the purchase of the brandy. In this eligible way I am now looking out for a vessel and in the directions I have given I am in hopes to succeed whereof I shall give you the speediest intimation and in the meantime I suspend your having any reference to my further directions to you about purchasing brandy and refer to what hereafter I shall occasionally write to you. On this opportunity the sundry small articles must wait'. [Peter Berail, 19 September 1758]

The Double Order

On 20 December 1758 Moore wrote to both George Ainslie and to Richard Herries & Co in Barcelona. 'I do not understand how your friends in Barcelona come to write to you that there was no appearance of sending a vessel for this place. A few day ago my son-in-law, Mr Charles Kelly of Douglas, was with me here and telling me that he had just then received an account of some goods being shipped on board a vessel for this Isle lading brandy at Salloe. I have a letter of the 14th October from Messrs Robert Herries & Co in Barcelona, pressingly recommending their services and readiness to load brandy for me. They don't give room to expect any difficulty or delay in procuring a freight ... their words are 'several neutral vessels are arrived and expected here with fish etc not few of their captains we believe will incline to go your way under £3 10s sterling a tun or there abouts' and I am sure that several vessels have been freighted, loaded and discharged in this Isle with brandy from Salloe since you wrote to me that you had sent directions to your friends at Barcelona etc to freight a vessel for me so that I am astonished at the delay which has attended your directions'. [George Ainslie, 20 December 1759]

'Your inclination and manner of circumstances (are) so inviting I cheerfully apply to you for a cargo of brandy, which I desire you will engage the freight and order for my account. The vessel most suitable for this harbour is one with a small draft of water. Therefore a small vessel is to be preferred. If such you can meet with, by which I mean a vessel of 100 tuns burthen ... but I would not have you herein limited for I shall be satisfied with a vessel of 100 tuns with about three hundred pipes of brandy and, as I incline that no other brandy be shipped on this vessel (see John Allan in Chapter Sixteen) but for my account, if a few pipes more of brandy are wanted to complete the cargo let these be also added. The vessel to be freighted must be a neutral one with directions that if visited by a French ship of war that they declare as if bound for a neutral port or if visited by any English ship that they declare their real destination for this port, where the cargo is to be delivered. This appears to me a necessary caution but I refer to you to alter or direct as you think convenient or necessary in this particular and that the papers which you send by the vessel correspond'. [Richard Herries & Co, 20 December 1758]

'I am become engaged in another cargo of brandy with Herries & Co of Barcelona, which your letter of the 2nd December, had it been in time would have prevented'. [George Ainslie, 2 February 1759]. As one ship was en route, the only hope was to stop the other one. 'Some circumstances have since occurred which render it convenient to have said cargo postponed for some time. If this letter comes to your hand before you have concluded the agreement for freight, I desire you may defer this agreement and the subsequent purchase of brandy .... which in due time I shall acquaint you and renew the relative direction'. [Richard Herries & Co, 15 February 1759]

The *Ceres*
'I observe that the *Ceres*, Jurgen Andriesson master, has sailed from Salloe. I am every day expecting the arrival of this vessel ... I have received an exceeding good character of the gentlemen at Barcelona who you employed about said brandy and however I have complained of the delay which attended the loading thereof it's probable that it could not be prevented for I apprehend on arrival of the neutral vessels the English factors settled at Barcelona, being in opposite interests, circumvent and exert themselves to obtain a preference to freight'. [George Ainslie, 1 March 1759]

There was a good reason for the *Ceres*'s non-arrival. 'On the 9th inst was driven ashore about three miles from hence the *Ceres* snow, Captain Jurgen Andriesson master, from Salloe laden with two hundred and ninety-three pipes and twenty hogsheads brandy consigned to you by Don Domingo ye Geromiono Duran of Barcelona and for his account and risk as per bill of lading. The vessel is so terribly bilged that I have been obliged to land the cargo, having first had a proper survey by two captains and two ship builders ... the quantity saved is three hundred casks, notwithstanding the opposition of the country (people), which are generally very barbarous on these occasions. They are all put into a safe cellar and locked up with His Majesty's (Customs) and my keys. As the expense will be pretty large, I shall be glad to know how I am to act on this occasion and beg you will manage accordingly ... The captain is at present ill of a fever but it's hoped he will recover and also that we shall, wind and weather permitting, get the ship off again and put her in her former plight. I shall be glad of an answer by return of post'. [Richard Hall, Falmouth, to George Moore, 19 March 1759]

'By the last opportunity from Liverpool I have received your letter of the 19th ult confirming the account of the accident which has happened to the Ceres (he had also heard from a Thomas Moore in Falmouth, via Philip Moore & Sons in Douglas) ... I am obliged to the assistance you have given for preservation of the ship and cargo and doubt not but that you will continue to manage on this occasion for the benefit of all concerned in the best and frugalest manner where the circumstances of the accident and distress claim your favour. I shall herewith write a letter to Messrs Knox Craghead & Co merchants in London to represent the property of the cargo and in consequence thereof that they may reimburse the relative charges and occasionally correspond with you for the further preservation of the interests concerned until delivery of the cargo here ... so that in respect of any relative matter you'll please apply to and correspond with them'. [Richard Hall, 16 April 1759]

'I am very sorry an accident of this kind should have happened so near home but it remains that the best be done for preservation of whatever part of the cargo is landed and that this part, if allowed by the government to be reshipped to be landed here according to the original destination. For this purpose I write to you and to desire on behalf of Mr Ainslie that everything relative be under your direction and that you will take such measures as will be suitable to the occasion for the benefit of Mr Ainslie and the insurers'. [Knox Craghead & Co, 4 April 1759]

But according to their original agreement (see letter dated 24 December 1755) the brandy still belonged to Ainslie. 'This cargo of Spanish brandy gave rise to the last cargo of Bordeaux brandy which I wrote to you for and from blending the different pieces was the means whereby at any time I could propose benefit by the Bordeaux cargo. I may follow the example and relinquish the Bordeaux cargo by which means the produce of both cargoes will remain for your account which you are very welcome to or if you please may be for our joint account'. [George Ainslie, 6 June 1759]

Despite this Moore obviously expected that Ainslie would treat the brandy as his. 'I observe that you have wrote to Mr Richard Hall in Falmouth to use all diligence about the brandy by the *Ceres* in order that the vessel is enabled to proceed therewith to this port and discharge the same ... by what you mention I am in daily expectation of the arrival of this vessel which, how soon it happens, I shall acquaint you'. [Knox Craghead & Co, 26 May 1759]. The *Ceres* had still not arrived at Peel by 2 March 1760.

The Daniel & Nicholas

Robert Herries & Co wrote to Moore on 27 January, 10 February and 3 March that they were freighting the *Daniel & Nicholas*. She sailed from Salloe on 13 April 1759.

On 4 June 1759 Moore wrote to John Quayle, the comptroller of customs at Castletown (see Chapters Fourteen and Fifteen). 'The *Daniel & Nicholas* from Barcelona, Junis Engwers master, is just now arrived in the bay here on my account. Please send me an entry by the bearer for the cargo, being viz

three hundred and ninety-five casks containing one hundred tons brandy
ten casks containing sixteen hogsheads white wine
one box containing one hundred and twenty handkerchiefs

to be regulated as the manner whereby you do with others.

'I have for my wife on board said vessel:

one wax cloth parcel containing two silk gowns and six pairs of shapes for shoes, one case containing twelve bottles oil, six pots olives, two pots honey, two barrels anchovy

which I desire you will admit unentered and give order for as usual, no part of them being intended for sale. I have enclosed the invoice of the handkerchiefs, which you'll please mark and return me to be regulated as is necessary at meeting'.

Now all that Moore needed to do was recover from the financial problem of having to pay for two instead of one cargo.

Peter Berail was still hoping to renew the correspondence with Moore. But 'All vessels with French commodities on board for this Isle will surely be brought into port if visited on their passage by any British ship of war or letter of mark and if brought into port will be condemned, as all trade with France is prohibited. It follows that henceforth no directions for brandy to be purchased in any part of France can be attended with the appearance of safety. At least the common method is thus unsecure and I cannot yet make myself acquainted with a method whereby I have any hopes to succeed so that for the present I must suspend any favourite design of having brandy from Cette'. [Peter Berail, 14 November 1758]

The last letter to Berail states 'I observe that the price of brandy is very considerably risen with you but the difficulty and hazard to which all commerce with you is become subjected must, much against my inclination, deprive me of the pleasure of corresponding with you in the manner suitable to my occasions and this must therefore be postponed until the appearances of danger be removed. I return you many thanks for your readiness to oblige me which I shall always retain a grateful sense of '. [Peter Berail, 14 February 1759]

There is further information about Moore dealing in spirits in the next chapter.

THE STORY OF PAT WHITE, BENICARLO

'You will herewith receive a letter from my friend Mr William Snell in London acquainting you of my interest in two vessels that sailed some time ago to New England in order to load fish for the Straights. I expect their arrival will be early in the season ... I've directed said vessels to touch at Alicante, where if the market be inviting their cargo will be disposed of under direction of Mr John Blundell, merchant there, and the produce of the *Peggy*'s cargo I have desired be given Captain Pat Montgomerie in specie or, which I prefer, in bills on Madrid answerable to my directions of loading her with brandy under your address. In case the *Peggy*'s cargo is not disposed of at Alicante, I have directed Mr Pat Montgomerie to call at Benicarlo to be under your ... direction as to the sale thereof, which accordingly please attend to by disposing thereof with you, if the market be favourable, or directing the captain to proceed to whatever market you judge most fitting ... It is uncertain when the *Peggy* may arrive but as it cannot be expected before your ensuing vintage is over it will answer with my design of loading her with brandy, which in due time let be provided, namely forty pipes of double proof brandy and the remainder of single proof brandy ... You will please apply the produce of the cargo of the fish by the *Peggy* towards the purchase of said cargo brandy and what may be wanting for your reimbursement for this remainder please draw for two-thirds thereof on Mr William Snell in London for my account and for the other third part of said remainder draw in Messrs Claud Johnson & Son, merchants in London, for account of Messrs John Kelly & John Callin, where your bills will accordingly meet with due honour. The *Lilly*, Robert Montgomerie commander, is occasionally to touch at your port to serve the sale of the cargo fish wherein if you assist or can promote you will oblige me. The produce of the *Lilly*'s cargo is to be applied towards a cargo of brandy to be loaded at Cette under the care of Mr Peter Berail. I have confidence in your favourable transactions for me'. [1 July 1751]

'The vintage I hear with you is very promising this season so that I hope the purchase of the cargo of brandy intended by the *Peggy* will prove favourable ... They advise that a discretionary power be given to Captain Pat Montgomerie in the sale of the cargo of fish as well as the places where to load the cargo of brandy ... that the voyage may be conducted in the best way ... I have to desire the favour of you on your receipt hereof to write a letter to Pat Montgomerie and forward to the care of Mr John Blundell ... wherein write him what you can dispose of his fish for and the price of brandy clear on board you can furnish the cargo before mentioned to be shipped on the *Peggy* ...

'PS Should Mr Robert Montgomerie of the *Lilly* judge it useful to load his vessel ... under your address I give him a discretionary power to desire you may accordingly purchase and ship the same, in which case his cargo is to consist of thirty pipes double proof brandy and the remainder of the cargo to be single proof brandy. Let no casks be less than 50 gallons ... On your receipt hereof write to Robert Montgomerie the value of fish and the value of brandy per pipe clear on board with you for his government, forwarding the same to the care of Mr John Blundell'. [15 August 1751].

'I declined giving orders for the purchase of either their cargoes until their arrival at Alicante, where I directed they might give the speediest advices of to the gentlemen in whatever place they or either of them intended to load brandy, to the end the cargoes might be purchasing immediately following such advice. I have a particular liking to the Valencia brandy, which will influence one or both of said masters to apply to you, and I prefer having the purchase under your management and address ... The taste of the brandy is what I prize. Its having an amber colour is to me a matter quite indifferent so that having good colour is sufficient for my purpose'. [14 October 1751]. And 'I cannot add more ... than in my letter of the 14th October'. [22 November 1751]

Both the Montgomeries loaded their brandy with Green & Stanton in Barcelona 'which by your repetition I find proved a great disappointment to you and by your manner relying on the sales of the fish and which probably you had engaged. It is very likely the fish was sold much cheaper than you would have transacted so that I have thereby been a considerable sufferer. On my setting out on these adventures I think I gave you early intimation thereof and from the correspondence I had begun with you I was very well inclined that the same was to continue in any instance or occasions. To both the same time I gave them a discretionary power of proceeding in what part they received advice would be most for my interest as to the fish and as to the brandy ... on ... the advice they received from you and others on the coast they were herein to be determined and if in these respects your letters to them were not so inviting as those they received from the other parts on the coast of Spain they did as to them seemed for my interest so that I have no room to fix blame to their conduct'. [21 November 1752]

CHAPTER THREE: THE RUM TRADE

'It is the general complaint with gentlemen who deal in the import of rum that they lose by it and in some respects that I've been concerned in I join in the same opinion. Notwithstanding rum is imported and the importer continues to sell'. [Alexander Porterfield, 12 October 1751]

George Moore certainly experienced several difficulties over his rum importations. These came mainly from the West Indies but also from New England. The *Peggy* collected rum from Barbados on her maiden voyage (see Chapter Seven) while the *Lilly* took provisions to exchange for rum in the West Indies on two occasions and in New England once (see Chapter Eight). Moore was involved in several joint ventures, including the *Grizzy* and the *Kingston*. At one stage he stopped importing rum direct, deciding to be supplied by whatever was imported by others either to Glasgow or Dublin or directly to the Isle of Man. But even this could cause problems, as did his attempts to sell rum on behalf of others.

Problems with Price of Rum

The source of the rum, its availability, either in the West Indies or on the Isle of Man, and the relative situation with brandy all affected the price.

The Sources of Rum

Jamaica rum was believed to be superior. '(I) have directed my cooper to lay aside for you a dozen bottles of Jamaica rum, the same that I have for my own use, to be forwarded to you as opportunity to Liverpool from this offer'. [Robert Kennish, 14 April 1759]. But the majority of the imports came from Barbados, St Eustatius or Antigua. 'St Croix rum we think not inferior to St Christophers, the quality whereof has much declined within these few years or with proximity with St Eustatius has given occasion to think so'. [Richard Oswald 26 October 1757]

The difference between the quality of these rums becomes apparent in Moore's concern about the exact origin of any rum that he was offered on the Island. 'I met a young gentleman of your city, McGregor, stepping on board to return home. It was a short time to strike a bargain for 4 or 5, 000 gallons of rum, which I did on his telling me it was good Barbados. The price was 2/4 per gallon, 150 guineas in hand and the other half at six months. He went off and when I came to examine the rum it is very bad, not merchantable Barbados rum. Indeed I suspect it from some other island'. [Thomas Finlay & Robert Patrick, 1 October 1754]. Moore was more explicit in his letter to McGregor. 'You may remember that when you treated with me to purchase your rum you told me it was good Barbados, by which I understood it was of the growth and produce of Barbados and of a suitable quality. In faith of what you told me I immediately concluded an agreement. But on examining the rum I can by no means satisfy myself that it is Barbados rum as it is deficient in every of the known qualities of Barbados rum. Of the parcel there are a few puncheons tolerably merchantable, of which ... were the two tasted with you. So that I am disappointed in my bargain by confiding more than was meet. Between 4 and 5,000 gallons of good Barbados rum was what I bought from you ... (what is) lodged is 4,752 gallons of a quality so inferior to Barbados rum'. [John McGregor, 1 October 1754]

'New England rum is constantly dropping in and affects the price of good rum, otherways by this time the price of good rum would have considerably advanced'. And 'New England rum is become a ... drug or uncalculable commodity. Two cargoes were this season landed at Douglas but no buyers. They are under the necessity of being cellared. Another cargo was everywhere offered at 20d per gallon unsuccessfully so this was brought off the Isle to some other market ... A small parcel from Boston was lately landed in this town also cellared so that I cannot think it would be in Mr Logan's or your interest to attempt the market'. [William Rowan, Dublin, 8 October 1750]

From time to time Moore looked for alternative sources of rum. In 1752 he considered the possibility of importing French rum from John Stedman in Rotterdam. 'Pray what colour is the French rum and what kind of casks? What else you know of the quality advise me'. [28 July 1752]. He was also in contact with Stuckey & Co. But 'I see no encouragement of your French rum so that I decline having any speculation therein'. [Andrew Stuckey & Co, 20 February 1754]

John Mowat appears in Chapter Four. 'I observe you have rum from your brother, who is settled at Rio Esquebo, whose rum is made in quality preferable to that at Antigua or Barbados, and promise on my offer of purchasing, if encouraging, to order your brother to send me one hundred puncheons against September. At this distance in point of time it is hard to say what price rum will be in September so that making any offer might be inconvenient to me. But if you please to let me know the lowest price you will lay down here ... if the price be agreeable and the quality answerable to your description I shall agree or perhaps you may encourage my sending out a vessel to load rum under the address of your brother and in this light I would be glad to know the state of the market there. I take Rio Esquebo to be adjoining Asia, part of Tura Surinam. Is sugar planted there or have they the molasses from the Caribee Islands? Is there any of the produce of Great Britain or Ireland that you would advise to send out in order with the produce to buy rum?' [John Mowat, 24 April 1753].

On 12 August 1753 John Mowat reported on a cargo of the rum that he had received. 'The quality proves good, not inferior to Jamaica ... but the place of delivery differs. Formerly I apprehended you would deliver me the rum in this town and now you propose it deliverable at Campvere'. [John Mowat, 5 September 1753]

Availability in the West Indies
'The shortness of crops at Barbados and the Leeward Islands the last season has not yet affected the price of rum here, which rather depends on the quantities imported'. [John Rowe, 14 August 1754]. There is insufficient evidence to show what effect if any this had on the prices in 1755.

Rum Scarcity on the Isle of Man
'There has not been for some years so great a scarcity of rum in this Isle as now. However, the market does not bear 3s English per gallon at the mast for there is a small cargo belonging to Liverpool within these few days arrived at Douglas for which the above price is

demanded, ready money. But as there appears no purchasers, it's said the vessel with rum will proceed directly to Dublin'. [Thomas Finlay & Robert Patrick, 8 February 1752]. 'Rum is also so scarce here and we rely on some of the Leeward Island fleet for a supply'. [Haliday & Dunbar, 25 September 1758]

Rum Glut on the Isle of Man

'There have been two or three parcels of rum landed from your Island (St Eustatius) insomuch that our market is become quite overstocked with that kind of rum and hence the importers being unable to sell have been obliged to cellar their rum, which in my mind will be more than sufficient to answer the demand of the next season, which begins in September, and with a very uncertain prospect of the sales turning to a tolerable account this must effect any design I have of having rum from your Island this season and quite discouraging it ... I suppose your market is generally glutted with provisions so that no encouragement can arise from dealing in that article'. [Ralph Sampson, 7 March 1753]

Competition with Brandy

'The value of rum here bears some kind of proportion to brandy so that if brandy be low and a moderate quantity of rum imported the rum will not be bought if not in a proportionate way of sale with brandy. We have just now had a large shipment of brandy so that Spanish is selling for 20d per gallon and French for 22d. There is no rum now at market. If there were it would not now exceed 2/2'. [Richard Oswald 26 October 1757]

Rum by the *Peggy* and the *Lilly*: Richard Smith & Co, Barbados
The *Peggy*

Moore planned to import rum from Barbados on the *Peggy*'s maiden voyage from Boston. For this he turned to Richard Smith & Co, who had been introduced to him by Richard Smith in London. In a letter dated 8 November 1749 Moore instructed that most of his share of the cargo of rum (one hundred and fifty hogsheads) should be purchased in March, when the prices were lowest (at approximately 1/8 per gallon) and that the remainder (up to forty hogsheads) should be purchased when the vessel arrived.

The problem which developed is explained in a letter to Richard Smith in London, dated 6 November 1750. 'I have now received your favour of the 11th ult covering one the 6th August from your house at Barbados with advice of their determining to load the *Peggy* with rum ... which they expected to conclude at 2/4 per gallon ... I'm now come to that time wherein I'm certain that my interest in the rum does not answer my expectance or intentions and in whatever degree I'm herein disappointed I esteem it a reason of complaint so have equal hopes of being herein indemnified ...

'Preceding this time I cannot forget that our correspondence was begun on your assurance, which you repeated, that I might depend on having my commands of all kinds punctually complied with. In your answer to my November letter you were pleased to mention 'I have in the strongest terms recommended my partners to do everything to please so valuable a correspondent and I make not the least doubt of their exact compliance' ... My reason for writing in said manner arose from the experience I have had as to the precariousness of the price of rum at Barbados ... I have always held it a rule that it is not in my power to debit any account but with the person's consent to whom the charge is made ... I directed a partial purchase to be made in or before March last and the remainder of said purchase to be made on the vessel's arrival. For said purchases in March and on the vessel's arrival my account was by you accordingly to be debited. This describes the specific times when my account was to be debited and any variation herein made without my consent that tends or proves to my prejudice so far and in this instance I have reason of complaint and hence are my hopes of receiving restitution or indemnification ...

'Permit me to make use of a parallel instance wherein I pray how would you be determined. On the opposite side of this Isle we have a herring fishery, some seasons in a considerable degree. Supposing I heard that you wanted or dealt in herrings and making use of the prospect and other circumstances that I invited and encouraged your dealing this way, promising you in this case that my agent at Douglas should faithfully execute your orders. In consequence of this you addressed me and my agent at Douglas, before the season comes on, to engage and contract for a certain quantity or number of barrels in the month or season when the herrings are cheapest to buy the quantity. At the same time you tell me you have freighted a vessel that about a certain time will arrive at Douglas to receive said quantity, at which time should the vessel be able to carry a few barrels more, you desire that this remainder may be also purchased for your account at the then current price. Your letter to this purpose I admit I have received and that I return you answer your directions herein shall meet with the most exact compliance, making you my acknowledgments for this your act of confidence in me. Following this, on your behalf, I make proposals of contracting for your herrings but no one will engage. The season of fish too comes on and the month wherein there is the greatest plenty of fish to be had at a moderate price. This month or season of purchasing is delayed and no fish is bought for your account. Following this your vessel for the herrings arrives at a time that the price is advanced 70 or 80 per cent and at this advanced price I purchase and ship the vessel full lading for your account, said price becoming so considerable that at the destined market for them you must be a certain loser. Would not the circumstances of such a bargain incline you to let the herrings remain to my own account or to expect to be indemnified in a loss consequent or so unexpected a manner of purchasing?

'You will hence see my cause of complaint and hence my motive in this rum affair, wherein I'm content with the part which has been purchased under my direction, about forty hogsheads. The one hundred and twenty-five hogsheads which should have been bought in March I'm content to take them at the current price in March, which did not exceed 20d per gallon, or I'm content the difference be submitted to two merchants in the usual way to arbitrate herein and have desired Mr William Snell relatively to act in my behalf to the end a conclusion may be herein made in the speediest and most friendly way, which I flatter myself will contribute to and to remove any other arise or arising cause of complaint.'

Moore's concern was partially assuaged. 'They will make me restitution if the cause of my complaint be well grounded or if I have an equitable right. Mr Smith also takes notice in his letter of the charges incident on rum being purchased at Barbados in March to lie till August would be nigh equal to the difference between 20d and 2/4 per gallon.

This difference computed on one hundred and twenty-five hogsheads would be about £430, which in the case of having rum bought before the arrival I should be inclined to think a very extraordinary charge'. [William Snell 3 December 1750]

As a result 'I delayed answering (his letter dated 12 October 1751) until it would be convenient to me to write to your house in Barbados for rum. Proceeding from your inclination that I continue my corresponding and in respect of the former affair relying on your opinion they'll join you in making a consideration that may be pleasing to me my letter to your house is enclosed.' [Richard Smith, London, 30 December 1751]

The *Lilly*

'On your receipt hereof or in March next when the price of new rum is first struck I desire you will buy for my account two hundred hogsheads. The vessel I intend said rum to be shipped on board will not be in Barbados till May or June ... By this you will see that I have no other design in view than to purchase at the first price, which I have experienced at your market to be the cheapest. The storage and expense attending said rum from its purchase to its shipping you will debit me. I refer you to transact herein in the frugalest way for my account'. [Richard Smith & Co, Barbados, 30 December 1751]. The reason for this was because 'in May I apprehend the demand for rum is greatest and consequently the price must be at the highest, which is what I would avoid'. [Richard Smith, London, 27 January 1752]

All seemed to be going well. 'There is a great prospect of a good crop and rum may be procured earlier than usual. I am hence inclined to believe that by this time you have succeeded in purchasing'. [Richard Smith & Co, Barbados, 27 January 1752]. Robert Montgomerie had gone to Cork 'to take in some new butter, of the best sort made there, with a small quantity of other provisions, which I'm hopeful may come to a good market and answer my design. In the sale of said butter and provisions, I have directed that he apply to you, as the most favourable means whereby my interest therein can be served. The produce I expect you will apply to my credit and by so much lessen your drawing on Messrs William Snell & Co in London'. [Richard Smith & Co, 11 April 1752]

47

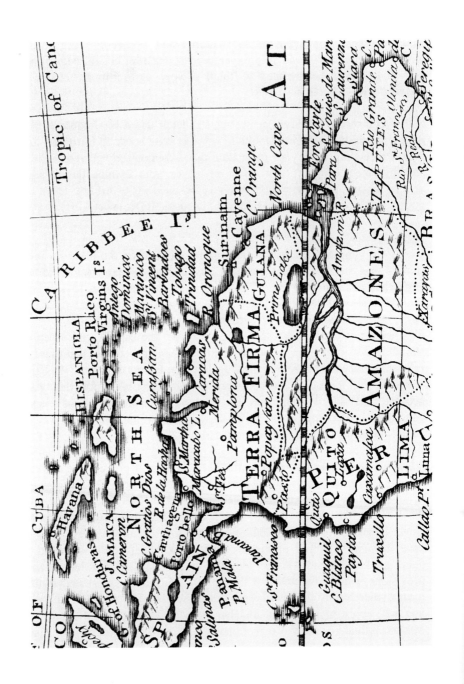

48

Figure 4: The West Indies

This information comes from 'A New Geographical Grammar: containing a comprehensive system of modern geography after a new and curious method' by Charles Vyse, 1779.

He lists the West Indian islands belonging to different European countries: **English**: Jamaica, Barbados, St Christophers (also known as St Kitts), Antigua, Nevis, Montserat, Barbuda, Anguilla, St Lucia, Dominica, St Vincent, Grenada, the Grenadines, Tobago; **Spanish**: Cuba, Hispaniola (or St Domingo), Porto Rico, Virgin Is, Trinidad, Margueretta, Juan Fernandes; **French**: greatest part of Hispaniola (or St Domingo), Martinico, Guadeloupe, St Bartholomew, Defeeda, Marigalante; **Dutch**: St Eustatius, Crueffon, Bonaire, Aruba, Saba and St Martins; **Danish**: St Thomas & St Croix

He then describes how long Barbados had been an English possession. 'Ever since the year 1625. When they first landed on the island there was not the least vestige of its having been inhabited, even by savages. There was no kind of beast, either of pasture or of prey. No fruit, no herb, no root proper for the subsistence of human life. The island was one continuous forest, the trees so large, and their wood so hard and stubborn, that the utmost labour was necessary to clear the ground. Some gentlemen of small fortune in England, by unremitted perseverance, however, surmounted every difficulty, and rendered the island a noble acquisition to their country'.

Finally he comments on hurricanes. 'They are indeed too common, as they often destroy in a moment the assiduous labour of many years, the hopes of the planter are wrested from him sometimes at the very moment when he thinks himself beyond the reach of fortune ... It is a violent gust of wind, rain, thunder and lightening, attended with a dreadful swelling of the sea, and sometimes with an earthquake; in a word, with every terrible and destructive circumstance the elements can assemble. As a prelude to the approaching havoc, the astonished planter sees who fields of sugar canes whirled into the air, and scattered over the face of the adjacent country. The strongest trees of the forest are torn up by the roots, and driven about like stubble; the windmills are swept away in a moment; their utensils, their fixtures, the ponderous copper boilers, and stills of several hundredweight are wrenched from the ground and battered to prices; their houses are no protection, the roofs are torn off with the first blast, while the rain rushes in upon them with a violence almost irresistible'.

On 10th March and 8th April 1752 Smith & Co in Barbados reported that they had purchased the two hundred hogsheads at 2s per gallon. 'I'm pleased with as I'm satisfied it has been little lower this season with you. Messrs Snell & Co ... advise me you have drawn on this account on them £1,800 they have accepted'. [Richard Smith & Co, Barbados, 25 July 1752]. In fact one hundred and ninety hogsheads, eighteen tierces and twenty casks of rum were shipped on board. 'Considering the circumstances of the *Lilly*'s arrival with you I was in hopes to have met a much better market for the butter'. [Richard Smith & Co, Barbados, 20 September 1752]

Then the problem started. 'When the Lilly left Barbados your friends had not quite finished the sales of the provisions from Cork but they expected doing so in a short time'. [Richard Smith, London, 23 November 1752]. 'I observe you have indulged the purchaser of the butter as he complained of his bargain. The price, namely 7d per lb, I believe is more than other cargoes since reached but considering the *Lilly*'s arrival was with the first new butter from Cork it cannot be thought a high price and had the *Lilly* proceeded to the Leeward Islands I apprehend it would have proved considerably to my advantage'. [Richard Smith & Co, Barbados, 7 March 1753]. 'The last letter I have received from your house in Barbados was dated the 10th January last .... but they make not the least mention of the account sales of the provisions the former voyage ... nor have I yet received my account current relative to that voyage. Why they thus long protract the settlement of that transaction, I dare say were the case yours you would think very disagreeable and were you concerned in new butter ... first arriving at the market in Barbados and selling as mine did there you would not esteem the price higher than the adventure merited or equal to countenance so extraordinary a delay. My occasions for the proceeds require my desiring you to give me leave to draw on you for what sum I compute due more or less to be accounted for'. [Richard Smith, London, 23 July 1753]

'I observe that Messrs Richard Smith & Co in Barbados have remitted you £228 18s 5d on my account. I'm amazed that these gentlemen use so retentive a facility in their dealings or that this long they have delayed to remit. But why they have not been pleased to advise me of this remittance and at same time transmitted me the accounts sales and my account current I have so repeatedly requested remains with me still some matter of surprise. A stagnation in business is always the consequence of people's differing in opinion in matters of mutual right or property'. [William Snell & Co, 4 December 1753]. 'Probably the closing of this account is owing to the gentlemen whom you have sent from your own counting house as assistants'. [Richard Smith, London, 20 February 1754].

'One of the partners Richard Smith & Co have been inviting me to renew my correspondence with them but circumstances are not favourable'. [William Snell & Co, 20 February 1754]. There is no further correspondence with the Smiths.

The *Grizzy*

This voyage became the subject of a major dispute with William Snell & Co in London (see Chapter Six). What happened to the vessel and her cargo of rum is described here. 'This winter I was one half concerned in a cargo of rum and other goods taken in at St Christophers and St Eustatius on a Scotch vessel named the *Grizzy*, John Ewing commander, who had also the direction for purchasing the cargo in said Islands. Ewing was very expeditious for he knew what benefit to the owners his expedition would prove. But unfortunately for the concerned on his return homewards ... with a fair brisk gale of wind 150 leagues to the westward of Ireland he struck on what in his protest he calls a rock. Be it rock or fish, he instantly with the next sea sailed over it. The effects of the stroke were instantly the vessel springing a leak and in less than half an hour there were five foot of water in the hold. But notwithstanding both pumps the water increased to seven foot. Then despairing of their lives the topmast and yards were cut away to keep by the vessel as long as possible from oversetting. The crew had the boat in readiness. Longer they could not stay with the vessel so betook themselves to the boat and the mercy of the seas and they were almost famished when providentially they were taken up by a vessel bound to Cork, where they landed the latter end of January last'. [Edward Kean, 21 March 1752]. 'After the accident ... the *Grizzy* ... floated to the Irish coast and was seen by some boat men, who towed her into a place called Schull. Some of the cargo of rum was on board. To satisfy the salvers and prevent the plunder of the country people the vessel and what was found on board has been disposed of under authority of the admiral'. [William Snell & Co, 15 April 1752]

'It remains that diligence be used for preservation of the ship and cargo. For this purpose I have wrote to Messrs Thomas Finlay and Robert Patrick to personate the interest of the cargo and do in every respect therein as were the care their own. Yet their applications may be aided and receive considerable weight from your influence. If you would desire a letter of recommendation from your neighbour, the speaker ... under such address our interest may be preserved or compassionated by the gentleman to whose lot or care it has happened'. [Edward Kean, 21 March 1752]. 'I received your favour the 22nd ult with the names of your friends in Cork to whom you had wrote that you had recommended them to me that I may mutually rely upon them in any instance I may have occasion to apply to them. I have to desire the favour of your assistance in a case of peculiar nature ... I'm not certain of the name of the port wherein the snow has been conducted but I apprehend it is in Cob Tonson, collector of Skibbereen, his district. As it may be expected he's now in Dublin a certain account from him may be received I have herewith sent you a copy of the master's protest'. [Thomas Finlay & Robert Patrick, 21 March 1752]

'I'm obliged to Mr Kean who has used his interest with the speaker to have the affair recommended to such as can be thought of any service. The accounts I've received of what is preserved of the cargo seems to differ. Should it promise any degree considerable the more friends the less hazard of abuse and I am well pleased your friend Mr Piersy is intimately acquainted with the BP of Cork as well as with the speaker. By a vessel just now arrived in our bay from Cork it is said that the *Grizzy* and cargo sold for about £800, that Ewing was left Cork and gone to Schull to make enquiries into the manner of the vessel's being brought there and the condition of the cargo. But for certainty herein or what success he has met with I must wait other accounts'. [Thomas Finlay & Robert Patrick, 11 April 1752]

Despite all this assistance 'The *Grizzy*'s affair I see yet remains unadjusted and by the delay which has already attended it may continue so for some time longer'. [James & George Piersy, 21 July 1753]. 'I see you are near the close of the accounts respecting the ship *Grizzy* and cargo and that a small pittance of the produce will remain to the proprietors. It is doubtless the commissioners' business to adhere to the collection of duties but to authorise a charge inconsistent with mutual justice ... I'm very much concerned for the trouble you have taken in this unfortunate affair'. [James & George Piersy, 15 October 1753]

At last, on 7 February 1755, the Piersys sent an abstract of the *Grizzy*'s account 'by which I see that the produce of the ship and cargo amounts to no more than £137 8s 3d, which the concerned must be content with. At same time I'm satisfied that you have done the utmost to favour their interest for which I'm obliged to you and thank you for declining any charge for your trouble'.

There were two outstanding problems. 'In Mr Finlay and Patrick's charge of £7 12s 3d there are five guineas they direct as a reward for their trouble. I make no kind of doubt but this reward they deserve or they would not direct its being charged. However from the situation and circumstances of this affair, where the utmost moderation was in some measure necessary to be contributed, from these considerations it is probable that the concerned had hopes of their waving a demand of this kind'. [James & George Piersy, 22 March 1755]

More concerning was John Ewing's viewpoint. His 'expectation that the whole produce is to be given him is something extraordinary but he cannot forget the recovery of the vessel and ascertaining his property in her was the sole and only motive that made him an adventurer to attempt it and for that purpose go to Cork ... As the recovery of the vessel was spur to his expedition I observe you have already paid him some money on this account, wherewith I am satisfied as you have allowed it off the produce of the ship and cargo'. [James & George Piersy, 22 March 1755]

'Your favour of the 15th August I duly received to advise that Captain Ewing is perpetually tiring you on the *Grizzy*'s affairs. To this purpose I had also a letter from Ewing in July last. But he was then setting out on a voyage, which he did without my having the opportunity of seeing him. I've this day wrote to his uncle, Mr Pat Ewing, who I think is the directing person on this occasion, mentioning your letter and his nephew's. I expect that as I have wrote very particularly on this subject it will influence his consent that you proceed to adjust the produce in proportions ... If this fails I shall in proper time acquaint you of my opinion how further to proceed'. [James & George Piersy, 9 October 1755]

Moore tried to explain the situation to Pat Ewing. 'The vessel by an unforeseen accident far distant from land met an accident that obliged the whole crew to abandon her and her cargo to the mercy of the sea and in that hopeless condition to betake themselves and trust to their small boat for the preservation of their lives. By the act of abandoning the vessel and the cargo the connection for the voyage became dissolved. No longer were either to be esteemed mutually bound as under the original destination until the safe delivery at the appointed port that tie became broken and in consequence thereof the dissolution separated the crew and the legal or equitable right that they or any of them as servants of the adventure had or could claim for wages. By their thus abandoning the vessel their right ceased and left not the shadow of a demand for wages or restitution. They by an act of providence were conducted safely to land and by an act of the same kind providence the abandoned wreck after several days floating in the waters was appointed to be drove on the western coast of Ireland and by the assistance of the inhabitants there to be conducted to a place of safety, where the remains of the vessel and the cargo was allowed to remain subject to the application of the different owners and their proof of their distinct property. This I take is a true narrative and I submit it to your consideration in your nephew's absence to the end that joining your own opinion to the opinion of his father and other his friends an unsatisfactory delay may not attend the application of the proceeds of said remains of the cargo of rum, which Messrs James and George Piersy write me they cannot apply as I have directed these are their words to me 'Captain Ewing ... insists on all and he seems to think you will assent to it but be that as it may he says he has a right by law to the whole from us and he has sent a power of attorney here to another to relieve from us the amounts of all'. [Pat Ewing, 9 October 1755]

As both these letters dated 9 October 1755 are crossed out in the letter-book and as there is no further correspondence on the subject, the end of this affair is not known.

The *Kingston*

Moore had a third interest in the freight of the *Kingston* brig, Captain Archibald Williamson master, to Barbados. The outward cargo was some herrings and other commodities to be sold at Madeira and proceeds invested in a cargo of rum. This was based on an agreement with Robert Arthur in Crawfordsdyke to transact the business of the outward and homeward cargo, inclusive of 5%. 'I hope this beginning may serve to introduce a correspondence that may prove to our mutual satisfaction'. [Hugh Clarkson, Barbados, 26 December 1758]

'As Mr Callin tells me it is necessary I have here enclosed two bills: £85 4s 10d, my draft on William Laing and Thomas Orr 23rd January at 14 days sight and £130 my draft on Alexander Morson, Glasgow at 10 days sight (£215 4s 10d) on account of my third part of the outward cargo per the *Kingston*. Equal to my interest therein I wrote to you to write to Messrs Richard Oswald & Co in London to insure for me. Hereon I rely. The condition of agreement I have made with Mr Callin for the freight of the *Kingston* is 7d per gallon of rum per invoice delivered here'. [Robert Arthur, 30 January 1759]

The next stage in the voyage is described in the Irvine custom house letter-books. 'Robert Arthur, merchant at Crawfordsdyke, upon 25 August 1757 did register at Irvine a square-sterned brigantine called the *Kingston* of 20 tons (built in New England in 1754) whereof James Ryburn was master and that Robert Arthur then obtained a certificate of that registration. This day Arthur went to the custom house to report that the vessel was lately taken at sea outward bound from Greenock, the master and some of the mariners being put on board the privateer, who took the vessel, and fourteen French mariners put on board in lieu of them to navigate the vessel and carry away their prize. But was afterwards taken and carried into Plymouth, where she now lies and is there to be fitted out for the West Indies.' [9 April 1759]

The Moore version of the event comes from three letters to Messrs Richard Oswald & Co. 'Mr John Callin of this place has received a letter from Hugh Paterson in Irvine of the 4th instant wherein are these words: 'No doubt you'll have heard of the misfortune of the *Kingston* being taken and retaken and carried into Plymouth, Captain Williamson and

Ryburn being both carried aboard the French privateer. Mr Arthur sent up James Montgomerie to take charge of her and to proceed her voyage'. What will be subsequent on this misfortune and the methods necessary to be observed for securing my interest in the cargo on board said *Kingston* I submit to you to direct for me as if for yourselves. But it occurs to me that if by this capture the voyage becomes ended I do not incline to be concerned or have any interest in a new or renewing the adventure. It seems to me eligible to abide by the first loss wherein my interest by your insuring for me is covered, which I mention to the end that you may please accordingly transact for me'. [9 April 1759]

'Messrs Arthur, Callin & Co are concerned in the cargo on the *Kingston* and to them the vessel belongs. Hence it is that they are inclined that the vessel and cargo proceed on the original destination. But with respect to the interest of the cargo circumstances are now greatly changed. At their intended departure from Scotland the season was inviting as well for the sales of the herrings as for the purchase of the rum. Should the vessel now proceed, the sales of the herrings must come to a late market and at a late market must the purchase of the rum lie. Therefore if I can consistently be disengaged from having any further interest in this adventure on these principles it was that in my last letter I mention of my inclination of having no further concern and so close the account. On this accident the others concerned are inclined to continue the destination and have wrote I believe to Messrs Claud Johnson & Son accordingly. If I can be got off pray do so for me. I shall be as well pleased if I cannot be got off this adventure and must abide by the original destination. I have herein forwarded copies of the letters which are now to be sent to the present master, James Montgomerie, being letters of credit and advice, the originals by Captain Williamson being probably lost'. [18 April 1759]

'I observe that the affair of the *Kingston* is settled and that she is to proceed on the intended voyage, notwithstanding your application and the attendant disagreeable prospects of facing the markets ... Robert Arthur's concern in the vessel has doubtless had its weight but I believe a settlement on the first loss would have proved advantageous to all concerned. In the event of said vessel's proceeding it is necessary that you forward by her the letters I forwarded you to Barbados in respect of my concern addressed to the gentlemen there. It would have given me great pleasure to have been taken off this voyage for really I have no great liking to my partners'. [28 May 1759]

Buying Rum on the Island

'The year or two past we have found to purchase rum here ... as it's clearly preferable to facing the market in any of the Caribbean Isles when outwards and homewards there is appearance of loss and no profit ... Another circumstance in the Douglas trade has kept me from intermeddling the wholesale way is all on credit six months is become the custom and no quantity can be sold but a considerable part thereof must be to the foreigners, who reside there. This is the check for one or two of them fail every year and complaints of losses are frequent'. [Thomas Finlay & Robert Patrick, 12 December 1754]

On 7 October 1758 Captain King, master of the *Gordon* brigantine from Montserat, offered Moore 3,793 gallons of rum. The next day Pat Boyd reported to Moore on some Antigua rum he had purchased in Dublin, which set the value of the *Gordon* rum at 2/4 per gallon. As a result Moore sent a bill to Ebenezer Munro, payable at the Old Bank office in Glasgow at 4 months - on 14 February 1759. 'You will I persuade myself be not displeased with this settlement of the price, as it may occur to you that the quality of Antigua rum is superior to Montserat rum and is accordingly more esteemed at Dublin'. [Ebenezer Munro, 21 November 1758]

However, Munro was not pleased. 'He says the price should be one penny per gallon more and the time of payment should not exceed two or three months'. [James Simson, 26 December 1758]. Moore's defence is of particular interest as it gives details of his current rum negotiations.

'What you say of my son's buying rum at Belfast is very true but it was Antigua rum and the price 2/8 per gallon was Irish currency. From these accounts and particularly that purchase of Mr Boyd's and the other ... from Barbados, for which he was then asked 2/5 but expected cheaper, seems testimony sufficient that 2/4 per gallon was an equitable price for Montserat rum, which on all hands is inferior to Barbados rum.

Mr Boyd's letter to me I see is dated the 12th of October which must comprehend the time of my agreement with Mr King, which was the 7th October, reciting the condition on time and at the price for which rum then sold at Dublin at the mast. The time whereon payment is to be made is four months on the purchaser, which Mr Boyd agreed in Dublin or London and accordingly on this precise time does our payment commence from the date of the delivery of the rum here. The *Industry*'s cargo of rum was brought here payable in London, of which Mr Callin and I had a part. When they called for my bills, looking over some Scots bank notes I then had by me I preferred giving them notes to giving my note at London and this accidentally was the cause why the payment was what you call ready money ... if the custom here was a rule, the general one is six months credit on which condition I bought a cargo of rum from Messrs Mitchell Orr & Co of Ayr the 4th of last month or that is the date of my bill. I am thus particular in order to satisfy you that the manner wherein I settled the price and payment of the rum was in a fair equitable way, as I promised Captain King. If yet you think otherwise I am satisfied that the difference be submitted to the determination of Mr Allan Dreghorn to whom let be communicated what I here wrote to you on this subject and the relative papers and Mr James Simson of the Old Bank will act accordingly for me'. [Ebenezer Munro, 26 December 1758]

There is nothing further in the letter-book about the problem. The tailpiece to this chapter describes another purchase of rum when the owner was not satisfied with the way Moore proceeded. The details of the method of payment have been included as an example of how the money was found on these occasions. Further details of Moore's banking arrangements are found in Chapter Six.

THE STORY OF ALEXANDER PORTERFIELD'S RUM

In January 1751 Alexander Porterfield directed Moore to dispose of his rum in Douglas not under 2/8 per gallon. 'I've offered your rum to severals but none will come up to your price (the current price was 2/5 per gallon in single pieces).' [Alexander Porterfield, 22 January 1751]. The rum was with Phil Moore & Sons in Douglas 'under the care of William Cannell a cooper, who gives due attendance to prevent leakage'. Moore offered David Forbes the rum at 2/6 per gallon, which he declined. 'He wrote me the enclosed answer by which you will see your rum is not likely to reach the price expected'. [Alexander Porterfield 1 February 1751]. In October 1751 John Finch, a Manx merchant, offered 2/4 per gallon for 20 pieces of the rum, part in hand and part in six months. 'I told him I did not chose to divide the parcel for he would expect the choice, which might perhaps prove of no service to the remainder and I was in hopes of a better price'. [Alexander Porterfield, 7 October 1751]

'There is just now in this harbour a Glasgow vessel (the *Industry*) discharging rum here from St Kitts. The master or supercargo took some time to try the market and was with several of the merchants. He at last agreed with me for eighty hogsheads, which is about three-fifths of his cargo. The condition is 2/3 at mast, one third the value on delivery, one third in four months and one third in six months. I'm to pay the duty and charges on landing, which is about 1d per gallon so the parcel will be about 2/4 per gallon lodged in my cellar'. [Alexander Porterfield, 7 October 1751]

In October 1751 Moore agreed 'to take to my own account your parcel of rum at 2/4 English per gallon per invoice measure'. Following this letter his son Phil was to deliver £165 in cash (see Chapters Nine and Fourteen). 'The remainder I shall pay you in six months ... The price I give corresponds or in some respect is not so advantageous to me as what I last bought here for the carriage to this town will lie me in about ½d per gallon'. [Alexander Porterfield, 12 October 1751]. The load totalled 4,138 gallons: £432 15s 4d of which £165 was paid already. 'I reckon charges of duty, which is 1d per gallon, of cellaring, porterage, coopering and for my commission, which would be nigh equal to 2d per gallon ... to what I've allowed is the price whereat I've offered rum to severals and no one would agree to give so that I persuade myself that what I've done herein will prove agreeable to you'. [Alexander Porterfield, 16 October 1751]

Inevitably this was not agreeable. 'You would not find the least cause of complaint to the time limited for the second payment were you accustomed with the custom in this Isle. This time I offered as often as I offered the sale of your rum so that I cannot be esteemed culpable in fixing a time for my payment which I readily would have accepted from any other and as to your expectance of my getting money at this season of the year for it give me leave to assure you that I do not expect in four months hence to receive as much money as I paid for the duty on landing and hence I hope you will be satisfied with waiting until the 19th day of April next that you may be than in cash and to accommodate the said payment in a mutual serviceable way I have herein enclosed you the bills for value following viz

£35 16s 6d Benjamin Bell on George Bell junior 30 November at 3 months
£28 17s 9d William Dickie 7th December at 3 months
£18 15s 5½d Malcolm Fisher 7th December at 3 months
£112 8s 10d John Kelly and John Callin on Ewing etc 27th December payable 3rd March
£43 7s 9d my draft on William Samson 31 December at 1 month
£78 9s 0d my draft on James Donald at 2 months
£317 16s 3½d
 which when paid, as I expect it will before the time limited, I have engaged for payment of your rum and will then serve to discharge the same. I've wrote to Samson & Donald in Ayr advising of my drafts on them. Theirs, Dickie's and Fisher's payment may perhaps be not very pointed but if they pay to answer my engagement as to time it will do if sooner the better'. [Alexander Porterfield, 31 December 1751]

'The bills I remitted you were such as I would have been very content to have received supposing I had sold your rum to any other in this Isle and waited their payment here ... I find the bills are returned to Messrs Peter & John Murdoch who write me they have intimated to you that if I am due you a sum equal to the sum of the bills they will pay it you on my account By this I suppose you have or will receive payment equal to your liking '. [Alexander Porterfield, 8 April 1752]. 'I'm obliged to you writing Mr Porterfield that you would pay him for me the balance for rum I owe him ...

'PS Since writing the above I've received yours of the 27th ult advising your having paid the money I was owing Mr Porterfield '. [Peter & John Murdoch, Glasgow, 8 April 1752]

CHAPTER FOUR: THE TEA TRADE

'The government in England have taken umbrage against the tea trade in this Isle, which is apprehended will end in a stoppage of that branch. Their dislike and the apparent great risk attending it was what made me decline being therein concerned'. [John Stedman, Rotterdam, 23 January 1751]

No eighteenth century merchant dealt directly with the East Indies for tea. Instead the importation of all goods from that part of the world was undertaken by a series of rival East India companies, based both in London and on the continent. The London company held a monopoly on all imports of East India goods into Britain so that they could control both prices and supplies. Yet it has been estimated that two thirds of the tea drunk in England, Scotland, Wales and Ireland during the mid eighteenth century came from Europe. Moore commissioned the purchase of tea at the East India sales in Amsterdam on 14 November 1757 and failing that at Middleburg, Zeeland, on 18 November or at Hoorn on 13 December. There are also references in the letter-book to the purchase of teas at the sales in Gothenburg.

As one of the main supply bases for this smuggled tea was the Isle of Man, the government attempted to control this by banning the import of tea into the Island (see below). The Manx trade is best described by Moore himself. In February 1752 John Stedman recommended to Marcus Ezechiel in Rotterdam that he should contact Moore about his proposal to set up 'a correspondence in the tea way, wherein I observe you have a very considerable interest and hence the facility you would have in supplying with importations the trade of this Isle, answering to the prevailing sorts in demand. I'm very sorry my knowledge in this article of trade is so confined that whatever account I give you of it may appear an imperfect one. For indeed it is very rarely I have any dealings in cha and these inconsiderable, as my friend Mr Stedman knows. The great demand in this Isle for teas is at Douglas, where the lower priced teas are in repute to accommodate those set of low people who deal with this Isle. These deal all on credit, as do those who supply them ... so that the whole of the tea affair in this Isle seems a trade of credit. The buyers from the importers have four months, which is the usual time they require and is generally given. Following this the importer, when his money is paid, must be content to have his specie, if it be a considerable sum, to some port in Britain. Liverpool is the general one wherewith bills on London are purchased for in this Isle. We have no traffic to establish a bourse of exchange, an inconvenience this which must be submitted to. I apprehend that the profit on teas is in measure answerable to these inconveniences as well as to the apparency of risk, which attend this trade.

'The risk is the motive that has withdrawn my concern in the trade, which though it's likely you are acquainted, yet it is not unbecoming me to mention. By a British Act of Parliament no teas can be imported in this Isle. However, as this Act clashes with the Lord of this Isle's royalty or prerogative, he insists on his rights and all manner of teas or other India goods are admitted to entry. Yet if it should so happen that a vessel with tea on board visited at sea in this Channel by any of the cruisers and known to be destined for this Isle, it is brought into a port in Britain and will there, it's apprehended, be condemned. To obviate this foreign clearances and papers with the teas are used. For instance you take freight on a vessel and ship teas as if destined and bound for St Eustatius. The consequence seems plain, though the vessel be put into any port in Britain or Ireland or though visited by a cruiser in the Channel. Hence you see my timorous disposition, which I cannot yet prevail on myself to shake off. Therefore though you propose an interest with me in making a trial I for the present decline'. [Marcus Ezechiel, 25 February 1752]

Further details of the use of false papers appear in two letters to Bagge, Wilson & Pike in Gothenburg. 'For the future, when you ship teas on a British vessel, I think the clearances at the custom house had best be for Liverpool or Bristol. But no teas or India goods must be therein mentioned to avoid suspicion were the vessel visited in the Channel by a cruiser'. [3 December 1750]. And 'What I mentioned about an English vessel's clearance was only in a general way and if visited at sea by any cruiser would in my mind be less liable to suspicion than clearing from Lisbon, which the cruisers are well acquainted is only to colour the destination subject to the discovery of any of the crew'. [7 March 1751]

The following Table indicates the source of Moore's tea orders between 1750 and 1759.

GEORGE MOORE'S TEA ORDERS 1750 to 1759

Date	Source	Supplier	Type of Tea
1750	Gothenburg	Bagge, Wilson & Pike	Unspecified
1751	as above	as above	3 chests bohea, 1 chest singlo, 1 tub hyson
1753	as above	as above	3 chests bohea, 3 chests singlo, 1 tub hyson
1754	as above	as above	4 chests bohea, 1 half chest congo, 1 half chest singlo, 1 tub hyson
1754	Rotterdam	John Stedman	12 half chests bohea, 1 half chest singlo, 1 tub hyson
1755	as above	Isaac & Zachary Hope	10 chests bohea, 4 half chests singlo, 1 tub hyson
1757	as above	as above	4 half chests bohea, 1 tub hyson
1757	as above	Livingston & Symson	30 chests bohea, £100 singlo, 1 tub hyson
1757	Gothenburg	McFarlane & Scott	30 chests bohea, 4 chests green

Key to the types of tea: bohea and congo were black China teas and singlo and hyson were green China teas

Apart from the risks involved in the tea trade, Moore was also concerned about the location of Peel. 'I live in this town on the north side of this Isle, eight miles distant from Douglas (where the Manx tea sales were held). At Douglas I have no connection with the trade or next to none so that any goods sent me to dispose of at Douglas I must consign to another to transact. It's obvious to you that this is no encouragement to send me any goods ... I thank you for your willingness'. [John Arnall, 25 July 1752]. Whenever unsolicited cargoes of tea were delivered to Moore these were sent to his brother Philip Moore, in Douglas. As a result, it was to this source that he turned when his son, Phil, decided to adventure in the tea trade. 'My son Phil's desired I may write to you about buying half a chest of the second best sort of bohea tea from 20d to 24d per pound. If you can assist this intended purchase let me know. Regard is to be had to the time of payment and everything about this to be done in the frugalest way'. [Philip Moore & Son, 18 January 1753]

The Dutch Merchants

Moore was involved with three different Dutch merchants for direct ordering of tea supplies: John Stedman, the Hopes and Livingston & Symson. All these were based in Rotterdam.

John Stedman

'My occasions to Rotterdam have been so small as to cause an interruption in my correspondence with you and hence it is I find that I have been so long debtor to your favour of the 14th November 1752 ... I have now an inclination of dealing a little in some low priced bohea tea. By the first opportunity that offers for this Island I desire you will ship two large chests of bohea ... and a tub of good hyson ... by the second opportunity ... two large chests bohea tea of the same quality with the two former chests ... and by the third opportunity ... two large chests of bohea tea of the like quality and price with the preceding bohea and one half chest of good singlo or green tea ... By this means of three different opportunities, in which way and no other way I desire said teas be shipped for my account, the risk attending carriage to this Isle will be divided. If I have encouragement, as I expect, my dealing in this article may be enlarged. Making no doubt of your attention to the quality of the bohea in what degree the price will admit.

'PS On recollection I find it best to have the ... in half chests instead of two large chests so that you ship four half chests bohea on each opportunity, which you'll please observe'. [John Stedman, 3 May 1754]

The first consignment per the *Fortune*, Robert Lloyd master, arrived at Douglas in August 1754. Moore now ordered paper for making up the tea in single pound parcels and about £20 worth of the lowest priced china cups and saucers. Stedman had died in July but his executors continued to ship his orders: four half chests of bohea on the *Young Theodore*, Jacob Wartha master, in October 1754 and four half chests of bohea and the paper on the *Vreide*, Michael Jompier master in December.

The Hopes

Despite Stedman's death, Moore declined an offer of trade from Livingston & Symson, 'giving me the prices of a variety of commodities with you'. [1 October 1754] Instead, on the recommendation of Thomas Arthur in Douglas, he turned to Isaac and Zachary Hope. Considering the subsequent events, the letter from Thomas Arthur to the Hopes dated 12 October 1755 is somewhat strange, as Moore himself recognised. 'By this you may observe that the condition of my dealing with you was literally specified and ascertained by the manner and intent of Mr Arthur's engagement on your behalf so as to leave no doubt about my receiving satisfaction, if by any accident I should have cause of complaint in the article of my trade with you, which he encouraged and became responsible for, assuring me in the most explicit manner of occasional recourse on him in such circumstances ... I confess to you that I am not acquainted with Mr Arthur's motives for so peculiarly ascertaining me against accidents in the course of my trade with you nor know I if it was by your appointment or what reply you made to him on your receipt of his letter ... It is sufficient now for me to know that Mr Arthur has indemnified me in respect of any injurious accident happening in my trade with you'. [Isaac & Zachary Hope, 20 March 1759]

Because of his fear of an imminent war with France (see Chapter One) Moore delayed from March to December before writing to the Hopes with an order for tea and other small articles to be shipped on the first Dutch vessel bound to the Isle of Man. The tea was to include: ten half chests bohea from 14 to 16 shillings per lb; five whole chests bohea from 16 to 17 shillings; five whole chests bohea from 20 to 21 shillings; one tub best hyson from 60 to 70 shillings; two half chests singlo from 20 to 24 shillings and two half chests singlo from 28 to 34 shillings [24 December 1755]

There was a problems with this order. 'My silence proceeds from the disappointment I have met with in the quality of the green (singlo) tea - the bale containing four quarter chests, which have been all examined and found alike. Had there been damage it must have affected the different quarter chests more or less ... after being unable myself to dispose of them I left directions with my friends in Douglas to part with them at any price. I have not to this day had advice they could sell them'. [Isaac & Zachary Hope, 14 July 1757]. In a postscript dated 29 August 1757 he added 'The green tea remains on hand so unsaleable that I know not what to do with it'.

Despite this Moore ordered a further twenty-four chests of bohea and one tub of hyson. The new teas arrived in October 1757. 'I'm just now sending my son to Douglas to qualify the teas and accordingly to dispose of them, wherein I expect he will succeed as you recommend'. Without waiting for a report from Phil, Moore continued 'By the first vessel, a neutral bottom, bound to this Isle I desire you will ship ten large chests of good bohea tea ... and I rely that the quality will answer the price'. [Isaac & Zachary Hope, 26 October 1757]

In fact there was already a problem. 'The last teas these gentlemen (the Hopes) shipped for me ... are so bad stuff that I'm ashamed to offer and appear in the sale of it. Everyone tells me they have imposed on me'. [Richard Oswald & Co, 3 November 1757]. As a result Moore refused to pay the price demanded by the Hopes for their teas (see tailpiece to this chapter).

The final letter on the subject is to Thomas Arthur. 'The dispute I have with Messrs Hopes in Rotterdam seems to be drawing near a conclusion as Mr Jolie in Dublin for them agreed with me in submitting it to reference in London, where I am preparing to send the relative papers. The recourse I refer to and rest on is founded on your recommendation and the terms thereof, contained in your letter to them dated the 12th October 1755 ... and in their letter to me they add these words 'we say that we hope you will think us capable to answer for ourself' from which I infer that they become with you principals in the terms of your letter ... To clear up this matter I think it will be necessary to have what they wrote to you in answer to your letter ... which I desire the favour of your sending to me a copy by the bearer or so soon as you can'. [Thomas Arthur, 14 July 1760]. There is no information about the end of the dispute.

Livingston & Symson

By November 1757 Moore was looking for a new tea supplier in Rotterdam. Having seen a letter from Livingston & Symson to John Callin & Co, Moore wrote to them with a request to purchase teas at the East India sales in Amsterdam, Zeeland or Hoorn as 'under your direction I persuade myself of being well used in respect of price and quality and on this I rely. The quantity I want is thirty whole chests of good sound china bohea, or thereabouts, or said quantity may consist of whole chests and half chests, as the lots happen. Of good, sound singlo tea I want a quantity not exceeding £100 sterling worth' He expected that the sales would be over at Amsterdam but hoped that he would be in time for Zeeland. 'If you can find a neutral vessel wherein to ship said teas at Zeeland to this town, or any other port in this Isle, it would be best to have this done as several articles of expense would thereby be saved. But if no opportunity of a neutral vessel offers at Zeeland and it is necessary to have the teas brought to Rotterdam to be shipped there, in that case I would prefer that the quantity was divided and I desire may be shipped on the first and second neutral vessel in the berth taking in goods of any part of this Isle'. He also ordered a tub of hyson. [Livingston & Symson, 3 November 1757]

Moore enclosed the letter to Livingston & Symson with one to Richard Oswald in London. In the postscript he added 'Had I known the name of your friend or friends at Rotterdam in whom you think I might confide I should make use of them or if you incline to my dealing with them you may revoke my letter to Messrs Livingston & Symson and write to your friends to transact in their stead for me'. [Richard Oswald & Co, 3 November 1757]. His concern was assuaged. Richard Oswald wrote on 22 November 1757 'acquainting me of your friends' kind mention and recommendation of Livingston & Symson'. [Richard Oswald & Co, 2 January 1758]

Although Moore's letter was too late for the sales at Middleburg, Livingston & Symson had purchased more than they required there so they shipped on the *Sarah*, Captain Berkhill, bound for Douglas, approximately half his order. But 'the vessel in her passage was visited by some of the Dover craft, who the master says forcibly entered into the hold and took out the most convenient packages for carriage. By that means I have lost the tub of hyson and one of the casks. It is some satisfaction to me that the value of the tub of hyson was insured. The remaining four tubs of bohea I observe are to be shipped by Captain Wolfers ... if you can obtain a secure place in his hold I desire you'll ship one tub of good hyson tea in room of that which has been pillaged or, if not by Wolfers, by the first following opportunity for this Isle ... I have not yet seen the quality of any of the goods by the *Sarah* but I persuade myself that they will give satisfaction'. [Livingston & Symson, 29 March 1758]. To Richard Oswald he added 'I find they have mostly concluded the purchase and have drawn two bills on you ... Their thus drawing is expeditious but I suppose it necessary'. [Richard Oswald & Co, 2 January 1758]. 'It seems strange that notwithstanding so many repeated complaints against these rovers, the government have not fallen on an effectual method to prevent such pilferings'. [Richard Oswald & Co, 29 March 1758]

Unsolicited Teas

Moore was approached by several Dutch merchants, offering to establish a trade in tea. Three examples of this have been selected to illustrate the types of problem involved.

Marcus Ezechiel, Rotterdam

The first part of Moore's letter to Marcus Ezechiel was quoted in introduction to this Chapter. He continued 'If you are disposed to make an experiment of the market in this Isle and address the teas to me what I shall do with them will be with the same caution and care as if they were my own. On which footing you may, if you please, make an experiment of about sterling £600 worth one third at 15d per pound, one third at about 20d and one third from 25d to 28d per pound. In which case send two invoices, one whereunto I must swear, therefore a genuine one for the payment of the duties, the other let the weight be alike exact but with an addition in the price of about 10%, which occasionally I may refer to. The whole parcel I would advise be bohea teas.

'PS Severals have applied to me to accept commissions in the tea way which I have hither declined. This beginning, if it prove one, may turn out to our mutual satisfaction, which so far as relates me I shall try to improve ... For the foresaid trial of tea you may lessen or enlarge the quantity as you think fit'. [Marcus Ezechiel, 25 February 1752]

As a result Ezechiel sent to Moore by the *Stadholder*, Johnson master, four whole chests and four half chests of bohea, six tubs of singlo and four half chests of hyson and by the *Vreide*, Jan Wolfers master, four whole and three half chests of bohea and thirty-two tubs of singlo. This was not the type of tea that Moore had suggested, as it included hyson and singlo with the bohea. But there were other problems, as Ezechiel wanted him to be responsible for the total debt 'remitting you the value of your teas before I myself am in cash for them. Therefore you must excuse my declining to accept said condition you propose. It follows that your teas must wait your further orders in respect of my disposal of them'. [Marcus Ezechiel, 15 April 1752].

When no reply was received and as he was about to set off for Scotland Moore wrote 'Whatever directions you give about the teas I have left to the observance of my brother, Phil Moore, who will act with the same caution as were I present'. [Marcus Ezechiel, 18 May 1752]. By 28 July 1752 six half chests of bohea and eight tubs of singlo were still unsold. The quality of the bohea was very bad and there was no demand for green teas. Moore wrote on 20 November 1752 'From this specimen of my dealing in commissioned teas at Douglas I find it does not answer your expectance and as it gives me great concern it does not prove mutually agreeable. I must therefore desire you will relinquish the thought of any further experiment this way'. As Moore had addressed the sale of the teas to Phil Moore & Sons (in Douglas) 'I have desired them to correspond with you on all occasions pertinent to the further remittance and sales. As teas lie much in their way I have hopes that your correspondence with them may be mutually improved'. [Marcus Ezechiel, 5 March 1753]. Some of the teas were still at Douglas in 1755. 'You'll observe they (Phil Moore & Sons) say they cannot sell your bad teas nor expect it on any other manner than by public auction for which they are, it seems, waiting your orders'. [Marcus Ezechiel 13 February 1755]

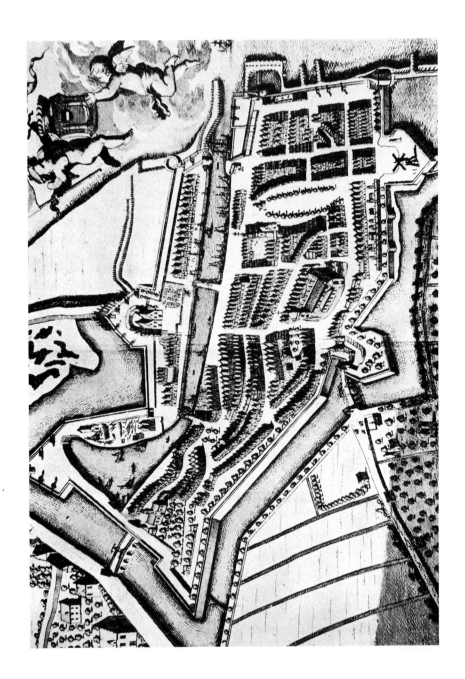

Figure 5: Campvere in the Eighteenth Century: John Mowat

In December 1750 John Mowat in Campvere consigned some teas to Mr Duthie but he had left the Isle of Man for Dublin. George Moore was requested to take over the sale of the four boxes of bohea and hyson. 'The teas are lodged in the public storehouse at Douglas to wait their invoice, which must be sent to be sworn to previous to their being admitted to entry ... I went to Douglas to try to sell them... but I could not meet with a purchaser'. [John Mowat, 23 January 1751]

Mowat wrote to Moore on 11 April 1751 but he did not reply until his return from Scotland in August. In the meantime, still without the weight of the four boxes, Moore had sold all of them to John Callin. 'I saw Mr Callin lately in Scotland, when he took the opportunity of telling me that on my word of the teas being alike in quality he was greatly deceived in one of the last boxes, which proved of quality so very mean as to give him too sufficient cause of complaint'. [John Mowat, 6 August 1751]. Moore was also 'embarrassed with our collector, as to the duty which arises payable per invoice'. With no response from Mowat, the problem continued. Callin 'makes loud complaints of the quality, that the teas, namely three boxes, did not answer the character I gave of them in pursuance of yours'. [John Mowat, 3 September 1751]

In 1753 Abraham James Hillhouse forewarned Moore about Mowat. 'I did not hear any flaw in his dealings but as you mention he is reinstated in business we are exchanging letters'. [Abraham James Hillhouse, 24 April 1753] 'My concern with Mr John Mowat is only speculatively (re his brother at Rio Esquebo and rum - see Chapter Three)' [Abraham James Hillhouse, 24 July 1753]

Further information about Mowat's financial situation comes from archives held in Rotterdam. The 'reinstatement' appears to have followed an explanation by Alexander Symson of Livingston & Symson on 14 March 1753 that John Mowat had become bankrupt. His continuation in trade was short-lived. On 15 November 1757 there was a further statement from Alexander Symson that he and David Gavin of Middleburg were sureties for the payment in equal amount of all Mowat's debts.

Theobald Dillon, Rotterdam

Moore had been recommended to Dillon by Abraham James Hillhouse in London. As a result Dillon sent, apparently uninvited, nine whole and six quarter chests of tea by the *Marquis of Bonnac*, Jan Wolfers master. 'The vessel was arrived at Douglas some time before your letter came to hand. The teas are landed in good order. By this and another vessel lately from Rotterdam I find that large quantities are imported in so much that (there are) no buyers for your parcel and I dare say were I now to press to sale it would not reach the first cost. I must therefore wait a little in hopes of a more favourable season of sale'. [Theobald Dillon, 5 February 1755]. In fact Jan Wolfers had also shipped in the *Marquis of Bonnac* thirty-five chests of bohea, thirty-five boxes of green tea and four tubs of hyson for Ross, Black & Christian and Phil Larson (13 January 1755), nine chests bohea, a half chest green tea, a half chest chouson and a tub of hyson for John Allan (23 January 1755) and a further fifteen chests and twelve boxes bohea for Ross, Black & Christian on 1 February 1755. Finally, on 17 February 1755 William Tiar imported one hundred chests of bohea on the *Prince William* from Gothenburg.

John Callin & Co and Phil Moore & Sons purchased the teas from Dillon. 'I might have sold ... at something a higher price for payment at six months in this Isle, which is the commonest method, but I preferred dealing with people on whom I can depend ... the bohea proves tolerable good ... but I cannot say so much for the green, the qualities of which were much objected to. If you like to continue in this way I shall use all necessary caution for your interest'. [Theobald Dillon, 27 March 1755]

This lack of enthusiasm for dealing with Dillon may have been emphasised by Moore's problems with Abraham James Hillhouse (see Chapter Six).

David Nathan, Rotterdam

This was another occasion when Moore passed on unwanted teas to his brother Phil in Douglas. By the time the tea arrived in the Isle of Man, David Nathan was dead so that all Moore's correspondence was with the executors. He referred to their letter of 6 June 1752 'accompanying invoice and bill of lading of six chests green tea and a box of china per *Vreide*, Jan Wolfers master, which in my absence from here were lodged in the custom house ... I have given directions they be sold in the same manner as if they were my own, which is the rule I observe in these matters' However, Moore was surprised 'How Mr Ballentine or Captain Jan Wolfers recommended me'. [10 July 1752] 'Your teas are of so low a quality they cannot be disposed of in the common way .. if you approve I shall set them up at public auction and give notice of the sale in the different towns in the Isle'. [14 October 1752]. On 5 March 1753 he reported that he had passed the teas to his brother, Phil Moore, in Douglas.

The story of John Mowat is told in Figure 5, showing Campvere in the eighteenth century.

The next chapter also describes an area of trade where Moore appears as a support for his son Phil and where Holland is also involved.

THE STORY OF THE HOPES' BAD TEAS

'I have had at sundry times some teas from Messrs Isaac & Zachary Hope ... The quality of some had proved so mean that in my opinion and in the opinion of several merchants in Douglas, who compared the price per invoice with the quality on landing, that some error had been made in the charge. This has occasioned my writing to those gentlemen that their adjustment of our account will depend on their declaration, in your presence, before a magistrate ... wherewith I shall abide'. [Livingston & Symson, 5 September 1758]. 'The circumstance most striking is that, pending my complaint of their sending me some bad tea, they sent me one whole parcel of very bad tea'. [Livingston & Symson, 29 November 1758]

The Hopes were not happy about the involvement of Livingston & Symson. 'In similar cases were you transacting any manner of business with a foreign merchant ... I persuade myself that you would think it lawful and equitable to expect and abide by similar recourse ... Nor did it ever enter into my mind that it was derogatory to any person's character or honour to swear to what such person had said or committed to writing on any occasion tending to obviate a dispute ... I subjoin the instances or causes of complaint

'1756 December one bale containing four quarter chests green tea sold to Thomas Cunningham and John Alder, quantity 246 lbs at 4/3d per pound £52 5s 6d. The two quarter chests sold to Cunningham are lying in his hands quite unsaleable and he will therefore pay nothing. On the two quarter chests sold to Alder, after various alterations, he paid me £11 18s 11d so that by the insufficiency of the tea in said bale I have cause to complain of having lost £40 6s 9d.

'1757 November having agreed for the sale of ten chests bohea by the *Bonnac* at 2/8 per lb but on examining the quality proved so bad that the buyer relinquished and to get the tea off my hands I was forced to sell said ten chests at 2/1 per lb so that on the sale of these ten chests I have cause to complain of having lost on the weight 2760 lbs at 7d per lb £80 10s.

'By which specification it appears that the injury I have received amounts to £120 16s 7d sterling value for which, as Mr Arthur has engaged, I expect that you will make me entire satisfaction'. [Isaac & Zachary Hope, 20 March 1759]

CHAPTER FIVE: TOBACCO

'You may remember I was speaking to you of having some leaf tobacco when I last had the pleasure of seeing you in Glasgow and, having further a mind to join with my son, Philip, and make a business in this way, I'm to desire you'll let me know the price of your tobacco fit for making rolls and your terms of payment. I design the tobacco by way of Campvere ... please let me know if you can accommodate me herein ... I'm thinking to make a beginning with fifty or sixty hogsheads but I defer this until I receive your answer. Phil has a great mind of having some of the tobacco spun as roll ... For this he wants spinners and presses. In these can you give him assistance for he's looking towards your help, which in this instance is necessary?' [Colin Dunlop, 30 November 1753]

As George Moore was determined to set up Phil's tobacco manufactory in the best, and frugalest, way, he was involved in the initial negotiations. This has resulted in sufficient information to reconstruct the beginnings, at least, of the business.

Without going into details of the somewhat complicated tobacco smuggling trade, suffice it to say that:

- tobacco from the colonies had to be landed at a British port before it could be re-exported to the continent; on landing a bond, with securities, had to be given for payment of duties; should any of this tobacco be re-exported then there was a drawback of these duties; the common practice of the tobacco merchants was to load a vessel for exportation, claim the drawback and then reland the tobacco, clandestinely, this time duty-free. Sometimes the tobacco vessels did go as far as Campvere. The same cargo was then reshipped on another vessel to be run on the Scottish coast. On other occasions the tobacco only went a few miles before being relanded. Examples of both these systems will be seen in this chapter.

The tailpiece quotes relevant parts of the 1751 Tobacco Act.

A MAP of the most INHABITED part of VIRGINIA containing the whole PROVINCE of MARYLAND with Part of PENSILVANIA, NEW JERSEY and NORTH CAROLINA. Drawn by Joshua Fry & Peter Jefferson in 1775.

76

Figure 6: The Virginia Tobacco Trade : James Orr of Irvine

'I'm pleased to see you have engaged your vessel to take onboard a cargo from Campvere for my account to this place. Accordingly I have wrote to Messrs David & John Gregory, merchants there, to ship on your vessel eighty hogsheads of tobacco ...

'On your passage homeward I would have you avoid if possible touching or going into any port in Britain or Ireland. But should necessity oblige you, let your report be made to the custom house within twenty-four hours following your arrival in the port. You are by all means to take care that no manner of East India goods of what kind soever be shipped on your vessel at Campvere for your own account or for any of the crew's or for account of any other person to avoid any delay or damages, which having East India goods on board might subject you or make you liable to'. [James Orr, Campvere, 3 May 1754]

James Orr's name appears frequently in the Port Glasgow custom house letter-books, as master of the *Concord* and the *Prince William* of Glasgow, both importing tobacco from Virginia. In March 1757 he petitioned for the delivery of the *Prince William*'s yoal 'which was seized by Daniel Campbell, commander of the Rothesay wherry, for being employed in running tobacco from said ship by the sailors coming up the river ... on his (Mr Campbell's) making towards the *Prince William* ... in order to board her, most of the sailors made off with the yoal towards Inverkip, near which the ship then was, and that he thereupon made after them. They, reaching the shore before him, began immediately to put on shore a considerable quantity of box and babbie tobacco, which they carried with them from the ship. That on his attempting to go ashore and seize it, and having only four of his hands with him, the sailors, being fourteen in number, threatened them. Finding it in vain to make any further attempt and the sailors leaving the yoal he carried her off with him'. [Collector at Port Glasgow to the Board, 26 March 1757]

This is the final reference. 'Mr James Donald, merchant in Greenock, & Co having informed us that they had an express last night from Islay, acquainting them that the brigantine *Elizabeth & Janet* of Irvine, James Orr (washed overboard in the passage) late master, from Virginia for Clyde, with one hundred and forty-four hogsheads of tobacco is put on shore on the north side of Islay and beat to pieces, by which her whole cargo is lost except about twenty hogsheads, and only part of that dry'. [Collector at Port Glasgow to the Board of Customs, 15 February 1758]

The Source of Tobacco

Figure 6 illustrates the tobacco trade of Virginia. This was the main source of supply for the tobacco imported into Glasgow and it was from this secondary source, indirectly, that the tobacco for Phil's manufactory had to be obtained. Colin Dunlop replied to the letter at the head of this chapter on 21 December 1753, informing Moore of the type of tobacco generally supplied to the Isle of Man; that the payments were usually 'one half in ten the other in thirteen months; that the tobacco is shipped to Campvere and insured by the seller, who in case of loss has recourse on the insurer, so that you can provide and ship the tobacco to Campvere, consigning it to my order, without any other charge until the arrival at Campvere, where my friend must pay the freight and follow what other orders are relative. I thank you for your favour and readiness to oblige my son, who is become very fond of this tobacco scheme, so that if it answers and appearances are favourable this may be an introduction of dealing more extensively this way. His inclination and mine agree with having what relates at Glasgow under your direction. In pursuance of this design I desire you will provide and ship off fifty or sixty hogsheads of good leaf tobacco by the first opportunity to Campvere, where having no particular acquaintance let this tobacco be addressed to any house wherein you think I may confide or, if you have not such knowledge at Campvere, let the tobacco be addressed to Mr John Mowat, merchant there (see Figure 5), with whom I have some small correspondence. But this certainty of having the tobacco shipped there remains to be provided for. This my son hopes you may appoint by directing to some other person in Glasgow to take care to engage freight thence in such manner as that it may not long lie in Campvere, which would subject it to waste and unnecessary charge. The quality of the tobacco is referred to you and in this I confide and rely ... remembering what you told me that you could at any time furnish me with tobacco I understood to be out of your own cellars. The first sort of tobacco I suppose to be what you have for inland sale, the second sort to be that wherewith the Irish market is supplied. As to the payment you may depend on its being made in the limited time or sooner'. [Colin Dunlop, 17 January 1754]

Dunlop's reply, dated 28 January 1754, was not received by Moore until late February. He replied on 1 March 'I see the kind of tobacco necessary for my purpose is become scarce at Glasgow by the sundry demands which have been made for the uses in this Isle ... I observe that of some cargoes now discharged you intend buying my quantity and conclude ere this the purchase is completed. If you cannot supply me with tobacco of your own importation, as I expected, you make the charge of 2½ per cent commission which I submit and shall with pleasure pay you ... It is necessary that samples or draft hands of each hogshead be with the tobacco in a box or made up in one of the hogsheads. You'll please direct it remains that the shipping the tobacco for Campvere be with the first opportunity and agreeable with your opinion I have herein wrote a letter to David & John Gregory, merchants there, with regard to their management'. [Colin Dunlop, 1 March 1754]

The letter to the Gregories stated 'On recommendation of some of your friends in Glasgow, who have acquainted me that you do the business of landing and shipping tobacco, I take the liberty to send to your care fifty or sixty hogsheads ... for the advance of freight of the tobacco, the duty and cellarage, please reimburse yourselves by drafts on Mr Abraham James Hillhouse merchant in London. You'll please alter the marks and numbers of the hogsheads, striking the old off and marking them from No 1, No 2 so on to the last number and send me in a letter by way of London to the care of Mr Hillhouse the numbers old and new'. [David & John Gregory, 1 March 1754]

At the same time, Moore wrote to Joseph Scott in Glasgow, asking him to ship twenty or thirty hogsheads of leaf tobacco to the Gregories, with that from Colin Dunlop, and to engage a vessel on freight to return with the total tobacco cargo to Peel. Again he asked for samples of each hogshead. 'There is no risk with tobacco from Holland to this Isle as there is no law forbidding this trade'. [Joseph Scott, 1 March 1754]

By 4 April 1754 Moore had found the master of the vessel from Campvere to Peel: Captain James Orr of Irvine (see Figure 6), whose vessel, the *Concord*, was '70 tons or upwards so that no objection will arise to the ship's tonnage (if stopped at sea - see tailpiece to this chapter)'. [Colin Dunlop, 10 April 1754]. But there had been an unexpected development. 'My last letter to you was the 1st last month. At same time I wrote to Mr Joseph Scott about spinners and, as I thought that he or his brother Mr Robert was extensively in the tobacco trade, I wrote him for some tobacco to be shipped with the parcel from you ... I have now received a letter from Mr Scott by way of Liverpool ... Mr Scott also writes me that he has very little knowledge of tobacco and its quality and to prevent any inconvenience from this circumstance that he has applied to you to get the number of hogsheads I wrote him for on which account I am very much obliged to him'. [Colin Dunlop, 10 April 1754]

In April 1754 ninety-two hogsheads of tobacco were shipped on the *Haughton*, Andrew Brown master, for Campvere. The invoice amounted to £864 7s 10d 'in which I observe is included commission of your purchase of the whole tobacco so that no part of it was your own, as I expected. Mr Simson has paid you £834 0s 10d, which, with the discount for prompt payment £30 7s, discharges the value'. [Colin Dunlop, 13 August 1754]

This was re-shipped by James Orr, who arrived at Peel in August 1754. The insurance, which also covered geneva and other goods totalling £184 12s 4d, was £20 4s 6d. 'But the samples you sent Messrs Gregory packed up in two boxes are not (on board). Orr says they were not shipped nor did he hear anything of them, which proves of great inconvenience and the more so as Messrs Gregories' letters with the new numbers of the tobacco is not yet come to hand'. [Colin Dunlop, 13 August 1754]

The only other details of a tobacco shipment to the Isle of Man relate to the *Neptune*, Bound Paterson master. This vessel sailed in ballast from Douglas to Clyde in September 1758. 'I expect that the price of tobacco is a little advanced but the quality is necessary to be attended to, in which particular I rely on Mr Sangster's choice. Should it happen that you cannot propose to supply the tobacco for Captain Paterson's cargo, my agreement of freight with him becomes void, in which case he will have to look out for another freight and in this alternative I recommend him to you'. [Colin Dunlop, 18 September 1758]

A cargo was available. 'Mr Colin Dunlop writes to me that the tobacco must be shipped on account and risk of Messrs Gregories, which he writes he will note to you to regulate you as to insurance. The tobacco which said Gregories are to ship for me at Campvere if you think had best be in theirs or in the name of Charles Kelly & Co, for whose account the same is, I desire you to direct accordingly and that they make the insurance homewards, if it can be done cheaper in Holland than with you in London'. [Richard Oswald & Co, 23 October 1758]. The insurance on the *Neptune* from Clyde to Campvere totalled £92 12s 6d. The voyage seemed to take an exceptional length of time, as she did not arrive in Campvere until January 1759. The insurance to Peel totalled £149 14s 6d. Times had changed.

The Manufactory

Having, he hoped, sorted out the tobacco supply, Moore then needed to set up the manufactory 'If matters are such as I expect, I come now to write you of the proposed manufactory, of which the best account I can give is as follows: five men and a roller is a number sufficient for the beginning. These have five shillings sterling per hundred on the leaf taken into the work house. This is four shillings to the spinners and one shilling to the roller and these give some small gratuity to a master who teaches the boys to read, without which instruction the tobacco boys are not to be had here. On this footing it is that the spinning of tobacco is done in this town and affords, I apprehend, encouragement sufficient for your engaging for me said six men.

'The presses necessary for this are to be four finishing presses, each one hundred and eight rolls, three rolls deep, three catches each forty-eight rolls and one pair of plates per thirty-two rolls. He that tells me this says that James Muirhead in the Gorbals has the best work in Glasgow for this purpose and that Alexander Rae and James Gill, blacksmiths, are the best for making the iron work.

'Accordingly I desire you will engage five spinners and a roller. One of the spinners or the roller may be as a foreman, who may have an eye to said different kinds of presses being well and truly made. You'll please also direct by the time the tobacco may be expected to arrive here that the men and said necessaries may be in readiness, when I shall direct a conveyance for them here. In the meantime I shall provide a house for the work. Phil joins his compliments with me.

'PS The person I speak with about my factory has given me some further directions about the four big presses - that runnels may be cut right and left and that the eight catches and plate be all cut on the right'. [Colin Dunlop, 17 January 1754]

Again there were problems. 'I'm sorry that spinners are so scarce with you that you have not been able to get the number I wrote you of. Notwithstanding it is necessary that the presses be made and therefore I pray you direct may be made so soon as conveniently the workmen can finish them. For I'm not without hopes of getting ... here spinners sufficient to answer my purpose. By spinners just now arrived here from Glasgow for a gentleman in Douglas I find that one thing is necessary, which not knowing I did not write you of in my last letter - some money in advance. This it seems is generally wanted to clear off old arrears and the money advanced to this spinner I'm writing of was five pounds by Mr Robert Arthur, who engaged him, and is to be allowed for the wages to become due on spinning by him. I was also told that the charge of passage to this Isle is at the expense of the proprietor of the manufactory'. [Colin Dunlop, 1 March 1754]

Inevitably Moore also wrote to Joseph Scott on the subject of spinners. 'I'm not without hopes of getting in this Isle the number of hands I wish to begin my factory, which is six. But I would be well pleased to have the five from Glasgow to avoid interference with the hands in factories in this Isle'. [Joseph Scott, 1 March 1754]

The identity of the head spinner, or foreman, was all important, because on this depended the success or otherwise of the whole operation. 'I am recommended to one Mr Watson, a spinner now or lately in the factory wherein Doctor Clark was concerned, and have herewith wrote him with intent to engage him. He lives near Mr Joseph Scott so that I've wrote to Mr Scott to hand him my letter. If Watson agrees to come he may perhaps fall on means to engage some other hands to come with him and Watson will be proper enough to inspect the making of the presses. If should he find to purchase any presses it will proportionately diminish the number of new presses and the necessity of having these made. By the latter end of May or beginning of June probably the presses will be in readiness and the spinners. This is about the time I expect being in Glasgow when I shall provide for their passage here, when the arrival from Campvere may be hoped for'. [Colin Dunlop, 1 March 1754]

The letter to Watson stated 'I'm about to engage in the spinning of roll tobacco here and am preparing ... necessaries for this purpose. I have been speaking with some of your friends here to know how I may get spinners. You have been recommended to me, particularly by Mr Mitchell, and as I hear my engaging you has all appearance of proving to our mutual advantage I have wrote to my friend Mr Joseph Scott in Glasgow to speak with you on this subject ... if you agree, as I hope you will, the presses to be made at Glasgow under the direction of Mr Colin Dunlop I beg you will superintend and have an eye that everything be done in a substantial way'. [Mr Watson, 1 March 1754]

It is clear that all Moore's information about the tobacco manufactory came from the tobacco spinner, Mitchell, on the Island. In the covering letter to Joseph Scott, Moore added 'Mitchell's design of coming to work with me he desires may be kept secret'. [Joseph Scott, 1 March 1754]

Watson was not interested in the job offer. 'I have now received a letter from Mr Scott by way of Liverpool, wherein he mentions he cannot get the man I wrote him about nor any other spinners can he meet with to engage so that now I have no expectance of having any hands from Glasgow and must apply some other way to be supplied'. [Colin Dunlop, 10 April 1754]. However, the presses were ready.

Moore's letter crossed with one from Colin Dunlop dated 6 April 'recommending my namesake for the purpose of my tobacco trading. I have this day concluded an agreement with him that he be the foreman of the work ... James Muir finds great fault with the presses I wrote to you about. As he understands what I'm wanting let him make what alterations he thinks necessary and be provided with what other materials he judges fitting for my purpose. For payment of these I've desired him to call on Mr James Simson at the Old Bank. But let Muir show you the account before he calls on Mr Simson for the money. On his leaving his family at Glasgow I have agreed that £8 or £10 sterling be advanced him ... and should be needed any advance money for the hands he expects to engage for me let that also be advanced'. [Colin Dunlop, 17 April 1754]

He gave detailed instructions to James Muir about the presses. 'Do you direct whatever alterations in said presses you think necessary so that by means thereof I may have materials for the factory in convenient good order or, if you can find to buy any secondhand press or presses that have been formerly used, I give you a discretionary power to buy these for me as you think proper. All the other materials you know I shall want I desire you will cause be provided so that I may expect to have everything in the best and in a frugal way. I desire you will also engage four spinners for the work. I think five spinners will be necessary and enough to begin with'. [James Muir, tobacconist, 17 April 1754]

On 28 August 1754 Colin Dunlop wrote to Moore 'giving me some account of James Muir's impertinent behaviour at Greenock, disagreeable to the gentlemen from whom you bought the tobacco and very much to me, as it creates noise that can have no good effect. But there is no remedy for that past indiscretion. There are some gentlemen at Glasgow less scrupulous than with whom you dealt for more than one at Glasgow offered to treat with me for tobacco of that kind I wanted, having the landing it at Campvere under their own direction'. [Colin Dunlop, 21 September 1754]

At last everything was ready. But 'James Muir by my direction lately wrote you about one of the screws, which broke so that until it's returned I lose the use of one of the presses, which proves extremely inconvenient and Muir also wants a pair of other screws and pins some how or other neglected, which adds to the inconvenience'. [Colin Dunlop, 21 September 1754]. In January 1755 Moore wrote to William Laing that his namesake in Glasgow had charged £9 3s 5d for a pair of screw nails. 'Pay him for me and get receipt according the sufficiency of his work for one year following that date. In this kind of work done for me at Glasgow I have been very much abused'. [William Laing, 15 January 1755]

Necessaries
Other things necessary for the manufactory included olive oil (from Cette), paper and bast. The paper was supplied from Holland and

Ireland. 'The only commission wherewith I have to trouble Peggy is to show McDonald a sheet of brown paper to know if he can make paper equal to that quality and at what price ... and if it answer I may probably recommend a great quantity in his way'. [John Onge, 25 March 1754]. Moore applied to James Crosbie in Liverpool to send him 'by the first opportunity two hundred weight of bast for putting up roll tobacco'. [James Crosbie, 21 August 1754]. This was not available. 'I thought the bast was a thing readily got in Liverpool or I should not have wrote to you about it for I'm sorry it should have occasioned your writing to Bristol. If it comes it's well. If it does not I pray give no mention of trouble as it's almost indifferent whether I get it or not'. [James Crosbie, 1 October 1754]

Others in the Trade

'There is a rumour here as if these factories were on a very uncertain establishment and unlikely to continue for that they give great umbrage to the merchants in Glasgow. As for my part I do not give credit to the circumstance of the storing for I conclude that were it of consequence that you would have favoured me with some intimation thereof nor can I think that the factories entirely supplied with tobacco from Glasgow give such cause of complaint to the importers of that commodity in Glasgow'. [Colin Dunlop, 4 May 1754]

Despite this, George Paterson of Kilmarnock wrote to Moore in 1754 for a supply of tobacco i.e. circumventing the Glasgow suppliers. 'The tobacco is under my son's management but he's so displeased with your dishonourng his former draft to Montgomerie that you must make up matters with him before he will send any tobacco'. [George Paterson, 19 November 1754]

Robert Arthur

As he was often in partnership with Callin, Robert Arthur of Crawfordsdyke was involved with the new tobacco venture. 'I have received sundry of your letters containing your approbation and consent with the tobacco business, on the new establishment and our opinion of another importation to serve the demands'. [Robert Arthur, 18 March 1755]. Arthur was well known to customs - as was the *Kingston* (see Chapter Three).

On 13 August 1757 the *Kingston* of Greenock, James Ryburn master, cleared out at Greenock for Christiansands in Norway with one hundred and twenty-seven hogsheads of tobacco, marked D, entered and shipped by James Dunlop & Co importers. It was believed that she was headed directly for the Isle of Man so 'we sent Captain Colin Campbell with the sloop under his command and the two wherries to Islay in quest (of her) ... Yesterday the wherry commanded by John Picken, which was also out on this service, returned to Greenock, by whom we are informed that the *Kingston* in her way out stopped some days at Campbeltown and then proceeded round the Mull of Kintyre to the northwards and that the sloops and wherries have examined all the most suspected creeks about Islay and the other islands and places thereabout but have not received any account of her ... very soon after the sloop and wherries went upon this service Mr Robert Arthur came to the custom house of Greenock and asked for the debenture for the tobacco shipped in the *Kingston*, when it was refused him. The very next day he set out for the Highlands, whence he is not yet returned, from which it is imagined he suspected a discovery and went himself express to order the *Kingston* to proceed to Norway'. [Collector at Port Glasgow to the Board, 29 September 1757]

The vessel arrived at Gourock, two miles below Greenock, on 30 October 1757 and on 31 October 'the master came to the custom house and offered to report her from the Isle of Man in ballast. But we refused to take his report unless he report her also from Norway, the foreign country for which he had cleared outwards with the tobacco ... and make mention of the cargo he has carried from thence to the Isle of Man, assigning as our reason for this refusal that we ought to be satisfied he had run no goods in Britain in his voyage from Norway to the Isle of Man, which we could not do without his also reporting from Norway ... As there is no doubt but she has brought back from Norway the very same tobacco to the Isle of Man and there landed it, we humbly beg your Honours directions whether we are not authorised still to insist on his reporting from Norway as well as the Isle of Man'. [Collector at Port Glasgow to the Board, 1 November 1757]

There is nothing further about this incident. But in May 1758 Arthur was quibbling about the payment of tobacco bonds (Nos. 1289, 1290, 1304, 1305 and 1306) entered into by him and others at Greenock and now in the solicitor's hands for non-payment. 'At the time we had these bonds returned us (by the Board) ... together with the debentures applicable to them, we made up a state ... we then showed Mr Arthur that state and proposed a settlement with him but he absolutely refused to do it, alleging he had been charged with much more interest than he ought to have been, particularly on the debentures on the *Betty*, on which interest had been charged to the time they were ordered by the Board to be expede, whereas he would have it charged to the time of shipping the tobacco only, without having any regard to the stop put to the passing of these debentures, as he was by the verdict of a jury entitled to payment as if no stop had been put on them. By reason of this and several other objections he started against the state, he declined to settle until such time as he would consult his lawyer at Edinburgh. On this account these bonds still remain on the list of the bonds in the solicitor's hands, Mr Arthur being from home at present. So soon as he returns we shall press him to a settlement'. [Collector at Port Glasgow to the Board, 20 May 1758]

Further references to Moore's involvement in tobacco importations are found in Chapter Seven, The *Peggy*.

Extracts from: An Act for the More Effectual Securing the Duties upon Tobacco (1751)

'Whereas, notwithstanding the laws heretofore made relating to the importation of tobacco into Great Britain, from His Majesty's Plantations in America, and for securing the duties due and payable thereon upon the importation thereof into Great Britain, and also with regard to the exportation of tobacco from Great Britain to foreign parts, many frauds and abuses are frequently contrived, committed, and carried on, by several ill-designing persons concerned in the different branches of business and trade in tobacco, to the great prejudice of His Majesty's revenue, and to the great loss and discouragement of the fair traders, so that it is become necessary that some further provision should be made for the more effectual preventing the same for the future; be it therefore enacted by the King's most excellent majesty, by and with the advice of the lords spiritual and temporal, and Commons, in this present parliament assembled, and by the authority of the same, that from and after the 25th day of May 1752 ...

'That from and after the 29th day of September 1751, no debenture shall be made forth for any tobacco imported into Great Britain after the said 29th day of September 1751, or any drawback be paid or allowed for the same when exported or entered outwards for exportation, to any part or parts beyond the seas, unless the same, and every part thereof, be shipped and exported from the very same port or place at which such tobacco was first originally imported into Great Britain, and no other ... no tobacco either manufactured or unmanufactured shall be entered or shipped for exportation to any part beyond the seas (Ireland only excepted) in any ship or vessel whatsoever, unless such ship or vessel shall be of the burthen of 70 tons or upwards; and if any officer or officers of the customs shall apprehend, or have reason to believe, that any such ship or vessel bound to foreign parts, and having tobacco on board her, shall not be of the burthen of 70 tons or upwards, it shall and may be lawful for such officer or officers to stop and detain such ship or vessel, and the whole cargo laden on board her, of tobacco, and all other goods, until he or they shall cause such ship or vessel to be admeasured ...'

Note: The whole Act covers twenty-nine pages.

CHAPTER SIX: THE BANKERS

'My trade is solely with the lowlands of Scotland, where the currency is influenced by the two banks established in Glasgow and such is the currency of their notes that all payments are made with them, which has introduced such a scarcity of money that actually there is almost wanting to serve our necessary occasions here'. [Thomas Finlay & Robert Patrick, 22 March 1755]

As there was no banking system on the Isle of Man (see Chapter Four), George Moore was dependent on bankers in Glasgow and London to undertake his financial negotiations. Apart from the logistical problem of ensuring that sufficient funds were available in the right place at the right time, there was the added complication of communication (see Chapter One).

The Glasgow Bankers

As he had well-established trade links with the Clyde, it was inevitable that Moore should use the Glasgow banks in preference to those at Liverpool. A history of the early banks in Glasgow is given in the tailpiece to this chapter.

Peter & John Murdoch (The Arms Bank)

At the beginning of the letter-book George Moore used Peter and John Murdoch, merchants in Glasgow, as his Scottish bankers. Although it is not actually stated, it is probable that it was in connection with their links with the second Glasgow bank, the Arms Bank (see Figure 7). The strongest proof of this comes in a letter relating to the dispute with Walter Logan (see below). 'How the account current was signed without mention of Logan I well remember. I desired you would cause have my account current in readiness as speedily as possible. The day it was in readiness you told me thereof, bid me call at your office and receive it from Mr Buchanan and take it with me to your accounting house to be signed. This was done and looking over the account when I received it from Mr Buchanan and the article of Mr Logan's drafts to the question put to Mr Buchanan as to Logan's probity he answered that I might be under no fear. Be this as it will even before my signing the account current you had wrote me these bills must be paid for my account ... the signing of your account current at your house in the country without mentioning Mr Logan's bill arose as well from company being present, when I thought it unreasonable to make objections'. [Peter & John Murdoch, 20 May 1752]. John Murdoch senior and junior, Peter Murdoch and Archibald Buchanan were all involved with the Arms Bank at some stage or other.

Moore certainly used the Murdochs for his banking business in Glasgow and there were frequent rumbling problems with them. 'I hope by this you have succeeded in remitting to Mr William Snell in London, where only I want to remit for it would be too chargeable by way of Messrs Murdochs.' [James Hutchison, 27 February 1751]. And, commenting on a remittance made to Robert Finlay, another merchant in Glasgow, 'The manner wherein that value was thence remitted to London proves so satisfactory to me that I would be very content what money is paid on my account in Scotland was remitted in the same channel, for which reason whenever you make another payment for me in Glasgow I desire it may be to Mr Robert Finlay, merchant there'. [William McClure, 11 November 1751].

But the real problem developed over Walter Logan (see Chapters One, Seven and Eight). Moore's complaint was that the Murdochs had introduced him to Logan, on several occasions they had reassured him about Logan's probity (see above), and, without Moore's directions, had accepted a draft worth £435 14s 6d from Logan, debiting his account with this sum.

'As this (Logan paying Robert Montgomerie 4s 6d sterling, towards what he owed Moore) differs greatly from my expectations arising through your recommendation and what you have severally wrote me on this subject, it remains that I point out the cause and the manner. I heard of Mr Logan's settlement at Boston and of his connection with you. Invited from this circumstance and a belief that his settlement as a factor there was subsequent to your permission, appointment or recommendation I willingly became one of his correspondents, which I did by sending him goods from Glasgow and with the proceeds directing him to build a vessel for me. So far I proceeded on his general character and his connection with you. I also had at the same time a design of sending goods from Liverpool, the produce whereof I intended to be applied towards purchasing a cargo at Boston to be shipped on said vessel. But before I proceeded in extending thus my correspondence with Mr Logan, I thought caution ... was necessary and I therefore wrote to you of what I had directed and intended to direct. By leaving to your perusal my letter to Mr Logan to the end that from the circumstance of his relation with you I might with confidence proceed and rely on the probity of our mutual correspondence or, if his settlement as a factor had not been with your appointment and recommendation, I might proceed with reserve ,,, Your answer I received pregnant with Mr Logan's probity and thanking me for thus making use of your friend. Without reserve or misapprehension I proceeded with my design of the goods from Liverpool ...

'What related the vessel's building I've had no objections to. But what related the cargo Mr Logan sent or shipped on the vessel the objections I had to this were various (see Chapter Eight) and, as I mentioned them to you, I would not repeat. It was obvious that in justice I might have left the cargo for account of Mr Logan answerable for my effects in his hands and that the bills he drew on you, as I gave him no manner of directions to draw on you or to you to accept and place to my debit, were without any degree of order. On stating you these objections, I prayed how would you manage were my case yours? Your answer to which contained an apology for his behaviour from a variety of circumstances, hoping that the event would be to my satisfaction, concluding that his bills were accepted, must be paid and would in course be placed to my debit. Under your thus appearance for him I respited exerting the power that was in my own hands, namely the power of holding the cargo answerable towards the value of my effects in his hands, and when I last signed an account current with you I respited requiring an explanation why my account was debited with the value of his bills, which should have been at that time mutually settled, had not Mr Buchanan's answer previous to the signing confirmed Mr Logan's probity or removed my suspicions thereof.

Figure 7: George Murdoch and the Arms Bank

'The success of the Ship (Bank) led to the formation of a second bank within the same year. The partners were twenty-six in number, and equally respectable. Their names were - Andrew Cochran, John Murdoch, **George Murdoch**, James Donald, William Crawford sen, William Crawford jun, Robert Scott sen, George Carmichael, Robert Christie, Thomas Dunmore, Archibald Ingram, John Campbell, John Jamieson, James Ritchie, John Murdoch jun, John Bowman, Archibald Buchanan, Laurence Dinwiddie, John Brown, Thomas Hopkirk, John Hamilton sen, John Glassford, and James Spreull, all merchants; Robert Findlay, tanner, Robert Barbour, weaver, and John Wardrop, writer, all in Glasgow.

'Of this influential company, seven gentlemen successively were Provosts of the city. The opening of the bank was announced in the *Glasgow Courant*, of 5th November 1750. The social firm was Cochran, Murdoch, & Co, and the name, 'The Glasgow Arms Bank.' The notes bore that emblem, and the city motto, rather tastefully executed. Their first cashier was Mr Laurence Scott'.

From: Banking in Glasgow during the Olden Time. Glasgow, Past and Present. 1862 (see also tailpiece to this chapter)

George Moore wrote three letters directly to George Murdoch. These concern a Portuguese schooner with a cargo of fruit and wine from Oporto. 'On receipt of your letter (dated 16 December 1757) I recommended Mr Marquise (Murdoch's agent) to my son-in-law, Charles Kelly in Douglas to make the necessary enquiries. The schooner was gone to Ramsey and both followed her for I apprehended some difficulty as it was said all the fruit and some of the wine were sold. They found the schooner at Ramsey'. [George Murdoch, 26 December 1757]. The rest of the story is unclear.

However, Moore does refer to 'Provost Murdoch' in his letters. 'I'm much obliged to Provost Murdoch's many civilities (in the context of son Phil's education at Glasgow)'. [Hercules Lindsay, 5 April 1751]

'Thus you may see my affair with Mr Logan differs greatly from what I've had reason to expect. He avoided making any returns for my effects in his hands, though I sent a vessel to Boston to accommodate this purpose. Were my case yours please tell me what you would expect from me? I must own that in every aspect of this transaction there appears hardships and losses, which without your intervention I should have escaped. Hence how far my expectance of your rendering me satisfaction is justifiable I would willingly accommodate in the most friendly way with you.' [Peter & John Murdoch, 8 April 1752]

The last letter to the Murdochs is dated 20 May 1752, reiterating many of the points in the previous letter, and closing 'I purpose speedily to go to Scotland, where I hope to see you and that this matter may be done away amicably'.

The Old (Ship) Bank
Moore was already in correspondence with Colin Dunlop. 'When I had the pleasure of seeing you in Glasgow we were communing about my ordering you the payments of some money to be remitted to my friends in London, Messrs William Snell & Co merchants there. I was telling you that the usual way I've of late been in is to have a bill on London for the exact sum paid in free of any manner of charges and for this the person with whom I dealt added some days to the bills so that the date of payment exceeded the ordinary course of exchange. I think you approved my dealing with you or in your bank or seemed to encourage it. If it be agreeable to you pray write me a line ... which I would choose to have for my future government. Should any money be paid you in the meantime for me let the equal value be remitted to my friends in London'. [Colin Dunlop, 7 July 1752]

'I received the favour of your letter of the 17th July last, which accidentally has been unanswered until now. The contents thereof answer my inclination and expectance and I abide thereby. In consequence whatever sums occasionally are sent to Glasgow for me shall be addressed to Mr James Simson, book keeper for you and Alexander Houston & Co. The remittances will be in specie and in such notes as are the currency, wherein my friends can have no choice ... by this means all janglings will be prevented, a circumstance this that gives me pleasure.

HOW MONEY WAS RECEIVED AT THE OLD (SHIP) BANK IN GLASGOW

'My commission with you is in consequence of an agreement Mr Colin Dunlop for himself and I made with me by his letter dated the 17th July (1752), I suppose he has acquainted you with. I have herein sent you: £83 6s 2d drawn on Thomas Gray, near Ayr, 7th inst at 20 days sight; £41 9s 6d drawn on James Young, Ayr, 7th inst at 30 days sight; £13 18s 0d on James Young, Ayr, 7th inst at 35 days sight; £16 8s 9½d on Malcolm Fisher, in Ayr, at 30 days; £118 11s 9d on James Allison, Ayr, at 30 days; £75 on Pat Douglas, Ayr, at 30 days; £280 Glasgow notes: £628 14s 2½d for my account.

'I have enclosed letters of advice to be forwarded to the persons on whom I have drawn, to the end they notice and be provided duly to pay. Should a few days following the date of their payment expire it's no matter nor need there be any expense of diligence, supposing to a month thereafter, though I'm persuaded all will pay at or near the time. My dealing here is with that part of Scotland where the Glasgow notes are chiefly current and being encouraged these have a circulation here. Hence you have the enclosed £280 (in notes). For whatever sums it (my account) may receive credit it may so remain till you receive from me how the same is to be remitted to London'. [James Simson, 13 November 1752]

'I'm under the necessity of having recourse on my friends by drawing on them for what they owe me so that I have to advise you of the following drafts payable to Mr James Simson, Glasgow. For value of goods per Henry Calvin, 26th June last £17 16s 5d; for value of goods per Thomas Costain, 29th July last £49 17s 7½d; for value of goods per John Cannell, 29th July last £15 12s 1½d to equal and discharge this sum, £83 6s 2d, I have this day drawn on you payable at 20 days sight. For value goods per Thomas Costain the 27th August £41 9s 6d to James Young and to you I've accordingly drawn payable at 30 days sight and for value of goods per John Cannell the 29th August £13 18s I have drawn on you at 35 days sight. I desire you will be careful to give due honour to my drafts as I rely thereon. Let this letter serve for advice to James Young of my drafts on him with you. Also I desire you will acquaint Malcolm Fisher of my having drawn on him for value of goods by Thomas Costain the 27th August £16 8s 9½d at 30 days sight to the order of James Simson that he duly honour the same'. [Thomas Gray, 7 November 1752]

'Should any sum be sent you for me let Mr Simson place accordingly to my credit'. [Colin Dunlop, 4 October 1752]

James Simson was a cashier at the Old Bank from 1752 to 1758 and during this time Moore wrote over seventy letters to him. The first financial arrangement was dated 13 November 1752 and is quoted in full (see insert) to give an indication of how the business was conducted. The arrangement was confirmed in a letter to Colin Dunlop. 'In consequence of our agreement I have begun a correspondence with Mr James Simson, book keeper at your bank, as by my letter to him dated the 13th this month. I intend making free with Mr Simson in this way to transact any business for me in Glasgow'. [Colin Dunlop, 23 November 1752]

Several attempts have been made, unsuccessfully, to reconstruct George Moore's account book. For example, in 1753 it is recorded that James Simson received payments totalling £3342 6s 5d while he was instructed to pay out £3904 18s 2d - yet Moore did not go bankrupt. The problem is that, apart from any crucial missing letters, there were too many private negotiations.

After several years of atypical non-acrimonious correspondence, on 29 December 1758 Colin Dunlop and Alexander Houston informed Moore 'that Mr James Simson was giving up the management of your banking business and that you had appointed Mr Alexander Morson to succeed him, with whom you desire my corresponding for the future in behalf of the bank'. [Colin Dunlop & Alexander Houston, 23 January 1759]. Moore wrote to Simson the same day. 'I observe that you have quitted your office in the bank and have joined in partnership with Mr George Buchanan. I wish you prosperity and very heartily that success your merit is entitled to. I make no doubt but that you have left a state of the debts owing to me with your successor, Mr Alexander Morson, and will occasionally assist him in any matters for me relative to them'. [James Simson, 23 January 1759].

Unfortunately all did not run smoothly for the new partnership. A vessel carrying wheat from Ireland to Glasgow was stranded at Ramsey and most of the cargo lost. Simson & Co appealed to Moore for his assistance but there was little that he could do. 'I'm sorry for the delay that has attended (the sale of what wheat could be salvaged) and that I could not do you any more service'. [James Simson, & Co, 31 May 1759]. In the meantime Moore continued his correspondence with Alexander Morson at the Old Bank.

The London Agents

There are no clear links between the merchants used by George Moore in London to transact his monetary affairs and actual banks so that the system is more suggestive of that during the early part of the eighteenth century in Glasgow (see tailpiece to this chapter).

William Snell & Co

At the beginning of the letter-book, George Moore's banker in London was William Snell, merchant. In 1752 Snell joined in company with William Perdon to form William Snell & Co. 'I wish you all success in your partnership'. [William Snell & Co, 27 January 1752]. The correspondence continued, apparently without problems, until the wreck of the *Grizzy* (see Chapter Three). One of the problems relating to this event was that the vessel had not been insured (see Chapter One). But it was a dispute over the payments of John Ewing's drafts, totalling £1,000, that caused the real rift.

The best summary of the subsequent events is in a letter to Phil Moore & Sons in Douglas. 'On the 3rd September 1751 I wrote to Messrs Snell & Co in these words: 'I'm about freighting a vessel, John Ewing master, to St Eustatius to load rum there or at Antigua. He will have directions from me to draw on you for my account, one half, which I compute will be about £700 or £800'. It happened that I made no mention in any response to Messrs Snell & Co until the 28th January or February following, at which time I wrote them a letter wherein are these words: 'I'm uncertain whether John Ewing, who is master of the *Grizzy* and has directions to load rum at St Kitts, Antigua or St Eustatius, will this season find to purchase as was expected. However when his bills appear I make no doubt you will honour them and at same time as usual make insurance.' It happened that Ewing loaded a cargo of rum and drew on Messrs Snell & Co £1000 for my account and on his voyage homewards met with the accident of loss of ship and cargo to the westward of Ireland. It also happened that Messrs Snell & Co accepted

Ewing's drafts for £1000 and did not insure this value. A dispute hence arose for whose account the acceptance of the £1000 be, the same being done and honoured before my letter of the 28th January or February came to the hands of Messrs Snell and Co.

'I shall not burden you with Mr Snell's opinion or my opinion on this subject, as doubtless what may be said on both sides may occur to you. Let it suffice that in our opinion differing we mutually agreed to accommodate it by a reference. For this purpose they named one in London. I disagreed with a reference in London and named one in Dublin ... however they disagreed with referring it in Dublin on which I wrote them I was satisfied that they consult the opinion of the attorney general or the solicitor general in London and which way soever either of these gentlemen give their opinion I mentioned I am satisfied that be the rule whereby we were mutually to abide and for this purpose I drew up a short narrative of the cause of difference on my side, to be laid before either of the gentlemen in order to receive their opinion ... Notwithstanding they delayed with consulting the opinion of the attorney or solicitor general in London, as if they were not as competent judges of mercantile disputes as merchants, and therefore they proposed a person in Amsterdam as reference there, a place wherein I have no correspondence. I declined and at same time asked them if they would agree to refer the dispute at Bordeaux, namely to Mr Ainslie, my referee there. This was in April 1753, the latter end of the month, when I wrote to them that I was soon to be from home and would make it my business to enquire about a referee at Amsterdam ... I went from home and returned in July, when I wrote to Messrs Snell & Co that I had consulted the opinion of some merchants in Dublin and Glasgow, who unanimously agreed that the reference of a dispute arisen here to merchants in Amsterdam or Bordeaux was applying for assistance in a foreign place and therefore to be avoided. To them it seemed odd that in a correspondence of so long uninterrupted a continuance a matter of difference arising could not be accommodated by themselves without the mediation of other persons, and this they recommended.

'On my return in July 1753 I therefore wrote to Messrs Snell & Co of my readiness to agree. I proposed to close the dispute on their allowing me £500 or at least £200 in terms of the credit established for

Ewing in terms of the first letter I wrote them on this subject, by which proposal they were to bear £200 and I to bear £800 of the value contained in Ewing's drafts and thus proportion the loss and obviate the obstruction to the renewal of our correspondence. Messrs Snell & Co decline this proposal but have offered me an allowance of £100 to be allowed or deducted off their arising profits from the renewal or continuance of their correspondence with me or mine with them and this their offer I have declined, as I still do their proposal of a reference at Amsterdam or Bordeaux ... I cannot close this letter without taking notice of the words they write the 29th March to you in a style warm, and seemingly too warm, if my claim be a most wrong one and it follows that theirs is a most right one. I'm still content to abide by the opinion of the solicitor or attorney general in London or the arbitrage of merchants in Dublin or Glasgow, whereby the distinction will be explained. You may if you please communicate to them what I write you. You may if you please intermediate an accommodation or you may if you please ... give me your opinion touching this matter of dispute, what you would do or what you would expect to have done to you were my case yours'. [Philip Moore & Sons, 6 May 1754]. Moore's confusion about the date of his second letter to William Snell & Co 'the 28th January or February following' can be explained by reference to the letter-book. The dates of letters over this period are: 27 January (5), 30 January, 7 February, 8 January, 8 February (3), 28 February, 11 February, 20 February.

At last it was agreed that there should be an arbitration at Dublin, Mat Weld, merchant, acting for Snell and Robert Patrick for Moore. The list of papers presented by Moore was impressive: copies of John Kelly & John Callin's letters to Pat Ewing, John Ewing and J Halliday & Co dated 4 September 1751; copies of Pat Ewing's letters to Kelly & Callin dated 16 September, 9 October and 22 November 1751; an estimate of the *Grizzy's* cargo, if bought at St Eustatius 1751; copy of account current with Robert Colhoun, St Christophers, 3 December 1751; copies of rum invoices at St Christophers dated 3 December 1751; copy of George Moore's letter to Ralph Sampson in St Eustatius dated 3 September 1751 with copies of all letters exchanged with Messrs Snell & Co relating to the dispute; copy of Messrs Snell & Co's state of the case given to Moore on 12 September 1755 and William Snell & Co's missive to submit the dispute also dated 12 September 1755.

In the meantime there had been a further complication as mentioned in a letter Moore wrote to William White & Co in Dublin. 'Your opinion of the dispute between Messrs William Snell & Co and me is precisely the same as my opinion of it. Namely that it unluckily happened. I still am heartily disposed that it be done away and therefore I cheerfully agreed to the arbitration in Dublin. My health, which has been not in a good state, made me less active in preparing matters necessary to lay before the gentlemen arbitrators than the nature of them required. However what I had to lay before said gentlemen should have been in Dublin before this time had not a fresh matter occurred which it became also necessary for me to arbitrate.

'It seems that Mr Snell, when he was in Douglas, took occasion to speak of a transaction I was concerned in in the year 1746. This related to a French vessel that I had with brandy shipwrecked at Derbyhaven, where the vessel and a great deal of the cargo was lost. On this subject Mr Snell said that I had insured the value in Holland, that I had bought the cargo of brandy at Derbyhaven at cant at a very low rate, part of it so low as 4d per gallon ... and that I had made a great deal of money by that enterprise (selling the brandy at 3/6 per gallon). This he said publicly to some (including Hugh Connor, merchant in Douglas) that he was a stranger to and never had any manner of correspondence with. With how much more freedom it may be presumed he spoke of this matter to gentlemen whom he was intimate with or were his correspondents and friends. As with these last mentioned you are justly ranked, I appeal to your Mr White and hope he will do me the justice to let me know if he, Mr Snell, did not tell him on the subject of the insurance, on my manner of management thereof and on the considerable deal of money I had made for that enterprise. In the same manner or to that purpose which I now write you that I've told to some gentlemen in Douglas I further appeal to you of the waiting several days to inform myself herein and to remove the influence the impression of such an account tended to create was not cause sufficient for me to employ those days for that purpose to the end that all such like impressions may find no place in the depending dispute. This is now done and all my papers are now in readiness to be sent to my son, who will embrace the first opportunity that offers for Dublin'. [William White & Co, 26 October 1755].

To Thomas Finlay he added 'My state of health is such that I'm at this season of the year afraid to attempt a sea passage or I surely would wait on the sitting and determination of the gentlemen arbitrators. I must therefore make use of my son to send by him the papers and my state of the case relative to the dispute. But he's too young to say anything nor can it be expected he can properly appear for me before the arbitrators or if his uncle Onge's appearing with him for me sufficient. This I'm undetermined about as he's a counsellor by profession, which perhaps merchants will not like to see on an arbitration. However give me leave to desire the favour of your appearing for me before the arbitrators, if you think it consistent or that you will direct this for me. From the papers which my son has may be seen all that I have to say and with what I've submitted I'm determined to be satisfied with what the arbitrators shall please to answer. I lately received a letter from Messrs William White & Co to acquaint me that they have delivered Messrs Snell & Co's papers to Mr Weld and that nothing could be done until papers were sent to Mr Patrick ... I am amazed at what in all the world could Snell mean by his slander or has he dreamed and believed it and so introducing this calamity into our dispute privately endeavour to injure it as well as injure my character. Hence this matter is headlong brought into our dispute and becomes a part thereof as the wiping of any slur on my character is essentially necessary to that equality of opinion which the arbitrators are to exercise. The matter of the insurance is quite cleared up by my correspondence in Amsterdam on that occasion, whose letters are herewith and two letters from Mr Hugh Connor in Douglas, the gentleman to whom Mr Snell vented himself ... Pray do you be pleased to act for me on this occasion in every respect in whatever manner is becoming the merits of my cause and as there will be a necessary expense attending the sitting of the arbitrators do this for me in your own good way and debit my account accordingly'. [Thomas Finlay, 26 October 1755]

Moore had tried to cover all eventualities. 'I've desired Phil to go to Mr Thomas Finlay, who will I hope direct him in the best way for me. As Mr Finlay is partner with Mr Patrick perhaps he himself will not incline to appear for me. I was thinking to desire the favour of you and whether merchants on an arbitration would like the appearance of a counsellor. This I know not but if it be allowed I would be glad you were with Phil at their first meeting, as it may give benefit or be of some service'. [John Onge, 26 October 1755]

'Since my young arbitrator went off I have not had a line from him so do not know what is yet done or concluded in respect of the dispute'. [Thomas Finlay & Robert Patrick, 10 November 1755]. The silence continued for many weeks. 'My son is returned from Dublin and acquaints me of the proceedings in the arbitration. He says that you have taken a great deal of pains to search into the nature of the dispute, to have a thorough knowledge thereof, to bring it to the speediest conclusion, which is extremely kind and merits my warmest acknowledgments. I find that Mr John Callin in this town designs soon for Ireland, he says towards the latter end of this week. He was the principal mover in the undertaking of that unlucky adventure and no one has a more intimate knowledge of all the circumstances relating it than he. What I know is already communicated in the state. As to other circumstances I'm entirely unacquainted with and an utter stranger to. If any matter on my side requires your further light or examining into I would refer to him. This perhaps you will think not improper as he is no ways concerned in the dispute nor can gain or lose whether Messrs Snell & Co or I prevail therein. I would therefore for this purpose that you have reference to Mr Callin. He will be in Dublin to transact some business with Mr Francis Moore ... I resent Mr Snell's discourse with Mr Connor at my expense. Every one is alarmed with my design of justifying myself in a public manner so that the scandal is hushed to prevent being introduced as an evidence against Snell. However I am yet with hopes that I may find out one to join or corroborate Mr Connor and if I succeed herein I shall try what I can do to receive satisfaction. Pray what do you think of it or what would you advise me to do?' [Thomas Finlay and Robert Patrick, 1 December 1755]

'I observe that the opinion of the arbitrators will be determined by Mr Snell's answer to some queries they have of him. Nothing less than an arbitration would please Snell and so he was positive in his opinion and inflexible. I was the more cautious in naming a friend in whom I could confide that the matter of dispute would be attended to and that a decision would issue from the merits thereof in an impartial view'. [Thomas Finlay & Robert Patrick, 24 December 1755]

There are no further references to the dispute in the letter-book. Though there may be several reasons for this, there are no further letters to Finlay & Patrick, save one to Messrs Robert Patrick & Co dated 6 October 1759. Long before the dispute reached arbitration in Dublin Moore had ceased his correspondence with Snell.

Abraham James Hillhouse

Moore had been in correspondence with Abraham James Hillhouse previously but he was reintroduced to him by Finlay & Patrick in Dublin. 'I'm three-quarters concerned in a cargo of provisions shipping or shipped on the *Lilly*, Robert Montgomerie master, for Barbados or the Leeward Islands by Messrs Thomas Finlay and Robert Patrick ... They do not incline to exchange letters with Messrs William Snell & Co so have recommended my using you upon this occasion. I readily agreed therewith in consequence whereof I expect you have insured equal to my part of the value of the provisions and £600 on the snow *Lilly* outwards for my account. Rum is to be shipped on her at Barbados or the Leeward Islands, the difference between the provisions and the value of rum is to be drawn for on you one quarter for their account and three-quarters for my account, which in due time I shall cause be remitted you. I have herewith wrote to Mr James Simson, book keeper to Messrs Colin Dunlop and Alexander Houston & Co ... to remit you £100 for my account I expect accordingly'. [Abraham James Hillhouse, 13 November 1752]

'I'm pleased you express so much satisfaction in this renewal of correspondence with you and I rest satisfied with your assurance that in whatever instance I apply to you my interest will be attended to. Our mutual friends Messrs Thomas Finlay & Robert Patrick in Dublin have repeated their recommendation of your offices and friendship. As these circumstances are much to my inclination they will invite my further correspondence'. [Abraham James Hillhouse, 20 November 1752]

In March 1753 he transferred the *Peggy*'s accounts to Hillhouse. 'I'm five-eighths concerned in the snow *Peggy*, Pat Montgomerie master, with fish from Boston to discharge at Barcelona with Messrs Harris Crisp & Co there, who are to load a cargo of brandy, five-eighths to my account. What the value of said fish shall want of the value of the brandy

I shall direct their drafts on you, which in case they do you will please honour. I'm not certain they will draw on you for some time ago I directed this their drafts on Messrs William Snell & Co but at present I cause to make this alteration. You will please attend to and to making assurance on my five-eighths the value of the brandy in case they write you to this purpose'. [Abraham James Hillhouse, 7 March 1753]

The first hint of a problem with Hillhouse surfaced in mid 1754. 'There is another merchant which I must also write to you in confidence about. Mr Abraham James Hillhouse has of late transacted all business for me there (in London) and just now I have received some intimation no way favourable to his character for that trust I should necessarily confide in him. Now I must desire the favour of your writing to your friend in London, requesting his opinion of Mr Hillhouse's circumstances and manner of dealing, which I conclude he may do without giving the least offence. My correspondence with Mr Hillhouse began on the recommendation of Messrs Thomas Finlay & Robert Patrick ... but the continuance of it must depend on the certainty of safety or the appearance of certainty free from surprises'. [Colin Dunlop, 4 May 1754]

Dunlop's response can be guessed from the following letter to James Simson in Glasgow. 'I have not yet fixed a correspondence at London suitable to my inclination but I expect it will soon be fixed. In the meantime I have occasion to make use of a credit in London to serve to reimburse the value of some provisions I have directed in the *Lilly*, Robert Montgomerie master, who is now here and with the first wind is to proceed to Belfast or Cork. If the vessel goes to Cork the lading will be under the address of Messrs James and George Piersy, if to Belfast under the address of Mr John Gordon ... for the value shipped, I compute about £400, I have directed the draft on your friends in London, Messrs Andrew Drummond Esq & Co, to whom please write on your receipt hereof that due honour be given to the draft ... and do you debit my account accordingly. This I have directed in consequence of what Mr Colin Dunlop was pleased to give me leave to do and appoint when I was in Glasgow. I have also directed Robert Montgomerie to write a letter to Messrs Drummond to acquaint them of the value of the goods ... to be insured to Boston'. [James Simson, 20 August 1754]

No letters exist to Drummond & Co and there was a somewhat complicated overlap between them and Moore's next agents in London. If anything, the situation with Hillhouse was exacerbated by the problem of Theobald Dillon's tea (see Chapter Four). Hillhouse wrote to Moore on 5 and 20 December 1754 and 4 January 1755 advising him 'of Mr Theobald Dillon consigning me nine whole chests and six quarter chests by the *Marquis of Bonnac*, Jan Wolfers master ... I shall not fail embracing such an opportunity of sale be the profit small or great, I shall not fail to hold the proceeds to your order or remit you the value so soon as it is in my power to do so. If therefore you are inclined to accommodate Mr Dillon's inclination of having a part of the value remitted him, allowing interest for your advance, you see upon what security'. He then continued 'Such are my connections with what is called the Old Bank in Glasgow that all money transactions I direct by means of the cashier, Mr James Simson, are done for me without commission and this extends to their correspondents paying money for me at London. The consequence whereof is obvious to you so that what business I can appoint will there canter. You may hence see the consideration for which an alteration takes place in my manner of business on a principle of saving I could not otherwise expect. I shall always have a grateful remembrance of your inclination to oblige me'. [Abraham James Hillhouse, 5 February 1755]

Moore's last letter was dated November 1755. 'I received your favour of the 9th September acquainting me that you had received the policy of my fire insurance for one year from Michaelmas last. The cost, £9 10s, is accordingly placed to your credit ... I desire you will please send me abstract of my account current balanced. I remain very respectfully'. [Abraham James Hillhouse, 8 November 1755]

Richard Oswald & Co
Moore clearly asked all his Glasgow contacts about a new banker in London. 'On my mentioning the house of your friend Mr Richard Oswald in London and my inclination of dealing with them you were pleased to tell me that if I did so you would become security for them, answerable to their trust and confidence, which in course of correspondence I might have occasion to repose or lodge with them. These circumstances prevail with me to desire your answer on this

subject and therewith please let me know how to direct for Mr Oswald's house in London, to whom at same time you may write to introduce our correspondence'. [Richard & Alexander Oswald, 13 August 1754]

'If the goods from Cork by the *Lilly* fall short to purchase the fish (in Boston), for the difference Robert Montgomerie had directions to draw on you. Also to write you to insure the value of the cargo of fish from Boston to Alicante and other ports in Spain, where he may best meet a market. You'll be pleased accordingly do for me. This direction to Montgomerie was in consequence to my speaking to your friend, Mr Richard Oswald in Scotland, when he told me if I inclined for a correspondence with you he would recommend and introduce it'. [Richard Oswald & Co, 22 October 1754]

The same day Moore wrote to James Simson, to smooth over the changeover. 'I'm now favoured with yours of the 4th inst wherein you mention that Messrs A Drummond & Co would certainly make the insurance I ordered ... I've a letter at same time from Messrs Richard Oswald & Co in London, wherein they mention that by order of Robert Montgomerie they have insured £600 on the Lilly from Cork to Madeira, Barbados etc, where they concluded she was bound to. To regulate this I have wrote them and desired they may speak to Messrs A Drummond & Co'. [James Simson, 22 October 1754]

Despite a possible irregularity in the move to the new bankers, 'I wish I had seen your Mr Oswald in Scotland, as it had proved a more regular introduction to our correspondence. I'm obliged to your favour herein'. [Richard Oswald & Co, 5 February 1755]. There is no suggestion of a rift in their correspondence. The last letter to an agent in London, dated 6 June 1759, is addressed to them.

The next two chapters look in greater detail at Moore's two vessels, the *Peggy* and the *Lilly*.

GEORGE MOORE AND THE OLD (SHIP) BANK

'Prior to 1750 there were no banks in Glasgow. A certain description of monetary accommodation, however, had long prevailed. Merchants of known wealth and reputation dealt in bills of exchange, and received money from small traders and others on deposit, for which interest was allowed, according to bargain. In these transactions, specie was chiefly employed, the notes of the three Edinburgh banks then existing being comparatively little known, and paper-money not popular in the West country. Besides these first class merchants, money was received on deposit by most of the joint-stock companies which carried on business in Glasgow, of which there were a number. These companies were composed of merchants of high standing, including many of the tobacco lords, or Virginia Dons, who associated themselves for carrying on, apart from their ordinary business, the refining of sugar, tanning leather, manufacturing soap, and the like, under the immediate charge of practical managers ... The deposits received by some of the joint-stock companies ... were of large amount, and remained with them long after the establishment of banks in Glasgow ...

'At length the rapidly-increasing trade of Glasgow determined some of the most wealthy and influential merchants there to establish a local bank to meet the monetary exigencies of the city. Accordingly, six gentlemen formed themselves into a company for carrying on the trade of banking, including the issuing of notes. These were - William McDowall of Castlesemple; Andrew Buchanan of Drumpellier; Alan Dreghorn of Ruchill; Robert Dunlop, merchant; Colin Dunlop of Carmyle; and Alexander Houston of Jordanhill. The social firm was Dunlop, Houston, and Co, and the descriptive was that of the afterwards well-known 'Ship Bank.' The notes bore the figure of a ship under full sail, and were very plain. They were originally signed by Mr Colin Dunlop and Mr Houston.

'The office was in the east end of the Bridgegate, then a place of importance ... Their first cashier was Arthur Robertson, in whose property was the bank. The business commenced in January 1750. The office hours were from ten till twelve forenoon, and from three till five o'clock afternoon, except Saturdays, when the bank was open only from nine till eleven ...

'The first cashier, Mr Robertson, died about three years after and Mr James Simson was appointed his successor ...

L. 12 *Scots.*   *No.* ⅓⅓⅓

                GLASGOW, 2*d January* 1753.

I, JAMES SIMSON, *Cashier, appointed by* Colin Dunlop, Alexander Houston & Company, *Bankers in Glasgow, pursuant to powers from them, Promise to pay to* John Brown, *or the Bearer,* Twenty Shillings Sterling, *the date, number, and creditor's name, are inserted by me, and these presents signed by me, and the said* Colin Dunlop, *and* Alex. Houston.

                                                JAMES SIMSON.

COLIN DUNLOP.
ALEX. HOUSTON.

'Such is a list of the whole native private banks which issued notes in Glasgow during the last one hundred and twelve years. It seems worth while briefly to mention what became of them. 1. The Ship Bank existed from 1750 till 1836, a period of eighty-six years, under that descriptive title. But during that time several changes of the social firm took place, in consequence of the death or retirement of partners, and the assumption of others in their places. The first contract of copartnery was for twenty-five years, and expired in 1775. All the original partners then retired, and eight new ones carried on the business of the Ship, under the firm of Moores, Carrick, & Co. The new partners were **George Moore, Ballamore, Isle of Man; James Moore, merchant in Glasgow (relations of the celebrated Sir John Moore, who fell at Corunna)**; Robert Carrick, merchant; Thomas Brown, formerly surgeon in London, then residing at Aitkenhead, near Glasgow; Andrew Thomson of Faskin; John Brown of Langfine; Thomas Buchanan of Ardoch; and William Craig, merchant ... This new firm removed the bank office in 1776 from the Bridgegate to the antique-looking tenement, so well remembered, which faced Argyll Street, at the south-west angle of what is now Glassford Street, where the business was carried on during half-a-century. They purchased the tenement for £1700. About eight years after this second change of partners, a third took place (1783), and the firm was altered to Carrick, Brown, and Co ...

'The bank used to be closed from one till two o'clock daily; and it was part of the duty of the youngest apprentice to protect the treasure during the night, for which purpose he was armed with a gun, powder-horn, and a few charges of slugs, and locked in till morning, a 'box-bed' being fitted up in the telling-room for his convenience. A bugle lay beside him to sound an alarm'.

From: Banking in Glasgow during the Olden Time. Glasgow, Past and Present. 1862.

CHAPTER SEVEN: THE *PEGGY*

'I see that you approve of the scheme of making the *Peggy* a Dane. I have been speaking of it to Captain Weiergang, who makes no doubt but he can accomplish the matter. An absolute bill of sale is necessary be made to Weiergang and he must give a ... bond for the value, by which the vessel may continue under the direction of the original proprietors. The manner of doing this is referred to you and to him to perfect as you'll be best advised. However, to act with caution seems necessary for I would not by any means have it publicly known for that may do harm and can do no good in case we should have occasion in the course of trade to make use of your old register'. [Pat Montgomerie, 23 April 1759]

The Peggy was built in Boston during 1750 and was owned five-eighths by George Moore and three-eighths by Kelly and Callin. This meant that all arrangements for a voyage had to be sorted out between the two parties. 'It is now agreed (with Kelly & Callin) on you to load fish in New England suitable for the Straights market'. [Pat Montgomerie, 12 March 1751]. And 'Messrs Kelly & Callin have agreed with me that it's advisable you have a discretionary power as well in the choice of the port in Spain where to load (brandy) as in the sale of the fish so that in both respects the interest of your employers may be consulted'. [Pat Montgomerie, 15 August 1751]. A further complication was that Kelly & Callin dealt with Claud Johnson & Son in London while Moore's agents there have been discussed in Chapter Six.

Maiden Voyage

The *Peggy*'s maiden voyage was to take lumber from Boston to the West Indies, where a cargo of rum was to be ready at Barbados. The problems connected with this cargo were discussed in Chapter Three.

'I had a vessel lately from Barbados. In her way she put into Belfast, where the master ... having occasion for some necessaries, applied to Mr Daniel Musendine, who was kind to give him £10 16s 8d

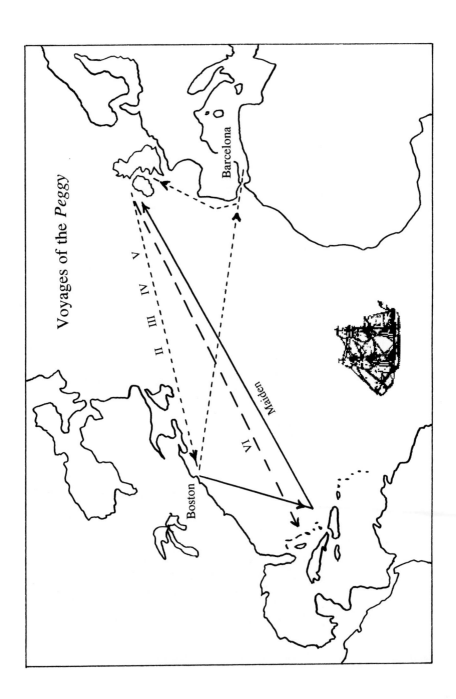

Voyages of the *Peggy*

Barcelona

Boston

Maiden

V

IV

III

II

VI

Figure 8: The Voyages of the *Peggy*

Maiden Voyage 1750: Boston to Barbados to Peel (but went into Belfast en route)

Boston: lumber to Barbados

Barbados (Richard Smith & Co): rum

Voyage II 1751 to 1752: Scotland to Boston to Barcelona (calling elsewhere in the Mediterranean en route)

Scotland (Joseph Scott & Co, Glasgow, Smellie & Hopkirk, Glasgow, Alan Glen, Irvine): manufactories

Boston (John Rowe, Henry Atkin, Aeneas Mackay & Co): rum (shipped back to the Isle of Man) and fish

Barcelona (Green, Stanton & Ford): brandy

Voyage III 1752 to 1753: Scotland to Boston to Barcelona

Scotland: manufactories

Boston (John Rowe): fish

Barcelona (Harris Crisp & Co): brandy, handkerchiefs etc

Voyage IV 1753 to 1754: Scotland to Boston to Barcelona

Scotland: manufactories

Boston (John Rowe): fish

Barcelona (Harris Crisp & Co): brandy and sundries

Voyage V 1754 to 1755: Scotland to Boston to Barcelona

Scotland: manufactories

Boston (John Rowe): fish

Barcelona (Harris Crisp & Co): brandy and sundries

Voyage VI 1757 to Barbados for rum (taken by a privateer)

Note: There are 'missing' voyages both between 1755 and 1757 and after 1757

111

on my account. Mr Musendine desires I may send him a bill on Dublin for said sum whereon to discharge Montgomerie's draft'. [Thomas Finlay, 22 November 1750]. When Moore discovered that Musendine had only given Pat Montgomerie £10, he applied to him for the 16s 8d balance.

This was not the only expense involved in the call at Ireland. On 6 August 1751 Moore wrote to the surveyor of customs at Donaghadee (see Figure 12), enclosing the following statement. 'November 1750 the snow *Peggy* ... was put into Belfast Lough, where two officers were shipped to attend her arrival in Peeltown. (Peter) Sidebotham came to George Moore and told him that he wanted some money to defray the expenses of said officers and his expense in coming to Peeltown about them. For this purpose Moore gave Sidebotham 20s English. Sidebotham died without payment and Moore wants the same'.

Moore added 'I desire you will do me the favour to acquaint your collector in Belfast how, as above, I want 20 English shillings, hoping by means of your application the same may be restored to, sir, your most humble servant'. [Surveyor of Customs at Donaghadee, 6 August 1751]

Voyage II
Moore was depending on Joseph Scott in Glasgow for the *Peggy*'s outward cargo for her next voyage. 'I do not forget the tender you made me of furnishing any my occasions for the Glasgow manufactory goods and the assurance you gave that you and your brother would herein accommodate me on as moderate terms as could be had in Glasgow. I promised to make all experiment of your favours so agreeable to my inclination and an opportunity now presents. The bearer of this letter, Mr Pat Montgomerie ... is in my employ. I design a voyage to Boston. For this voyage ... I have recommended him to you to be supplied with what goods are in your way and what goods are not in your way you will direct he be furnished with to the value above mentioned (£800). The snow is to lie at Irvine so that the goods are to be sent there. Mr Montgomerie has the direction and choice of what goods he esteems most suitable for the market'. [Joseph Scott, 10 December 1750]. Goods were also supplied by Smellie & Hopkirk. A description of the Glasgow manufactories is found in Figure 9.

The *Peggy* was to load fish at Boston. Moore believed that she would hold about thirty hundred quintals (one quintal was equivalent to 100 lbs) of dried cod fish. 'I have since received your letters of the 22nd May and 17th June at Boston. I find you have sold the most part of the outward cargo for fish. The price you mention is very low but I make no doubt you did the best that could be done, as the reasons are they must be submitted to. I presume you met no difficult in disposing of the remainder of your outward cargo on the same terms. It would be rather agreeable to have all sold than to have any part remaining in that country unsold'. [Pat Montgomerie, 15 August 1751]

Moore already had a problem about money still in Boston. 'In the hands of Mr Logan I have effects to a considerable value. The account I have desired he may adjust and settle. I've also desired him to give you and to the commander of the *Lilly* the value of said effects in his hands. If he can so behave as to give the proceeds in the value of fish or any part thereof I desire you may settle with him for me in this or any other manner. By this means you may have effects more than sufficient for the *Peggy*'s loading of fish. The value of such remaining effects let be remitted to me by bills of exchange or by rum to be bought and shipped while you are in New England or let such effects be lodged with the gentleman in Boston to whom Mr Scott's letter of recommendation may be directed'. [Pat Montgomerie, 12 March 1751]

The problems with Walter Logan were discussed in Chapter One. As he did not co-operate, Pat Montgomerie sold his manufactory goods to Captain Henry Atkin and to John Rowe, from whom he purchased the fish. Henry Atkin was supposed to pass his payment to Aeneas Mackay & Co but he delayed as 'the same has reference to the return of some vessels you had on sale'. [Henry Atkin, 13 July 1752]. Aeneas Mackay & Co supplied thirteen hogsheads of rum for Pat Montgomerie and another five hogsheads 'to replace the balance due the freighters of Captain Montgomerie's vessel on account of snuff he sold you belonging to his outward cargo'. [Aeneas Mackay & Co, 18 May 1752]

On 23 July Montgomerie informed Moore 'You expected half your load on board by the first of August and the remainder by the first of September'. [Pat Montgomerie, 14 October 1751]. Montgomerie's initial instructions were to sell the fish at either Alicante or Benicarlo, where he was to load his cargo of brandy under Pat White (see Chapter Two). Because of the rapid changes in the prices of brandy, in August 1751 he was given a discretionary power to find the best markets himself (see above). But advice was still forthcoming. 'By all accounts Valencia brandy is the best made in Spain and this is the sort which I've wrote to Mr White in Benicarlo about, so that it is most likely you will apply to him for the cargo'. [Pat Montgomerie, 14 October 1751]. And 'From the high price which brandy is risen to in Spain I've directed Robert Montgomerie to proceed to load in Cette ... which I mention for your government should this come in time to regulate your and his lading brandy for, at the advanced price of brandy in Spain, one Spanish cargo will be sufficient'. [Pat Montgomerie, 28 December 1751]

Green & Stanton in Barcelona wrote to Moore on 6 November and 4 December 1751. 'I observe with pleasure the arrival of the *Peggy* ... at your port, that he (Pat Montgomerie) applied to you for the disposal of the cargo of fish ... though this seems a very great deduction, I'm satisfied therewith and that you have herein acted in the best way to serve the interest of the concerned. Mr Montgomerie's proceeding directly to your port appears attended with no other inconveniency than the delay or what arises from his waiting the letters I wrote him about loading brandy, forwarded to Mr John Blundell, merchant in Alicante. By your writing to him I expect in course of post Mr Montgomerie would receive my letter. He has thereby a discretionary power of loading brandy in what port in Spain he could best find to do the same for his employers, applying the proceeds of the cargo of fish to the value of brandy and for the remaining value of brandy by bills on London namely two-thirds this remainder on Mr William Snell in my account and one-third this remainder in Messrs Claud Johnson & Son on account of Messrs John Kelly & John Callin which is hereby also confirmed'. [Green & Stanton, 27 December 1751]. The section in this letter underlined by the author is the only clue why Moore did not use Green, Stanton & Ford again but turned to other brandy suppliers in Barcelona instead.

'Make what haste you possibly can to return with your cargo of brandy. Should you touch in any part of Ireland be very cautious that none of the crew offer to run any small quantity for a vessel is seized there laden with rum bound for this Isle on account, as we hear, of one of the crew's running a few gallons of rum'. [Pat Montgomerie, 28 December 1751]

The *Peggy* arrived at Peel in April 1752, some fifteen months after she had sailed from Irvine.

Voyage III

For this voyage the outward cargo from Boston was to be the same (see Figure 9). Moore wrote to John Rowe 'I find that Captain Pat Montgomerie had dealings with you last year in the sale of the goods he had with him from Glasgow and in the purchase of the fish he loaded on the snow *Peggy*. Mr Samuel Crisp of London ... has made mention of you and in so favourable a way that I'm hence invited to recommend the bearer, Captain Pat Montgomerie, who, as last year, intends this year to Boston in the same manner with factory goods to sell and to purchase fish and some rum. I beg the favour of you to do him what friendly offices is in your power and your assistance in whatever instance is necessary'. [John Rowe, 13 July 1752]

In October 1752 and January 1753 Moore complained to William Snell & Co in London that he had not heard of the *Peggy*'s arrival in Boston. In fact letters were on the way. 'I'm favoured with yours of the 8th January letting me know that Captain Montgomerie had then 2,000 quintals of fish onboard. By his letter to me of the 22nd January he writes he had further received 500 quintals and expected the remainder the first dry weather. I'm very much afraid that the delay which has attended on the shipping the fish will be of great injury to his voyage for if the season of Lent be over before he arrives in Spain the price there will be lower'. [John Rowe, 24 April 1753]

In the meantime Moore had written two letters dated 14 October 1752 to await Pat Montgomerie at Alicante and Barcelona. 'I've lately received a letter from Mr John Blundell in Alicante, which gives a poor prospect of the sale of fish there the ensuing season so that I'm apprehensive you will have directly to proceed to Barcelona'. And 'This is under cover to Messrs Harris Crisp & Co in Barcelona to whom I have wrote in regard to my interest in the *Peggy*'s cargo out and home. To

Figure 9: The Fish Trade and Glasgow Manufactories

The fish was loaded in New England, usually at Boston. 'Selling a part (en route to the Straights) would lessen and be of service I think to the preservation of the remainder ... Pray take great care that your cargo of fish be taken on board in dry good order for on the quality of the fish depends the success of the voyage'. [Pat Montgomerie, 12 March 1751]

'What I mean by meeting with a favourable market at Alicante or elsewhere you may hence judge: if it answers the cost of the cargo and also a moderate freight I would have you agree and close with the market, particularly if it offers at Alicante for the market there for fish is the most considerable one in the Mediterranean ... Two or three months credit may be of great service to me, which no one can be safe in giving but one that is resident and thereby has an acquaintance of the solvency of the person with whom he deals'. [Robert Montgomerie 1 July 1751]

'My being concerned this year in Glasgow factory goods arises from the certainty I have that few or no goods have been this year exported thence and no exports was intended so that the small quantity wherein I'm concerned has the fairer prospect of turning out well'. [Henry Atkin, 13 July 1752]

'The directions which Mr Rowe gives for the choice of these goods is that there be no stripped or checked Hollands nor diapers but that they chiefly consist of even eighths or yard wide checks of the Glasgow sort from 12d to 20d per yard that the others be 3/4 common checks and red ticks and a few pieces of plaids'. [Pat Montgomerie, 23 July 1753]. 'Let these be made into three or four different packages sorted for the convenience of selling and consign them to Robert Montgomerie, master of the Lilly in Boston, giving them into Mr Pat Montgomerie's care for me'. [Joseph Scott & Co, 23 July 1753]

Moore was offered various other commodities. 'I've been speaking to Pat Montgomerie as it was very much my inclination to encourage your shoe factory but he says they are an article which no way suit the market he intends for so that he does not purpose taking with him one pair'. [Dr Moor, Kilmarnock, 23 July 1753] them I have applied and addressed my five-eighths of the cargo of fish to sell for me and to load five-eighths of the cargo of brandy to be loaded on the *Peggy* there or on that coast to be discharged here. You have a commission from my young family to buy fifty Barcelona handkerchiefs of the largest size and different colours ... I've this day been speaking with Messrs Kelly & Callin, who will I suppose write to you to the care of their friend in Barcelona and direct about their concern in the outward and homeward cargoes'. [Pat Montgomerie, 14 October 1752]

In April 1753 (some ten months after she had been in Scotland collecting the outward cargo) Moore wrote 'I do not hear of the arrival of the *Peggy* ... at Barcelona. Messrs Harris Crisp & Co respite buying brandy for her until she arrives there'. [Abraham James Hillhouse, 24 April 1753]

Four problems developed from this first contact with Harris Crisp & Co. Five butts of brandy fell into the harbour while being rafted to the *Peggy*. 'I understood them not all at my risk or account as well from the practice of the other shippers of Montgomerie's cargo as in the common acceptation of the manner generally used in debiting the invoice for butts of brandy clear on board. No words can stronger imply your delivering or my acceptation of the delivery and if so surely I'm exonerated of any intermediate risk in the present instance, as well as in any future one'. [Harris Crisp & Co, 30 October 1753]

As there was a deadlock in the dispute, Harris Crisp referred it to arbitration. 'I am now favoured with yours of the 22nd March to advise me of the determination of the lawsuit ... whereby you are sentenced to bear half the loss and the rafters the other half in consequence whereof you have debited my account 88 dollars. You are fully acquainted already with my sentiments on this subject. It remains that I rest satisfied with whatever be the rule you are pleased to establish as a precedent but at present it seems to me an establishment of a point that requires being obviated and must suspend any further remarks on this business until I see Captain Montgomerie'. [Harris Crisp & Co, 4 May 1754]

'The loss on the five butts of brandy I observe still remains in suspense but I can see no reason why Captain Montgomerie does use a different language or have contrary opinions when he communes with you and with me on that subject. The matter in dispute seems to be the establishing of a precedent whereby to be regulated in any future the like accidents of loss ... I hope you will not take it amiss that our sentiments on this subject be implicit and mutually understood. The practice should be the rule. Now in this Isle it is foreign to have any other opinion of the practice than that used by the houses in Barcelona with whom the merchants in this Isle correspond. This correspondence you know has solely circulated in yours and in Messrs Green, Stanton & Ford's house. They entirely give up the matter or occasion of dispute and you affect to divide it so that in any future the like accidents of loss the practice would be similar and thereby the rule in your house and the rule in their house be very different. There is another house setting or set up in Barcelona in the name of Messrs Robert Herries & Co. Herries has a personal acquaintance with several persons in this Isle who seem to have a great regard for him. I have been speaking of the loss of the five butts of brandy and asking them what would Herries & Co agree to in the like case. They told me that the practice used by Messrs Green, Stanton & Ford should be the rule with them and which they for Herries & Co would promise. If hence I am to form an opinion you see upon what foundation it is determined'. [Harris Crisp & Co, 13 December 1754]

'I am now to own receipt of your favour the 21 December and 18 January in which you are pleased to give up the 44 dollars stated to my debit in my former account ... I observe your admitting the precedent as a rule on any future the like occasions but are not satisfied with the justice whereby it is expected at this distance. The practice established in other houses seems enough to ascertain it but if the rafters are engaged by contract or by custom to make good such kind of damages that may happen it is plain that this is the factor's recourse wherein he is to rely and to expect recourse in another channel might be looked on as a double security. I should not have troubled you so long on this subject were it not from the motive of establishing a precedent, which were you in my stead I persuade myself you would alike urge'. [Harris Crisp & Co, 24 March 1755]

'I observe your acquiescence with my debiting your account with 44 dollars ... and of the precedent hereby established with this reserve that hereafter they are at the ship's risk from the time of the rafts being alongside. How far a vessel may be thus held liable I apprehend requires a general custom to support or must depend on a condition expressed in the charter party'. [Harris Crisp & Co, 15 August 1755]

The second problem related to the handkerchiefs mentioned in the letter to Pat Montgomerie dated 14 October 1752. 'As to the handkerchiefs ... he will satisfy you that what were charged, the large sort which he saw in Barcelona, were not in the box when he opened it for me on board his vessel ... the quantity was exact but the whole handkerchiefs of one sort'. [Harris Crisp & Co, 30 October 1753]

Next there was the port charge of 23.11 dollars at Barcelona. 'I have demanded this ... from Montgomerie. He has refused to pay and shows his having paid this sum to William Pollard, vice consul, as from his receipt the 18th April specifying to article of paid charges and would have allowed it until he see you but he declines as in his words paying money twice. This therefore with your leave I shall debit your account'. [Harris Crisp & Co, 15 August 1754]. The problem was still continuing in 1755.

Finally 'Pat Montgomerie told me it would be very inconvenient for him to take one part of his cargo in at Salloe and proceed to any other port for the remainder. I must therefore leave this to his determination'. [Harris Crisp & Co 30 October 1753]

The *Peggy* arrived from Salloe, with information about all these problems, in July 1753.

Voyage IV

In September 1753 Pat Montgomerie was in readiness to set sail for Boston with Glasgow manufactories. 'I am very glad to hear that your state of health gives every appearance of recovery and would admit of your proceeding on the voyage. For from what I heard I concluded you would not be able to proceed'. [Pat Montgomerie, 30 October 1753]. Montgomerie had on board £100 worth of goods for the Lilly (see Chapter Eight) but as they did not meet up in Boston John Rowe used the proceeds to ship ten hogsheads of rum on the *Caledonia*.

On 24 January 1754 Montgomerie wrote from Boston 'He was clear to sail with a full cargo of excellent fish. I compute his arrival at Alicante, where he would first call, was in March and that there or on the coast he has by this time concluded the sales of the cargo or fish'. [Harris Crisp & Co, 4 May 1754]. The letter Montgomerie received from Harris Crisp & Co at Alicante must have been persuasive because 'I believe you exerted yourselves for my interest. Circumstances must be submitted to however. Montgomerie may complain that he left Alicante and came up to Barcelona, thereby injuring the sale of the fish by leaving a better and coming to a worse market.

'I've tasted a good deal of the brandy and think that the quality in general is unexceptionable comparatively with the quality I've formerly had from you. Your brandies are improving and if with the flavour you add proof it will the more establish a character, which no doubt with you will prove a general utility. I cannot say so much in favour of your casks. These indeed are miserably bad. No less than ten casks were used to fill up my five-eighths the *Peggy*'s cargo. Severals onboard and on shore were obliged to be run off into other casks for preservation of the brandy'. [Harris Crisp & Co, 15 August 1754]. 'I observe it is not in your power to remedy the badness or insufficiency of the butts used to contain the brandy. The complaint must be doubtless general, which may as it ought contribute to a general establishment'. [Harris Crisp & Co, 13 December 1754]

Voyage V

Once again Montgomerie was to take manufactured goods to Boston for fish. The biggest difference first appears in a letter dated August 1754. 'You have herewith my draft on Mr John Rowe old tender £571 15s 5d or lawful money £77 11s 5d which, with the proceeds of the sale of my Negro Douglas, let be applied towards my part of the cargo of fish to serve by so much to lessen your drawing for me'. [Pat Montgomerie, 14 August 1754]. And 'I expect you have disposed of my Negro Douglas because his face I never want to see. If he be not sold, sell him in Spain for what you can get for him'. [Pat Montgomerie, 4 November 1754]. There is no further information about what happened to Douglas.

Again the brandy came from Harris Crisp & Co. The correspondence about the rafting problem had continued throughout Voyages IV and V - the first reference to Robert Herries & Co was in a letter dated 13 December 1754. This was the last time Moore used Harris Crisp & Co for his Barcelona brandy (see Chapter Two).

The missing years

The gap in the letter-book makes it difficult to trace what the *Peggy* was doing between the end of Voyage V and May 1757. On 30 August 1755 Moore wrote to John Brown about payment for goods from the factory taken by Pat Montgomerie valued at £106 3s. 'I remember the gentlemen of your company told me they would deal with me in as good terms as any in Scotland'. [John Brown, Ayr, 30 August 1755]. In January 1756 Moore wrote to Pat Montgomerie 'I wish you would look out or enquire among your friends at Glasgow for a freight for the *Peggy* and let me know if you can agree or can expect it'. [Pat Montgomerie, 7 January 1756]. The next relevant letter is dated May 1757.

Voyage VI: Taken by a Privateer

'On the 15th this month Messrs John Callin & Co, who have an interest in the *Peggy* ... forwarded a letter they received from Messrs Stevenson & Sons, Barbados, to acquaint that the *Peggy* near that island was taken into a French port by a privateer and in about seventy hours the vessel was retaken again and with the privateer carried into Barbados. Callin's letter was to Messrs Claud Johnson & Son, who are desired to acquaint you therewith that proper intimation of the loss might be made to the insurers and in case that bills were drawn to re-establish the loss the word or writing would provide to honour them, which in so obvious an instance it is hoped they will agree to'. [Richard Oswald & Co, 31 May 1757]. The Gentleman's Magazine lists the vessels taken both by and from the French for each month during 1757 but there is no mention of this incident.

'How Pat Montgomerie ... will proceed is uncertain. He may load a cargo of rum at Barbados or one of the Leeward Islands. In this case my part of the cargo will be about one hundred and seventeen hogsheads equal to 17/49 parts of the three hundred and thirty hogsheads computed for her cargo. The settlement of the loss outwards may effect the extent of his bills for the purchase of said cargo rum. Montgomerie may not perhaps be exact in his manner of drawing therefore please when his bills appear so let them be compared with the sum he draws on Messrs Johnsons so that your payment for me may not exceed my part of the cargo.' [Richard Oswald & Co, 1 June 1757]. The uncertainty continued. 'I'm surprised at the occasion of the silence attending the *Peggy* at Barbados. Not a word about her have we had since Messrs Stevensons advice of her arrival so that I cannot determine anything or write with certainty about her'. [Richard Oswald & Co, 14 July 1757]

Then there was news at last. 'Yesterday arrived the *Peggy* ... from Barbados, which she left in convoy of the *Anson* and other men of war and parted them at Cape Fear. I find that Messrs Stevenson & Sons have drawn on you for a much greater sum than my interest in the cargo, namely £135/.10.1 ... Captain Montgomerie says that he forwarded by the Anson the vouchers of capture to Messrs Johnson & Son and that by a Liverpool ship in the Channel he wrote them advice of his arrival, I suppose they have received and intimated to you'. [Richard Oswald & Co, 25 July 1757].

This letter contains information about the respective shares in the cargo, which should have been:

John Kelly	£356 13s 4d	9/49
Pat Montgomerie	£276 10s 1d	6/49
J Callin & Co	£757 18s 4d	17/49
George Moore	£757 18s 4d	17/49

More missing years

The next gap is partially filled by the Ayr custom house letter-books. On 6 May 1758 the *Peggy* of Irvine, Pat Montgomerie master, arrived from Virginia with two hundred and seventy-eight hogsheads of tobacco. This fits in with a letter from Moore to Hugh Paterson, dated 15 December 1757, referring to £40 owed for an outfit to Virginia. On 29 December 1758 the *Peggy* was reported as being in quarantine at Lamlash, 'waiting the spring tides' with two hundred and eighty-six hogsheads on board. This voyage is referred to by Moore. 'I received your letter of the 29th January acquainting of the delivery of the cargo of tobacco in much better order than you thought or could be expected from so hazardous a voyage. I hope there will be no such trouble attending the payment of this freight as there has been with Mr Galloway's (see Chapter Eleven), whose delay has been such as I never believed he would have permitted, especially as he knows that I had passed his bill for value and the gentleman to whom I endorsed it passed it to the Bank at Glasgow, where lying unpaid and protested I was under the necessity of repaying the value to the Bank'. [Pat Montgomerie, 23 April 1759]

The Plot

'A favourite scheme of Mr Callin's for the *Peggy* has been for some time waited on, but it has turned out to be too hazardous and impracticable, or so I am advised. Since then we are quite at a loss how to frame a voyage. I have been this day with Mr Callin. Probably this evening or tomorrow we may come to some resolutions ... so soon as we resolve on what's best to be done we shall soon acquaint you'. [Pat Montgomerie, 19 March 1759]

While there are no details of this 'favourite scheme'. Moore described an alternative solution, which was to register the *Peggy* either in Norway or Denmark as a Danish vessel (see the heading to this chapter). She would take an outward cargo of tobacco, preferably from David Galloway. 'It will help an old score for my friends have got no money from him yet on account of the tobacco freight. But if you cannot get any tobacco from Galloway you must get it elsewhere as you best can for the benefit of the concerned'. [Pat Montgomerie, 23 April 1759]

'What we intended first with the *Peggy* was to bring here a lading of timber from 8 to 10 inches square and 40 feet long, which is wanted for the new quay we intend here (see Chapter Seventeen). This Captain Weiergang says is only or best to be had at Riga, Dantzig or Koningsberg and may be proceeded for from Norway, where he thinks it's best to manage about the Danish scheme. Following this the vessel may proceed to the Straights ... I have been thinking that, if you find any great inconvenience in sending the vessel for that kind of timber we want, and no other will do, in that case would you approve of lading deals in Norway and proceeding to a market in Ireland, following which would you approve of taking out a cargo for Boston to load fish to Spain and there here with brandy in the old way? As a British vessel to America and to Gibraltar, when doubtless convoys up the Straight may be expected frequently to offer and from Barcelona the vessel may return a Dane. I refer to you to conclude in this matter as you think best for the benefit of the concerned.

'I cannot have the pleasure or hopes of success in this expedition unless you yourself conduct it and on the whole I think that you will run no great risk ... It will occur to you that it's necessary to make insurance on the value of the tobacco and for the value of the present outfit, my part whereof being five-eighths parts I desire you will write to my friends in London Messrs Richard Oswald & Co to insure for me and for Messrs Kelly and Callin's part they desire you'll in like manner cause insurance be done for them on the value of the tobacco and outfit as you do for yourself ... Captain Weiergang will probably want a little money for necessaries which you'll let him have in the general account'. [Pat Montgomerie, 23 April 1759]

According to the Ayr custom house letter-books, on 24 May 1759 the *Peggy*, Pat Montgomerie master, sailed for Norway. The next detailed reference to Montgomerie is included in the tailpiece to this chapter. But it is possible to identify some of his other voyages. By 1765 he was clearly working for Oliphant & Co, wine merchants in Ayr. He was master of their *Isabella* on at least three occasions between 1765 and 1767. By the 1770s he was master of the *Beggars Benson* on familiar cross-Atlantic journeys. In 1781 he was master of the *Fox* of Irvine, a ship of 160 to 180 tons built in Maryland in 1780 and owned by Arthur McClure & Co of Irvine, on a voyage from Greenock to New York (personal communication from Eric Graham).

A STORY OF PAT MONTGOMERIE

'The fraudulent practices of many of the traders here occasions continued vexation'. The collector was concerned about 'the insolence and incorrigibleness of these persons (smugglers) and even some of eight others of a professed higher degree that lately assumed the name and firm of Alexander Oliphant & Co. After they had run ashore eight pipes of Portugal wine in this harbour out of the hold of the ship *Isabella* of Irvine, Patrick Montgomerie master, from Oporto the 16th October last and lodged the wine in their cellar where we found it ... they had the boldness to enter a claim to the wine on the credit of some old importations from Lisbon, from the evidence of John Kean and Dick Caskell, two porters they brought hither from the Isle of Man at the commencement of their partnership in trade and who were employed in bringing that wine out of the ship and rolling the pipes into their warehouse. That a few days after the seizure was made these merchants sent away the two porters out of this town to Ireland, or the Isle of Man, and maintained their wives and children here in their absence. But when ever the trial in the exchequer was over the 19th of last month they sent for these porters, that before were not to be found in the kingdom and who are now again in their service in this town. This piece of management is so glaring and notorious in this place that we have presumed to notice it and that without their evidence in court of the running and lodging the eight pipes of wine it was fully proven to the satisfaction of the jury, who gave a verdict for the Crown but had not those two porters been stolen or put out of the way for seven months (of which the solicitor has an affidavit) tis more than probable there would have been no trial and thereby saved the expense and such trouble by the perverseness of that Company'. [Collector at Ayr to the Board, 4 July 1767]

'The seizure lately tried (may be seen) in another, and better view, for the owners of the eight pipes wine are well known and upon record ... and in corresponding with the collector at Belfast whereby a fraud was discovered in the shipmaster by reporting a considerable quantity of goods short at Ayr, of which he really brought from Oporto and had onboard when he left Belfast and came hither. We must submit ... that Montgomerie the shipmaster has incurred the penalty ... for making a false report which may be clearly proved by the officers and books both here and at Belfast'. [Collector at Ayr to the Board, 4 July 1767]

CHAPTER EIGHT: THE *LILLY*

'I was this day on board her with Mr Thomas Orr, looking at her hold. She is every way to my liking'. [William Laing, 11 February 1751]

The *Lilly* was to have been George Moore's pride and joy. A snow, burthen about 120 tons, she was built in Boston during 1750. The maiden voyage was a near disaster and Moore seriously considered selling the snow. Instead he found a new master and there were five subsequent comparatively successful voyages (see Figure 10). An over-extended stay at Antigua in 1752 resulted in an infestation of ship worm (see tailpiece to this chapter) but these were dealt with and the vessel returned to Boston, where she was sheathed. Finally in 1754 she was wrecked at Cape Cod and within months her master, who appears to have held Moore's great esteem - he sold Robert Montgomerie a quarter of the vessel after her first voyage - drops from the letters.

The Funding of the *Lilly* and her Maiden Voyage

Within months of the launch of the *Peggy* at Boston the *Lilly* was also launched there. To fund this project, and to pay for a homeward cargo of rum, Moore sent cargoes of goods from Glasgow and Liverpool to Boston (see Chapter Six). The resultant problems with Walter Logan are summarised in a letter to the Murdochs.

'In September 1749 I wrote Mr Logan a letter to be forwarded with some goods from Glasgow, which you shipped, desiring on their coming to hand he would dispose of them to the best advantage for my account, answerable towards building a vessel, as I directed, and goods in return, as I should hereafter write to him. On December the 19th (1749) I wrote by Captain Laing, intended master of the new vessel, with goods from Liverpool, desiring their disposal for my account to be added to the sales of the goods from Glasgow, whereof the expense incident in building the new vessel to be deducted and the remaining produce to be applied to

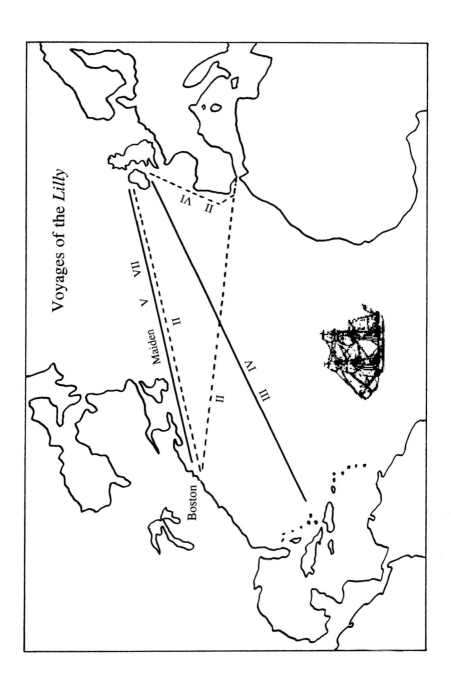

Voyages of the *Lilly*

Figure 10: The Voyages of the *Lilly*

Maiden Voyage 1751 Boston to Peel, John Laing master

Boston (Walter Logan): timber, lumber, rum

Voyage II: 1751 to 1752 Scotland to Peel to Boston to the Straights Robert Montgomerie master

Scotland (Joseph Scott, Glasgow): manufactory goods

Boston (Aeneas MacKay & Co and Henry Atkin): fish

Gibraltar (James Reid) and Alicante (John Blundell): fish sold

Barcelona (Green, Stanton & Ford): brandy and wine

Voyage III: 1752 Scotland to Cork to the West Indies Robert Montgomerie master

Irvine: coals

Cork (James & George Piersy): butter, beef and pork

Barbados (Richard Smith & Co): rum

Voyage IV: 1753 Scotland to Peel to Belfast to Dublin to the West Indies to Dublin

Dublin (Thomas Finlay & Robert Patrick): butter and beef

Antigua & St Eustatius (Halliday & Bros): rum

Voyage V: 1753 Scotland to Cork to Boston

Cork (James & George Piersy): butter and linen

Boston: rum

Voyage VI: 1754 Scotland to the Straights

Ayr: coals

Gibraltar (James Reid): coals sold

Cette (Peter Berail): brandy

Voyage VII: 1754 Scotland to Cork to Boston

Cork (James & George Piersy): butter

Boston (John Rowe): fish

Wrecked at Cape Cod

129

purchase one hundred and sixty hogsheads of rum, some hops, if to be had, and filling up the hold with white wood hogshead staves and for what he might be in advance on this purchase, desiring him to draw on me. December the 26th (1749) I wrote by Laing to Mr Logan, referring to my former (letter) and therein mentioning I might have some occasion to make some alteration in the homeward voyage, which if it should so happen I should write him by way of London. The 26th March (1750) Mr Logan advises of the receipt of the goods from Glasgow, value £571 10s 6d sterling, which he mentions have come to a pretty good market. He therein also refers to some necessaries for the vessel with the master and goods from Liverpool ... and gives me leave to depend on all diligence and dispatch. On his receipt of my orders on the 5th of June (1750) Mr Logan advises of the master's arrival and of the goods from Liverpool, value £1071 11s 2½d, that the snow will be launched in six days, that he's preparing for her lading ... On the 23rd July (1750) he writes that the Liverpool goods are a bad assortment, some charged high, and only fit for the winter season, adding these goods will be a small assistance in loading the snow, that the cargo by her will amount to £1600 or £1700 sterling and that he will be obliged to draw on me £1300 sterling. The circumstances this far are agreeable. The Glasgow goods are sold at a good market, the Liverpool goods by their assortment have produced £300 or £400 and I expected the vessel was to be instantly dispatched or, should the vessel be detained, I expected that his drafts for said homeward cargo would be lessened in proportion to the sale of the remainder of the Liverpool goods and in this channel the transaction would have given content.

'But Mr Logan makes herein a variation. On the 5th December last (1750) Mr Logan writes me a letter covering bill of sale of the vessel, costs and incidents (this document exists at the Manx National Heritage library and provides intimate details of the building of the snow from the price of her hull to that of her six foot woman figurehead to the rum paid the carpenters) ... At same time of my receipt hereof I received others his letters advising he had drawn on me £40 odd sterling in August, favour of John Cain, and in November £435 14s 6d sterling in your favour. This transaction imports very differently from his preceding designed one in July. Timber boards and oars are shipped for this place, where they cannot be sold and must be purposely sent to seek a market elsewhere.

Mr Logan has dispensed with detaining the vessel five or six months, burthened with the expense of a crew sent out from Glasgow and has at last shipped a cargo unconformable with the terms of my letter, yet has reconciled himself with drawing bills to such an extent. And to add to the perplexity hence arising he permits me to be unacquainted with what part of the outward goods were sold to their produce. From an estimate I have made of the value of the ship and amount of the cargo by her it falls short of the value of the goods sold the 23rd July. I've been severally concerned in goods last summer at Boston ... at which price I find Mr Logan purchased from Captain Pat Montgomerie, with whom I was chiefly concerned. This would appear as a rule for said estimate, which you have herewith. By Mr Logan's keeping the vessel so long as the 5th last month instead of drawing on me it might be expected he would have remitted me bills for the remainder of the Liverpool goods. As to the acceptance of these bills I'm in suspense which way to determine. For in my mind if I accept them it is for his honour and not occasionally for my interest or to serve as necessary to reimburse his layings out on my account. And by accepting them I must have recourse to the value of effects in Boston greater than I intended, expected or is convenient, and in the hands of a gentleman with whom I've not experienced a equal commercial correspondence.

'Pray how would you manage were my case yours? You'll oblige me in giving your opinion'. [Peter & John Murdoch, 17 January 1751]

The reasons why Walter Logan changed Moore's instructions were contained in a letter dated 26 October 1750 'giving me an account of bad news you had received of the sales of rum in Ireland and that therefore you had detained the snow in expectance you would receive from me a countermand my former orders. I have hereon to acquaint you that in the year 1749 I knew that Boston rum sold low in Ireland. I also know it sold low there in 1750 and I dare mutual to say that Boston rum will be sold at a lower price in Ireland in 1751, all which with respect to my concern at Boston I never intended having any reference to. ... Notwithstanding that the snow, under the constant expense of a full crew, was detained waiting so far down in the winter season as until the 5th day of December. I'm not master of figures whereby I can reconcile myself with this your transactions for me and as you have forwarded several your letters to me to the perusal of our mutual friends Messrs Peter & John Murdoch in Glasgow, who have referred thereto and to your management for me, it hence becomes necessary to give them my opinion. Said Messrs Murdoch advise me of their having credited your account and debited mine with your drafts on them for my account. Arthur Young has forwarded your draft unendorsed so that no one for him can receive the value'. [Walter Logan 12 March 1751]

The story is continued in letters to William Laing, the master's brother, and James Crosbie in Liverpool. 'The *Lilly* is not yet arrived and I am surprised what has so long detained her. I begin to suspect that she did not sail from Boston at the time I expected and that the gentleman who was to load her there has taken advantage of Mr Laing's easy temper to influence his stay. How the voyage will turn out I cannot say but it has not now a good prospect'. [William Laing, 10 December 1750]. Moore wrote the following month. 'The *Lilly* is arrived with a cargo very improper for this market, mostly lumber which cannot here be sold, so that I must send her to Liverpool, where if circumstances are agreeable she will take a cargo for the Straights'. [William Laing, 15 January 1751].

'I have no manner of satisfaction by Mr Laing, as to the quality of the goods you shipped. Nor has Mr Logan made any the least returns for their proceeds. Mr Logan to add to this disagreeableness has sent me by her 50 tons of square oak timber by clearance to be landed here. This timber will not sell here so it must be sent elsewhere to a market. I'm thinking of Greenock or Irvine for this purpose'. [James Crosbie, 23 January 1751]. The price of the rum on board was 'extravagantly dear. It stands me in English 2/6 per gallon so that I will not sell it under that price at least while the market continues high here, which from every appearance like to be for some time'. [William Laing, 15 January 1751]

Moore had various alternatives. His first recourse was to Pat Ewing, his agent in Fairlie, but the long and detailed letter, dated 30 January 1751, was crossed out and appears not to have been sent. According to this he would order Laing to anchor in Fairlie road and proceed to discharge the cargo. But before he could do this Moore wanted Ewing to go to Irvine and consult with Pat Montgomerie. If the timber market was alike at Greenock and Irvine then it should be discharged at Irvine. 'By the *Lilly*'s anchoring at Fairlie she will be in safety until you are satisfied ... of no risks being run on entering from Boston, for I am not quite satisfied if any difficulty attends the delivery of a part of the cargo in this port and proceeding with the remainder part to Britain. Yet I think the uniform practice is in my favour but I would run no risk. What remains of the staves let remain on board. They may serve for discharge hereafter. The charge of outfit and coals let be deducted off the proceeds of the timber or I shall account with you accordingly'. [Pat Ewing, 30 January 1751 - crossed out]. His final decision is recorded in a letter to the Murdochs. 'The oak timber I was necessitated to land here as a risk attended from this Isle'. But he wrote to James Crosbie on 7 March 1751 the result of this was that the timber must 'meet with a hideous sale'.

To add to this, there were labour problems. 'I had no kind of expectance but that the crew would have stayed another voyage with me in hopes I might with them get something to make amends for the last voyage and I would have been very content therewith, as on such a voyage nothing but the master's care in navigating the vessel would be necessary. In a day or two after I wrote you my letter (dated 15 January) Mr John Laing told me that none of the crew would agree to go to Liverpool and that herein they were so positive that they had already sent their chests home. Hence I'm forced to the necessity of sending the *Lilly* to Scotland and what there to do best I cannot well tell. For rum I have no kind of thoughts being that way already concerned with Pat Montgomerie. Under these circumstances I must either sell the snow or look out for another master, whom it will I find be always proper to give some discretionary power of the cargo. Nothing should depart me from Mr Laing, whom I'm satisfied is very diligent and honest. You will hence I hope not take amiss that I have come to a resolution of sending the snow on a voyage to Boston and thence to the Straights, ship and cargo to be under the sole direction of the master. For this you see the necessity I'm under of providing another master suitable for such a charge, which your brother has told me he would not undertake ... So I'm where I first set out to look out a proper master. On delivery of the cargo in Scotland the wages etc due the master and crew is £98 18s 6d with £28 10s formerly paid ... John Laing tells me the crew expects wages here and going to Scotland, which is very odd for when I spoke to them they told

133

me they were only hired for this voyage and that they were clear to leave the snow on her arrival here. I told Mr Laing if they insisted on this I would clear them all off, find out another crew more compliable to my intention of directing her. But if they stayed, in consideration of the trouble they would have in discharging the lumber, I would desire you to give them something, which accordingly please do for me. I would be content you permitted Jamie Laing, if he pleases, to stay with the *Lilly* and go on her next voyage and I shall take proper care to give proper directions about him'. [William Laing, 30 January 1751]. 'Mr John Laing and the mate (William Laing's son, Jamie) have not mentioned anything how they are to be paid during the *Lilly*'s lying here and until her arrival in Scotland. I must refer to you that they be paid to their satisfaction. So soon as you have settled with them let me know that I may bring the same to account accordingly'. [William Laing, 11 February 1751]

To Find a New Master

'It will be the discretest way not to acquaint Mr Laing or let anyone know that I intend a new master till the present cargo is discharged and so long after as may be convenient. When John Laing leaves the *Lilly*, you will take care that the ship's register be left on board to serve the succeeding master. All things on board and in the cabin belong to the *Lilly*. Let the two apprentices (John Cowle and Mathew Quirk) on board be taken care of till the new master comes on board'. [Pat Ewing, 30 January 1751 - crossed out]

Moore turned to Pat Montgomerie and, in case he had sailed for Boston, to Joseph Scott in Glasgow to find the new master. Montgomerie clearly recommended Robert Montgomerie (it has been impossible to confirm the relationship between these two men - were they brothers or father and son?) and, for most of the time covered by the letter-books, the Montgomeries were masters of the *Peggy* and the *Lilly*.

Voyage II

Robert Montgomerie received his instructions for this voyage in an open letter to the new master, dated 21 January 1751, and when he arrived at Peel for supplies. 'By vessels from England write me to the care of Mr James Crosbie, merchant in Liverpool, and by vessels to Scotland write me to the care of Messrs Peter & John Murdoch, merchants in Glasgow, for it will be pleasurable and of satisfaction often to hear from you and how you are proceeding. I wish you a good voyage'. [Robert Montgomerie, 12 March 1751]

Moore had hoped that Walter Logan would have sufficient funds (from the final sales of the Liverpool goods) to provide the balance between the outward cargo and the load of fish. In fact only £2 5s old tender (4/6 sterling) was forthcoming. 'Mr Robert Mountgomerie writes me that he could not get the value I expected from Mr Logan so that my design in sending that vessel to Boston is baffled and how to behave next in this intricate affair I'm in great measure at loss'. [Peter & John Murdoch, 22 January 1752].

In fact Montgomerie turned to Aeneas MacKay & Co and Henry Atkin, both in Boston. 'On settling my account with him (Montgomerie) I found he charged me with 50 quintals of fish at Boston more than he took in, for which I hold him accountable to me in the sum of £212 10s your old tender. This he told me arises from an error which you made in the value of fish wherewith you charged him. He was noisy and complained on this subject. I adventured to pacify him by assuring him were you made acquainted with this error you would regulate it to his satisfaction. He told me he had wrote you two letters (one from Gibraltar) about it, to which I must refer you'. [Aeneas Mackay & Co, 18 May 1752]. Montgomerie was on his next voyage when Moore received a reply from Hugh Mackay & Co (Aeneas had died in Greenock) dated 21 September 1752. 'As all mistakes should be allowed they should in like manner be reciprocally known ... I have been looking over his account charges at Boston. I see therein a charge for pilotage up and down so that if you paid his pilot and hold me to pay the same charge of pilotage by me it will be twice paid. I wish that Montgomerie had been more distinct in his accounts and thereby have prevented any mistakes and the occasions of writing about them. I have at any time with pleasure made good for mistakes in the same manner that I would expect them to be made good were the mistakes to my prejudice'. [Hugh Mackay & Co, 23 November 1752]

To complicate matters 'The fish season in New England has been a very backward one. Hence it's scarce to be had and the scarcity has enhanced the value'. [John Blundell, Alicante, 3 September 1751]. This led to a major delay and, as was seen in Chapter Two, in the meantime there were dramatic changes in the relative prices of brandy in France and Spain. As a result of these problems, Montgomerie was bombarded with letters - 1 July, 15 August, 14 October and 27 December 1751. He loaded his cargo of brandy with Green, Stanton & Ford in Barcelona.

Voyage III

This second Robert Montgomerie voyage was not from Scotland to Boston to the Straights but set a pattern for subsequent voyages, as Montgomerie was instructed to take coals from Ayrshire as ballast and load provisions for the outward cargo in Ireland for the West Indies. On this occasion he loaded butter, beef and other provisions with James & George Piersy at Cork (see Figure 11).

The next stage of the journey depended on whether or not Richard Smith & Co in Barbados had obeyed Moore's instructions. 'On your receipt hereof, or in March next when the price of new rum is first struck, I desire you will buy for my account two hundred hogsheads (of rum). The vessel I intend said rum to be shipped on board will not be in Barbados till May or June ... By this you will see that I have no other design in view than to purchase at the first price, which I have experienced at your market to be the cheapest. The storage and expense attending said rum from its purchase to its shipping you will debit me. I refer you to transact herein in the frugalest way for my account. With the compliments of the season'. [Richard Smith & Co, 30 December 1751]. Montgomerie was given various options. 'When in readiness (at Cork), as dispatch is necessary, proceed to Barbados and deliver the letter for Messrs Richard Smith & Co merchants there (marked 1). On delivery of this letter enquire of them if they have in readiness the two hundred hogsheads of rum I some time ago wrote them for. You need not tell them you have any provisions or butter on board. On their answer you will know what to do. If the two hundred hogsheads are a part or bought give them the other letter, which is also directed for said Richard Smith & Co. In this last letter I have told them you have on board some new Cork butter of the best sort made there with a small quantity of other provisions for my account, for making the best sales whereof I have directed that you apply to them, as the most favourable means whereby my interest therein can be served. So with them consult the best means of disposing of the butter and provisions to the end that the produce of them may be given to said Messrs Smith & Co and by so much less in their drawing on Messrs William Smith & Co ... for the value of the rum, and if said Richard Smith & Co have already drawn for the value of the rum the proceeds of the butter and provisions are to be remitted to Messrs William Snell & Co ... by bills for my account, which you may do, or if you yourself cannot find to do have in the care of Messrs Richard Smith & Co to remit for me'. [Robert Montgomerie, 11 April 1752]

If Richard Smith & Co had not obeyed Moore's instructions, or if the price of rum was over 2 shillings a gallon in Barbados, then Montgomerie was to go to St Kitts (St Christophers), where he was to contact Robert Colhoun for half his cargo of rum. Colhoun would charge 5% commission for advancing money and this should be remembered when proceeding to St Eustatius, where the rum would probably be 3d per gallon cheaper, and where he was to contact Ralph Sampson for the other half of the cargo. Alternatively, should any French rum arrive at St Eustatius while he was there, then he should buy a parcel of it, up to 5,000 gallons.

Finally 'Take notice that the duties of rum are payable 90 gallons for a hogshead lacks of a lower denomination, namely tierces and barrels. The duties are payable in the like proportion at $4\frac{1}{2}$ per cent. Some of the factors charge as above others charge $4\frac{1}{2}$ per cent on the whole number of gallons per invoice. Make yourself herein acquainted and so manage if you can for me that I may pay for no other duty than is payable at the custom house'. [Robert Montgomerie, 11 April 1752]

Everything appeared to go smoothly. 'I've just now received advice that the *Lilly* ... arrived at Barbados at about the beginning of July and as his cargo ... was lying waiting his arrival. He purposed lodging the Cork goods with Messrs Richard Smith & Co and immediately take on board the rum so that he expected to sail thence about the middle of July'. [William Snell & Co, 13 August 1752]. The problems over this second cargo of rum from Richard Smith & Co were discussed in Chapter Three.

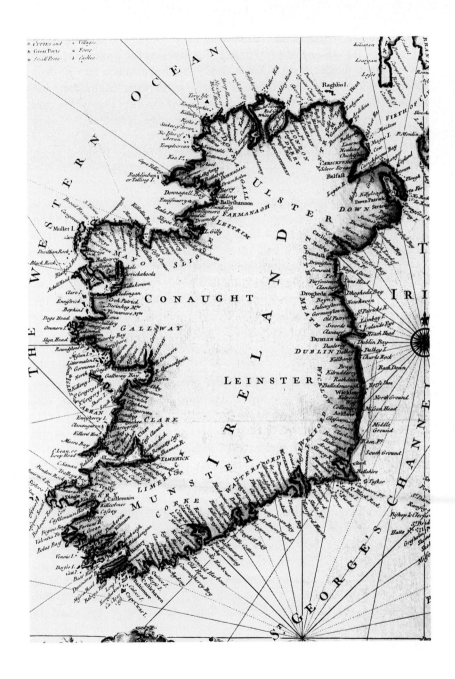

138

Figure 11: Provisions from Ireland

In 1752 Moore made his first experiment of sending provisions from Ireland to the West Indies. Robert Montgomerie was to try Barbados first. 'If you proceed to the Leeward Islands, dispose of the butter and provisions where you can best find to sell them. In this dispatch is necessary for other vessels with new butter from Ireland will be following so that you may sell at Barbados as you think the price inviting by all means'. [Robert Montgomerie, 11 April 1752]

'I observe the price of butter is very high, rather higher than I expected it would be. However I'm quite satisfied ... that everything was done in the best manner. The affair of dealing in butter I'm great measure unacquainted. From the experiment I've made I shall be better able to form a judgement how again to proceed thereon [James & George Piersy, 20 July 1752]

This experiment was not as successful as Moore had hoped. 'Though the *Lilly* happened first with a quantity of new butter to arrive at Barbados yet the sales of the butter did not answer the expectance arising from so favourable an incident. The whole was sold at 7d per lb and the other provisions in a way scarcely answerable to a freight, a proof that the markets there are well supplied'. [James & George Piersy, 23 October 1752]

Moore's next voyage was with Thomas Finlay & Robert Patrick in Dublin. But 'The outward cargo of provisions by the *Lilly* proves a miserable article so that a considerable loss attends the sale. One article therein seems circumstanced with cause of complaint. The sale of one hundred barrels at St Eustatius for £200 debited with a charge of freight at 2/3d per barrel, which leaves 37/9 and no more per barrel. If no more than this price could be had with you or at the time no more in the other Islands, wherein you advised me you had established houses to accommodate and encourage your friends, the owners must be content. But if a higher price was then given at any of the said Islands it will readily occur to you that they cannot be satisfied with your transporting one hundred barrels to St Eustatius and selling them at said price.' [John Halliday & Bros, Antigua, 21 July 1753]

'In two proceeding instances of provisions by the *Lilly* my expectation was not answered ... How willing soever I may be or any other is pressing with provisions to any of the Leeward Islands I do not experience that it is inviting to be concerned in this way but circumstances may change my opinion'. [James & George Piersy, 15 October 1753]

Voyage IV

For the third Robert Montgomerie voyage, Moore agreed to a partnership (75:25) with Thomas Finlay and Robert Patrick, merchants in Dublin. By this agreement, dated 20 September 1752, provisions were to be shipped at Dublin and taken to the West Indies for a cargo of rum to be landed part in Ireland and part in the Isle of Man or wholly at either place.

Moore nominated four alternative rum sources: Richard Smith & Co in Barbados, John Halliday & Co in Antigua, Robert Colhoun in St Kitts and an open letter 'undirected occasionally for you to direct as you find necessary as to serve the interest of the sales of the provisions and purchase of a cargo of rum'. [Robert Montgomerie, 20 September 1752]

The problems started at the very beginning. 'Montgomerie has been patiently waiting here a fair wind for Dublin. Last night it seemed southeast so he parted this and is just now put back into our bay. It proved that he could not fetch much to windward of Belfast. He could not turn this Isle so as to get to the other side, where if he wanted he might have the chance of getting herrings and to lie in this bay or go to leeward seems best to be avoided. I've thought he had best run down to Belfast and on his arrival to forward you this letter by post'. [Thomas Finlay & Robert Patrick, 28 September 1752]. Moore had hoped that to save time the provisions might be loaded at Belfast. Instead Finlay & Patrick needed more time than expected to provide the cargo at Dublin. Moore was looking for another banker in London (see Chapter Six) and the Dublin merchants recommended Abraham James Hillhouse. They also suggested that if the *Lilly* went to Antigua then the rum should come from John Hillhouse.

'I have no pure connection with the Hallidays of Antigua further than bargaining with them ... so that if your friend Mr John Hillhouse will transact on the same footing that they have agreed to I would rather incline being in the circle of your acquaintance. One of the Hallidays was here since I last wrote you telling me that his company had established a house at St Christophers and one at Montserat so that there and Antigua they proposed alike doing business'. [Thomas Finlay & Robert Patrick, 10 October 1752]. 'I'm not sure whether your friend at Antigua will do business as the Hallidays have agreed. If he does at your instance I'm content that he have the preference, which in my directions to Montgomerie I have desired. I have had some experience of Montgomerie's diligence and hence am encouraged to place confidence in him - I expect he'll use to our mutual advantage'. [Thomas Finlay & Robert Patrick, 13 October 1752]

One final instruction to Montgomerie was sent to Dublin. 'My son is returned from Scotland. His commission to you is that you buy him 5 or 6 hundredweight of coffee beans, if this you can and without injury to the cargo'. [Robert Montgomerie, 13 October 1752]

Montgomerie wrote from Antigua on 7 January 1753 'by which you will see his proceeding and manner of acting for our interest'. [Thomas Finlay & Robert Patrick, 19 April 1753]. Further letters were received from Montgomerie from Barbados and Antigua. 'Considering the circumstances, the manner of the disposal of the outward cargo at Antigua seems the best you were able to direct and I hope it will turn out to some advantage '. [Robert Montgomerie, at Dublin, 23 May 1753]

On 3 March and 16 May 1753 John Halliday & Brothers wrote from Antigua with 'accounts sales of the provisions of the *Lilly* ... and invoice of rum you shipped ... Montgomerie is arrived here and has discharged the rum in good order, namely one quarter in Dublin and three-quarters in this town'. [John Halliday & Bros, 21 July 1753] But 'The *Lilly* is so worm eaten by her long lying at Antigua that she cannot proceed on that voyage I had destined her. I must send her to be sheathed (see tailpiece to this chapter). To do this in the frugalest way I've directed her to Boston'. [Thomas Finlay & Robert Patrick, 21 July 1753].

Voyage V

For this voyage Montgomerie was back with the Piersys in Cork, where he was to load linen and butter. But 'You are not to ship on board any other linen or butter ... at Cork but what is answer for my account'. [Robert Montgomerie 21 July 1753]. Moore instructed him to take this to John Rowe in Boston, where he was to purchase rum at 14s or 15s old tender per gallon 'as many hogsheads as you can stow in your lower hold' and for between decks about 50 quintals of fish, wood staves and three or four dozen oak oars 'such as will serve our Manx boats'. [Robert Montgomerie, 21 July 1753]. If there was no New England rum to be had then Montgomerie was to take a full cargo of fish to the Mediterranean.

£120 worth of Glasgow manufactory goods were to be included in the *Peggy*'s cargo to contribute towards the *Lilly*'s costs at Boston (which included sheathing). For some reason Montgomerie did not go to Boston or contact Rowe (so missing the goods per the *Peggy*). 'By what he writes me of his conduct there (New England), he has been acting quite different from my intention. I wonder he refused your offer for the butter but I cannot recall any directions to him or renew them'. [John Rowe, 4 December 1753]

No reference has been traced to the name of the merchant who supplied the cargo of New England rum. 'He (Montgomerie) makes no computation of what sum he will draw on you. In one of his letters he says it will be a small bill. What he means by this will soon be known'. [Abraham James Hillhouse, 4 December 1753]. Montgomerie arrived at Ramsey on 17 December 1753.

Moore was so depressed about the losses associated with the rum trade that 'I'm determined this season to try to supply myself with rum by purchasing on arrival here'. [Thomas Finlay & Robert Patrick, 11 February 1754] (see Chapter Three)

Voyage VI
'The vessel I wrote you about a freight to Hamburgh is arrived. As you have not engaged for me I wave the thoughts of sending her there and being told that freight for Philadelphia at this season is frequently to be met with at Liverpool I'm very willing to take freight there and I write this letter on purpose to desire if you can engage a freight accordingly that you will please do so. The vessel is to be here to wait your answer.

'PS Since writing the above Robert Montgomerie, who is master of the vessel, has desired ... to see his friends in Scotland, which I have agreed with as his return will be probably before I receive the favour of your answer'. [James Crosbie, 14 January 1754]

During this visit to Scotland, Robert Montgomerie went on the debt collecting expedition (see Chapter Nine). In the meantime Moore changed his plans and instructed Montgomerie to load coals at Ayr. 'Montgomerie has directions to touch at Gibraltar and Port Mahon for to sell the coals and so soon as he arrives on the coast he is to give you the speediest advice. You will therefore please proceed to have his brandy in readiness so that the shipping it may be accommodated with great dispatch. I'm under apprehensions Montgomerie will be difficulted in the stowage of the lower hold, which is but a little above 6 feet deep, and for this reason it was that in my former letter I desired you favour regard to get the casks of the smallest size'. [Peter Berail, 20 February 1754].

Montgomerie did load the brandy at Cette. There is no record as to whether or not he also succeeded in another commission. 'If anywhere you can meet with the large kind of Barbary fowls, bring me a cock and three or four hens'. [Robert Montgomerie, 16 January 1754].

Voyage VII

This time Moore instructed Montgomerie to take linen cloth from Scotland and butter etc from Cork. 'So soon as you arrive at Boston consult the best manner you can for the sale of the said goods outwards. If the season will permit your lading fish and you can think of being in the Straights in time to answer the market, you may buy a cargo or as much as you can stow in the hold, filling between decks with whatever goods you think fit for me. Or you may take in goods suitable for the market in Surinam, to which place you may proceed to load molasses for the Boston market. Or you may load flaxseed on my account or partly on freight or should any other incident of freight or lading happen or occur whereby you think I may be benefited I herein give you a discretionary power to act for me as you think best or are advised on any occasion of advice. I have wrote to Mr John Rowe and hope he will favour my request of doing you any civilities ... If you load with fish I shall write to meet your arrival at Alicante and following the sale what is next to be done (Moore planned that he should load brandy with Peter Berail at Cette). If you proceed to Surinam and bring molasses to Boston you will be difficulted in what manner to dispose of the proceeds for I believe you cannot meet with bills on London. Supposing you meet a freight homewards I would not by any means leave any effects behind you in the country so that I think best way would be to proceed to Philadelphia to load flour for Dublin. If you take part freight and part goods on my account where you are freighted to must also determine the place of discharging. Whatever flaxseed or other goods you take on board for my account or if you load flaxseed entirely on my account I'm apprehensive such a quantity will be too much at once at any market in Scotland so that it would be best first to touch at Dublin to try the market there. Boston rum is a commodity at present in great disrepute here so that I would not by any means you load rum'. [Robert Montgomerie, 20 August 1754]. All these complicated instructions were unnecessary, as Montgomerie took on board a cargo of fish.

Then disaster struck. 'On the 3rd March in company with several other vessels they (the *Peggy* and the *Lilly*) both left Boston. On the day following the *Lilly* was drove ashore to the south and eastward of Cape Cod and with difficulty the crew saved their lives. Robert Montgomerie writes that he has applied to the admiralty at Boston for directions herein. His letters are dated 21st and 23rd March and mentions that they had ordered a survey on the ship and cargo and empowered Montgomerie to make the most of all the cargo and the ship. He writes that two-thirds of the fish was wet and the ship no hopes of getting off, being so exposed to the land, and adds that his last to me contained invoice bill of lading and account current by one Lusk for Clyde and that he had a letter by him to you insurance about £800 sterling on the cargo. These letters by Lusk are not yet come to hand so that my interest in the cargo is not fully covered by insurance as I intended, which is necessary to be observed. With respect to a proportion of the salvage you'll please intimate to the insurers what is necessary upon this unlucky occasion ... My former interest in ship and cargo is abandoned and in every respect relative to my interest herein be pleased act for me in the best manner'. [Richard Oswald & Co, 4 June 1755]

'Robert Montgomerie in the sloop he purchased at Boston touched here in his way to Clyde. He told me he found monies to pass his own bills payable in Scotland for what he wanted, which I understand did not exceed £100 ... *He is now no longer in my employ so that for the present my connection with him ceases.* Herewith you will receive Robert Montgomerie's protest with all the accounts relating to the shipwreck, duly done under the authority of the court of Boston'. [Richard Oswald & Co, 18 August 1755]

'I see you have accommodated matters with the insurers and adjusted the loss ... Your settlement with the insurers seems to be done in an equitable way and is agreeable to me. Any gratuity that might be expected for Captain Montgomerie, as it could not come under the name of a demand and was optional to the insurers to allow, was right you did not permit interfere with the account or create any delay'. [Richard Oswald & Co, 24 December 1755]

Moore wrote to Robert Montgomerie on 27 September 1755 'The kilt and jacket will be very agreeable but my wife is not at home to try them on the youngster.' His final letter to Montgomerie is dated 7 January 1756. 'Your letter of the 9th December was handed me by Robert Jones to whom I gave accordingly goods to £131. For this sum I have drawn on him and on you, as you mention, and have made the same payment to Mr Pat Montgomerie answerable for some arrears I am owing him'.

Robert Montgomerie appears in the Ayr custom house letter-books in November 1757 as master of the *Montgomerie*, loaded with tobacco from Virginia. Further references to him have been found in 1761 as master of the *Kingston* of Greenock, still owned by Robert Arthur and John Callin (see Chapater Three), and in 1768 as master of the *George & James* on a voyage from Leith to Boston (personal communication from Eric Graham).

THE STORY OF SHIP WORMS

The *Lilly* was infested with ship worms because she lay too long waiting for her cargo at Antigua in 1753. As a result the worms had to be killed and the vessel sheathed. Robert Montgomerie was instructed to proceed to Cork 'where you are first to get carpenters to warm the *Lilly*'s bottom so as to kill the worms and then paint her over, allowing for the expense of this ... Make what dispatch you can in Cork to proceed so soon as possible to Boston, where the snow must be sheathed. For this work buy a sufficient quantity of nails in Cork and brown paper to take with you. Brown paper I apprehend will be of the same service as hair would be for the sheathing'. [Robert Montgomerie, 21 July 1753]

There is evidence that wooden sheathing to protect a vessel from ship worm was first used in the fifteenth century. When it was discovered that contemporary Spanish vessels were using lead, this was adopted instead. Following an investigation in 1682 into the corrosive effects of lead it was officially banned by the Admiralty. By the eighteenth century wooden sheathing was in use again. In 1761 copper sheathing was introduced but its use was not universal at first. There were still some occasions when lead was used. The *Marlborough* had been sheathed in lead when she was built in 1768. But when she was in dock at Chatham a couple of years later it was discovered that 'the iron fastenings were found to be so deeply eaten away that the lead was stripped off and replaced with wooden sheathing'

During the sixteenth and seventeenth centuries wooden sheathing was put on over a layer of animal hair and tar. 'This was reported to prevent the worms from penetrating to the planking, although it greatly increased the cost of building'. The wooden sheathing was sometimes filled with iron or copper nails (see letter from George Moore) 'put in so closely that the heads were touching and formed a kind of metallic sheathing'. Sometimes the wooden sheathing was painted 'with various mixtures of tar and grease; with sulphur, oil, 'and other ingredients'; or with pitch, tar, and brimstone'.

Source: Marine Fouling and its Prevention. US Naval Institute Annapolis, Maryland 1752

THE SMUGGLERS

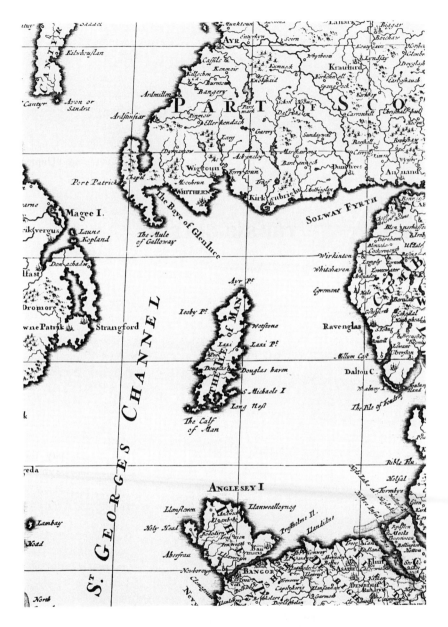

Figure 12: Location of the Isle of Man

CHAPTER NINE: THE SMUGGLING BUSINESS

'The season of the year is become so far advanced that it calls for the visit which is annually necessary to be made to my customers in Scotland'. [James Hutchison, 1 May 1759]

Although George Moore was by no means the only Manx merchant involved in the smuggling trade with Scotland, his letter-book provides a unique insight into the character of this trade and, possibly of greater significance, the individuals involved, his smuggling 'Friends'.

If anything, there was a surfeit of suppliers of smuggled goods on the Isle of Man. 'It proves unlucky that several others have begged the experiment of importing rum this season of the year into our Isle so that the market is quite overstocked'. [Robert Colhoun, 5 February 1753]. A problem over more than one supplier of goods in an area of Scotland is described in the tailpiece to this chapter.

Several of these other merchants failed (the stories of John Allan and Thomas Savage are told in Chapter Sixteen). 'A few days ago I heard that (John) Ross has failed and gone off this Island, owing a considerable sum to several. As I hear there are not effects sufficient to pay the natives, who have a preference, I have no expectance of the payment (£23 owed to Peter Mitchell of Ayr) when the bill falls due ... I am sorry I have this bad account to give you of Ross'. [David Mitchell, 30 January 1759]

Moore survived. This was probably a direct result of his business acumen. But, while his ability is not in question, there was a certain degree of luck involved. Some merchants failed simply because virtually all their smuggling wherries were wrecked or seized. Moore suffered several setbacks in the delivery of his goods but these were all at the risk of his customers. 'In the postscript of your letter you further desire me to send half a tun of brandy and rum in 5 gallon casks at your risk and mine. Sending any goods at my own risk is a condition that if I did or agreed with any one I should agree with you. But as I do not deal in any such way I hope you will excuse my declining any such risk'. [John Allan, Ballantrae, 26 March 1759]

At the same time he adhered to his own strict rules. 'As to the trade in this Isle, you are well acquainted with it. My manner is to have as good goods as my neighbours in this town and to sell as reasonably as they do or as I can, which I have done and continue to do. But I can by no means bring myself to follow the sales in Douglas or be ruled by any one price there, where it is publicly known that some sell considerably cheaper than they buy. I shall always remember the rule I mentioned to you and if I succeed in giving you content I shall be indifferent in making an apology to any other'. [John Munn, 7 January 1753]

Sadly the question still remains: how did Moore's smuggling business start? The earliest date quoted in the letters is 1739 (see Chapter Twelve) and frequent references are made to debts dating from the early and mid 1740s. Certainly by 1750 the network of agents and customers was well-established. This network stretched from Neil Beaton at Maryburgh near Fort William in the north to John McCulloch at Kirkcudbright in the south, a distance of only one hundred and fifty miles as the crow flies but, particularly towards the north, covering a coastline deeply indented by sea lochs, so greatly increasing the area (see Figure 13 in Chapter Ten). It included some sixteen agents, who were often merchants in their own right, and well over three hundred customers, from lairds and surgeons to local fishermen and labourers. Perhaps the most significant fact is that Moore appears to have known each one of these people individually.

Every summer Moore would spend a couple of months travelling round south-west Scotland and the southern Highlands, visiting all his contacts. On at least one occasion his trip started and ended in Galloway. 'I met the wherry at Portnessock I expected and by her my passage'. [William Kerr, 7 July 1752] 'When I got to Stranraer the wind turned fair to take my passage so that I delayed returning you a list of old debts owing me'. [William McClure, 29 July 1754]

He was certainly in Ayr more than once in 1754 and 1755. 'To have seen you when I was last in Ayr would have given me great pleasure but I suppose your business and hurry at the fair prevented it'. [Pat Douglas, 29 July 1754]. And 'In summer 1754, when I was in Ayr, I frequently sent my servant with a line and by word of mouth to desire the favour of seeing you and to receive the balance, £87 2s 6d, you then owed me. But I had the favour of no other answer than verbally, by the servant, that the balance should be paid me or remitted to Glasgow. On my return to this Isle towards the latter end of July 1754 I drew on you £87 2s 6d to Mr James Simson, which finding not paid in March last I delayed applying to you for the balance, £20, still owing me, until I came to Ayr, as I did in June and July last. At such times I severally applied to you by my servant to have the favour of seeing you and to receive satisfaction for said balance due me which I was not favoured with'. [Pat Douglas, 8 October 1755]

The circuit was fixed. 'John Orr from Inverkip, now residing in Gourock, owes me £20 on his bill 13 July 1745 and £10 8s 11½d for value delivered on his letter January 1747. By going to Gourock he's got out of my road when I'm in Scotland and declines seeing me, though I send for him. Pray enquire into his circumstances and, if he is able to pay, I would be content you would cause utmost diligence be raised to make out payment, if on fair means he refuses it (see Chapter Twelve)'. [Joseph Scott & Co, 26 September 1751]

There is also a hint that once in Cowal Moore travelled no further than absolutely necessary. 'I intend being in Scotland about the season I formerly have been there. Before I come over, if the payments were made you, it would look more custom-like and will be rather more agreeable to me than if delayed until I come to the Millhouse. In any respect I refer to you to do as you think proper'. [John Munn, 8 April 1752]

But he went to Inverary. 'On my return from Scotland I generally review my Highland debts and settle the payments that have been made me. The account you settled with me in July last in Inverary, I did not get an abstract of, which you said you would send me'. [John Marshall, 5 September 1755]. 'Two or three years ago I was at Inverary when my friend Mr James Campbell gave me up some papers in relation to a debt of mine he had raised diligence to recover'. [Hector McLean, 19 December 1758]. He was also in Kintyre (see below).

Details of the journey appear in a letter to Robert Montgomerie. 'You are next to face the Highlands, which I think will be best done by ferrying at Largs and landing at Blairs Ferry, near Barnaby Boyle's, a change house near the shore. He will supply you with a horse to ride to Kilfinan to John Munn, who receives money for me in that country. I have wrote to him to pay you what sum he has received or owes me. As I would have you get what possibly can be got there. Let him give notice to all the people who owe me that they come in to pay and appoint the meeting them where Mr Munn and you think most convenient. Should John Munn be from home, which I do not expect, his brother James Munn will assist you. The Highland expedition is the troublesome part but leave no money there that you can possibly get'. [Robert Montgomerie, 16 January 1754]

There is also a description of how Moore's son, Phil, was to deliver part of a rum payment in cash. 'Herein is a letter for Mr Alexander Porterfield, the gentleman at whose house you may remember we came on our way from Paisley to Greenock'. [Phil Moore, Glasgow, 12 October 1751]. 'In my letter to Phil are notes, value £165, to be given to Mr Alexander Porterfield ... I've desired Phil on his receipt of my letter to wait on Mr Porterfield if he be in Glasgow. Or if he be in the country that he hire a horse and take a guide with him to Mr Porterfield's house to deliver his letter'. [Hercules Lindsay, 12 October 1751]

On most occasions Moore undertook the debt collection himself. 'I was in hopes to have received this sum in Tarbert but I heard you were not at home so I had not the opportunity'. [James Stevenson, 7 July 1752]. Then in January 1754, when in urgent need of funds, he turned to the master of the *Lilly* (see above). 'Mr Robert Montgomerie, who is in my employ, is about to go to Scotland. I benefit by him to call on some my customers for money and have directed that whatever sum he receives that he take it with him to Glasgow to be paid you and placed to my credit'. [James Simson, 14 January 1754]

The instructions to Robert Montgomerie give another insight into the distances covered: Irvine - Loans - Irvine - Hunterston - Fairlie - Kilfinan - Inverkip - Glasgow - Ayr. It is hardly surprising 'Robert Montgomerie writes me that he was so tired with his Highland journey that he could not stay to receive any money for you (in Inverkip) to take with him to Glasgow, which he has left with you to receive in your own way'. [William Laing, 12 February 1754]. The situation was further complicated by the fact that during this time Robert Montgomerie got married (no record of this marriage has been found).

Phil undertook the journey in 1757. Inevitably 'My son had not the success in Scotland which I expected'. [Hector Bryce, 19 August 1757]. And 'I received yours of the 5th inst, acknowledging your remittance of the bills I sent I'm sorry you give so bad an account of them. It they prove as you say, I shall think Phil had bad luck in his first settlement of accounts at Old Kirk'. [William Laing, 12 September 1757]

The following year Moore was in Scotland himself again. 'I was in hopes to have seen you when I was last in Girvan'. [Thomas Craig, 21 August 1758]. And 'I had some hopes that if I had seen you in Ballantrae on my return from Glasgow that you would have settled ...' [John Allan, 25 August 1758]. But 'This is to be handed to you by the bearer, my son Philip, who goes to Scotland to settle my accounts and to receive the relative sums due me, which pray acquaint Mr William Allison of and accordingly let your and his account be settled and stated with him for me'. [James Hutchison, 30 May 1759]

In emergencies, Moore also tended to use anyone whom he could trust. 'Mr John Callin of this town going to Scotland gives me an opportunity of acquainting you how favourable it would be to pay him the value you are owing me ... his receipt shall be a sufficient discharge'. [John Blair, 18 August 1757]. Moore wrote to Callin 'On your arrival acquaint the above persons to pay as per the above accounts and bills enclosed and send off Mr Fearran's letter. On your arrival at Stranraer send off Mr Blair's letter and give my letter to Mr McKie. If any payment follows I desire you will give what you receive to Mr James Simson'. [John Callin (Peel), 18 August 1757]

Apart from settling old debts, the main purpose of the journey was to lay down the rules for future deliveries, to take out references on new customers and to accept orders for future deliveries.

Moore insisted that all orders should be in writing - a point of reference should there be a dispute in the future. 'I have wrote to Robert McLea to know why he refuses to accept my draft for goods delivered on his missive, which doubtless he knows is equally binding on him as if he had signed my draft'. [John Munn, 14 November 1752]. And 'I have wrote to John Moure in Girvan and sent him his account whereon is owing me besides the value of his bill the further sum of £4 1s 11d ... to remove any occasion of dispute I have also enclosed the missives wherewith I gave the goods conform to his orders. These show him when you deliver this letter and ask his acceptance of payment of my draft'. [William McClure, 29 July 1754]

Sometimes there were problems when someone else inherited debts. 'You desired me in Ayr that I would return you the missive letters I received from your late husband, Mr James Donald, on which I delivered the goods the value whereof you have accounted and paid me. Accordingly I have herein enclosed said letters being nine in number, namely: one letter dated June 11th 1753 answered June 25th 1753; one letter dated June 29th 1753 answered July 7th 1753; one letter dated July 13th 1753 answered July 24th 1753; one letter dated June 29th 1753 answered July 26th 1753; one letter dated august 9th 1753 answered August 17th 1753; one letter dated August 9th 1753 answered August 21st 1753; one letter dated August 24th 1753 answered September 9th 1753; one letter dated August 25th 1753 answered September 24th 1753 and one letter dated September 15th 1753 answered September 26th 1753, which I desire you'll be pleased examine and compare the accounts with the value you have paid me'. [Janet Donald, 18 August 1755]. Neither the original letters nor the replies have survived, possibly suggesting that such orders were transcribed in a separate account/letter-book.

There were other problems as well. 'Elizabeth Auld denies her having wrote by Adam Auld so here is one of the enclosed letters. If she swears it is not her writing or wrote by her direction I must have recourse on Adam Auld, who lives just opposite to your house. It's necessary to try her'. [James Hutchison, 24 August 1754]. The result of this is not known.

It is not often that Moore 'punishes' his customers as the result of the misdemeanours of one individual. 'Stewart about Ritchie's wherry has so disappointed me that my customers must excuse me I have not answered their letters by him. For really I cannot reconcile myself with being thus duped. Stewart paid or gave his security for a part of Ricthie's debt to Foley but to my concern he declared he would withstand an action I took out in our courts with so much warmth that I was determined to give him no goods on any account for himself or any other. The most of the letters I should other way have answered'. [John Munn, 9 November 1751]

The order was accepted on various conditions: the customer did not have outstanding debts - at one stage this was limited to £100; they were known to Moore; the goods were available on the Isle of Man, and reasonably priced, and delivery was possible.

Outstanding debts were a major problem when more goods were ordered. These letters were all to John Munn in Kilfinan. 'In the new list I've now sent I've got some new customers. I expect that these as well as the old will be punctual to pay their debts one month following the date for I shall not be forced to give large credit as I used to and therefore with severals shall only give new credit as the old is paid'. [14 November 1752]. The next two letters also relate to customers in the Cowal peninsula. 'Duncan Munn I find owes me the full contents of his bill in your hands £34 2s 7d. He also owes £17 18s by John McLachlane the 17th September last and without sending me the value or taking notice of these debts he writes me two or three different letters for fresh goods on credit. How willing soever I may be to oblige him or am satisfied that he is able to pay yet he's to consider that it's impossible for me to trade in giving credit so extensively and must excuse me in not answering these his last letters. At the same time I must desire he will no longer delay the payment of the value of his bill'. [7 November 1753]. 'Severals are disappointed in their letters to me as I do not choose dealing with those who let their old debts lie over unpaid'. [26 December 1754]

There were also problems elsewhere. 'My son has been telling me that you have wrote to me for some goods on credit. Now this is depending on our former account and having recourse to your account I observe that you are owing me on two bills with Mr Allison in Ayr £127 8s 7d and £100. As these are too large sums for one man to owe in my way of trade, you surely will not take amiss that I am cautious to extend this debt. Our trading should be mutual. That is, as well to your liking as mine. If you kept within the bounds of £100 credit this should be sum sufficient for both our occasions and if in this manner you can propose I should be content it were the rules as well with you as others'. [James McClure, 18 December 1758]

Moore kept a constant check on his customers. 'I'm very much surprised you have not been more successful in getting the sum owing me considering how liberal I was in giving them (his customers in Cowal) credit, most of them at a time when their credit was refused by others in this Isle and indeed from this circumstance I concluded they would have been very punctual in their paying off the credit which I gave them'. [John Munn, 8 April 1752]. And 'If there be any I deal with you have no good opinion of pray let me know for my government'. [John Munn, 9 November 1751]

He was also usually very circumspect about taking on new customers but, inevitably, sometimes problems developed. 'Do with Ben Graham as you best can. It's odd that I all along refused giving him any credit until the time he took me in. I was led to think he was an honest man or that his neighbours would not entrust him in the manner they did'. [Hector Bryce, 1 May 1759]

His worries about David Mill appear in three letters to James Hutchison at Ayr. 'I have dealings with two chaps in Kirklenzie with whom, however, I am not well-acquainted. I must therefore desire you'll have a particular eye to secure or get value of the sums they are owing me and by the first opportunity let me know what opinion you have of them or they have in the country'. [12 January 1753]. 'I'm obliged to the hint you gave me of David Mill for since then I have answered none of his letters. I'm not acquainted with Mill but he's not careful in his writing for goods. I suppose all my drafts on him are accepted. If he fails in payment let ultimate diligence be used to recover what he owes me. This I think is the best way while he has effects in his hands and doubtless will appear to maintain his credit in this Isle ... I mentioned to Philip Moore & Sons something about Mill but I think they did not mind me'. [27 February 1753]. And 'David Mill I see has given me cause to remember the caution that is necessary on giving credit. I was very accidentally drawn into a conversation with him and did not know him. I have applied to his credit some goods ... which have been lodged with me for his account. But the value falls greatly short of what he owes me. Have you found any means of securing any part for me?' [3 May 1753]

The smuggling business increased at such a rate that sometimes stocks were low on the Island. This, together with other factors noted in Chapters Two and Three, affected the price, sometimes putting it out of reach of the customers. 'The prices are risen to 3/4, which I take is high or considerably higher than you or any other of the rest expected. How long they may then continue is uncertain but in my mind they will not fall this season'. [John Munn, 9 November 1751]

It must have seemed to Moore that the complaints were endless. 'The price of brandy charged in the accounts to your place is exactly the same with the price to Old Kirk but I shall hereafter send Spanish brandy, which is cheaper and meaner in the quality'. [Robert Morris, 30 December 1758]

Another complaint was that of quality. Here, depending on his mood, the current situation on the Island, the quality of the overall produce and the length of time before the complaint was made, Moore agreed on an abatement, or insisted on the full payment. 'I do not know if you have made any difference in point of quality but I think that the goods from me has been of a better quality than those I've been told are sent to your place. But if mine deserves any distinction this I submit'. [John Dickie, 16 January 1754]

'I observe in these payments there are stoppages or deductions made on the rum, where the charge is 2/7 or on the brandy where it is charged 2/2 per gallon. When I was at Inverkip there were sundry complaints of the quality of the rum and I was telling that 1d per gallon was (the difference between) ... having rum which could be depended on would answer the market and that kind which is to us uncertain or would not answer the market. If from the experience of my rum it is not esteemed better or deserving this difference I also submit the difference of the penny per gallon on the parcels that remain unpaid. As to the brandy that was charged at 2/2 per gallon, I shall grudge to have any deduction made of the price for James Orr was here at the time and can tell how scarce brandy was in the place. He himself offered 2/ per gallon and Irish men offered me ready money 2/1 per gallon to whom I could have sold all the brandy I had but I then preferred keeping what I had to accommodate my customers. You may hence see that the charge of 2/2 per gallon was not unequal to what I might reasonably expect to get from whomsoever I sold brandy to at that juncture. Yet you may herein do ... as you please ... and settle with them at 2/3, at 2/ or as you can agree with them. But on all your receipts pray let the account be settled for you know it will be disagreeable as well to them as to me to meet hereafter to settle disputed balances and I would prefer all settlements at one without occasions of meeting and dispute. As there are none with whom I deal as I regard so much as the dealers in Old Kirk, I prefer that my accounts with them be settled to their satisfaction and so let them be done'. [William Laing, 12 February 1754]

Various factors affected the ability to deliver goods: the season, the availability of appropriate vessels and the presence of revenue cruisers both round the Island and off the Scottish coast. 'As the season is now so far advanced I cannot expect the particulars (of £223 8s 4d paid to James Simson, Glasgow) by any boat from your parts nor account of what further payments have been made you for me, which I make no doubt you have rendered all diligence to obtain'. [John Munn, 6 May 1755]. And later the same year 'Not a boat has gone to Scotland since I returned home. This letter is forwarded by a sloop for Campbeltown that has discharged some goods here'. [John Munn, 5 September 1755]

As soon as an order for goods left the quayside at Peel, they became the responsibility of the customer. This would produce problems, particularly when payment was expected for goods that had not been received. 'That account was founded on the sundry value of goods which from time to time I delivered your order by safe carriage or miscarriage, whereof you are satisfied I had no concern in as I could not be a loser or benifitter by either nor with any accident that followed my delivery of them, wherein originally my demand on you was founded'. [Pat Douglas, 8 October 1755]

'By your letter and the reading it seemed as if I had made no abatement on the lost goods but on looking over your account I find that I abated to you £5 4s answerable for the accustomed abatement I make in such cases and as I told you in Ballantrae. However, I have no mind that you be denied, as you expect a further abatement, and have therefore sent you two and a half dozen white Lisbon wine in a bag I hope will be agreeable to you'. [John Allan, 26 March 1759]

Although the terms varied both throughout the period and from area to area, Moore expected payment for goods in two or three regular instalments. The main problem with this was that further goods would have been delivered during the first, let alone the second, time period so that sums owing accumulated rapidly during the long-nighted winter months.

The effort involved in negotiating with each customer to pay their debts at Glasgow would have been counter-productive. As a result Moore appointed a series of agents, from Tarbert to Stranraer, whose main role was in collecting debts owing. These people are discussed in Chapter Ten while the customers appear in Chapter Eleven. It is in the identification of these customers, particularly in the local custom house letter-books that putting the 'flesh on the bones' of Moore's smuggling friends becomes possible. But the most detailed information about an individual's circumstances comes when ultimate diligence was used to obtain payment of long standing debts (see Chapter Twelve). Finally, the wherries which transported the goods from the Isle of Man to the Scottish coast are described in Chapter Thirteen.

THE STORY OF WILLIAM SOMERVILLE OF RENFREW

These letters come from the letter-book of another merchant, John Steuart of Inverness. In 1722 and 1723 there was contact with William Somerville of Renfrew over his fishing business. 'I am sorry you came to such a bad market for your herring at Stockholm and shall be glad to see you here this fishing season, which I hope may give you more profit than last. If you are to bring a ship about here soon I know nothing will do better than slate from the Isle of Mull'. [29 June 1723]

The problem between the two merchants began a few years later. 'The counties about Lochaber and Appin was glutted with wine and brandy by little Somerville of Renfrew in the month of April last, and has more still coming. But if we sell as cheap as any other, I find we will be preferred to any'. [Alexander Steuart, my son, 13 July 1728]

'Being advised of the 14th current that those I depended on in Argyllshire for taking a large quantity of brandy per Duncan Baillie are supplied by Somerville at 10s per gallon, and nine months for payment, which are terms I cannot go into, therefore I entreat how soon this comes to hand you forward the enclosed to Donald McIntyre, wherever you hear of him ... For I am now not inclined that the bark return to the Sound of Mull at this time, there being little good to be expected that way, besides a great deal of risk and charges. For you see Somerville has knocked that trade in the head by his Marseilles brandy, which can be sold much cheaper than that from Bordeaux. So, as I have said, if it be possible to sell anywhere about the Isle of Skye, I do not incline to send the bark, or any part of the cargo southward'. [John McLeod, Glenelg, 18 May 1730]

Note: William Somerville is referred to by Moore in the context of an outstanding debt (see Chapter Twelve).

From: Scottish History Society. *Letter-book of Bailie John Steuart of Inverness 1715-1752* Ed William Mackay Second Series No 9 Edinburgh 1915

CHAPTER TEN: THE SMUGGLING AGENTS

'I want a correspondent in your place in whom I may confide to receive sundry sums owing me or becoming due me at Largs and to remit the same to Glasgow and am thinking that you would answer to do me this favour. I therefore write to you to know your inclination and if it be agreeable to you pray write to me a line by Mr John Callin so that I may act therein when certain of your approbation'. [Hugh Morris, Largs, 19 August 1757]

The agents were an essential part of Moore's smuggling business. They were his point of reference in an area, the people who had the closest contact with his customers and those to whom he could turn, in theory, when attempting to raise money in a hurry at Glasgow to pay for a future supply of goods.

Moore's next letter to Largs is addressed to <u>Robert</u> Morris, who presumably had agreed to act as agent instead of Hugh. 'The above is list of sundry debts due me in Largs and at Fairlie, which I send to you to receive the value of for me, which I desire you will do so in due time and as soon as possible you can. I desire you will remit whatever sums you receive for me to Mr James Simson at the Old Bank office in Glasgow'. [Robert Morris, 20 November 1757]

The phrase 'my occasions in Glasgow' occurs frequently in the letters to the agents (see Chapter Six). On 7 November 1752 Moore used this phrase to James Allison (Ayr), James Hutchison (Ayr), William Kerr (Stranraer), William McClure (Drumbeg) and Janine Stewart (Girvan) and on 12 January 1753 to Hector Bryce (Dunure Main), John Dickie (Loans), James Donald (Ayr), Pat Ewing (Fairlie), James Hutchison (Ayr) and William McClure (Drumbeg).

Moore compensated the agents for their trouble in a variety of ways. John Dickie (Loans), James Allison (Ayr) and William Laing (Inverkip) received an abatement of 1d per gallon on their personal

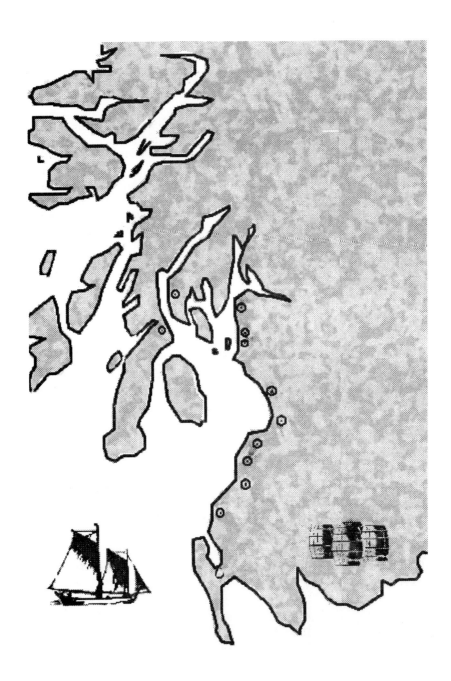

Figure 13: The Smuggling Agents

This sketch map indicates the location of Moore's more important agents from north to south of the area. Brief notes are given about each.

John Cowan, Tarbert: 5 letters between 1750 and 1754. 'I wonder Mr Cowan did not make some addition (to the payment Munn made to Glasgow) as I believe it was in his power so to do'. [John Munn, 8 November 1750]
John Munn, Kilfinan: 27 letters between 1750 and 1757. 'John Munn ... met with an accident falling off a horse, which has delayed the remittance I expected from him for he could not travel'. [James Simson, 12 March 1753]
William Laing, Inverkip: 32 letters between 1750 and 1759. 'I've bought the twenty deeping of herring nets you desired me but I do not know by what opportunity to forward them'. [8 May 1755]
Robert Morris, Largs: 4 letters in 1758 and 1759
Pat Ewing, Fairlie: 9 letters between 1750 and 1755. 'By the arbitration at Glasgow the Ayr merchants have got wind of us for which no help (no further details)'. [30 January 1751]
John Dickie, Loans: 17 letters between 1752 and 1758 (see tailpiece to this chapter)
James and William Allison, Correath: 17 letters 1751 to 1760. 'In all instances relative or in composition of any debt pray do for me as you would for yourself, wherewith I shall be satisfied'. [William Allison, 21 August 1758]
James Hutchison, Ayr: (see comments in this chapter)
James Donald and his wife Janet, Ayr: 12 letters 1751 to 1755. 'If the payments fail of success I have written them that there is no help for directing of diligence'. [Janet Donald, 10 December 1754]
Hector Bryce, Dunure Mains: 15 letters 1752 to 1759. 'I am obliged to you for the trouble you have taken to secure what can be of James Watt of Drumshang's debt'. [2 November 1758]
William McClure, Drumbeg: 21 letters 1750 to 1759, including those to his son Thomas
Janine Stewart, Girvan: 4 letters 1751 and 1752 (see this chapter)
John Allan, Ballantrae: 13 letters 1751 to 1759. A merchant - 'I think I mentioned to you that the price you set on your piece of cloth was too dear for no one has bought a yard at the price'. [12 March 1753]
William Kerr, Stranraer: 14 letters 1750 to 1754. No clue as to what happened after the last letter - 23 September 1754

orders. This did not seem to satisfy Dickie, as Moore wrote in January 1754. 'The value in list of accounts is always to you set down cheaper as to the others. In your letter to me you say I hold the goods too high ... My dealing to your place is in small sums. Were it in great sums whatever encouragement is in there given by anyone in this place I do assure you it should be given by me in the same way. If you please to let me know if you try it you shall find it'. [John Dickie, 16 January 1754]

Despite this 'In casting up your own account you will find an allowance equal to one penny per gallon as usual, I desire you may keep to yourself and I shall further gratify you for your trouble herein. I do not know what has happened to prevent your writing to me for goods as usual as I do not think you are supplied on better terms'. [John Dickie, 18 October 1757]

Sometimes alternative methods were imposed by the agents themselves. 'I've often thought of writing or speaking to you of an article in your account which I've some objection to. It is your charge of 1 per cent on collection of my money. I know the trouble that attends it. However no other person charges me more than ½ per cent. This objection of difference, if you please to remove it, may be of mutual service'. [James Hutchison, 28 November 1754]

In 1752 William Kerr complained about the lack of recompense for his trouble. 'As to making you any allowance, your remark is very just, which has been owing to an accident you did not attend to. On settlement of accounts with you it appeared to me that you had for some time before our settlement received money for me and on account hereof you were in use to give me a bill on Boyd in Kilmarnock. This bill I thought was owing you for value with him on account. The last bills on him you gave me I sent one to Kilmarnock to receive the value but put off the payment. I left word to remit the value to me in Glasgow but he never remitted it so that the value of these bills did not come into my remittance to London, which you know must be done by cash ... I left them in Glasgow to answer in some of the manufactory accounts. And for these I had other my own bills unpaid sufficiently answerable so that Boyd's bills I could not hold in the same light as payment, though I took care they were never returned you. However to make amends in this instance I have sent you with the bearer Robert Agnew a bag containing two dozen of white port and a bag containing two dozen of red port. Please accordingly accept. For the future I think our accounts should be mutually to our satisfaction so it would be best that the premium for your trouble be fixed. Whatever charges you lay out in receiving money for me, namely postages or expresses, let this be charged to my account and I'm further willing to allow you one pound for each hundred pound you receive and remit. If herewith you be satisfied please let me know'. [William Kerr, 20 November 1752]

The problem was sorted out within the year. 'I intended ere now to have sent you account of some tea in acknowledgment of your civilities to me but it happens that the tea I expected is not yet arrived and I have not a pound by me. When it arrives I shall send some to Ms McKie and by this bearer, John McDowall of High Portnessock, I have sent you a bag containing two and a half dozen of very good white Lisbon wine'. [William Kerr, 25 October 1753]

John Munn was also sent wine. In November 1752 he received one dozen red and one dozen white port 'to drink'. The following November 'I've not at present white wine but if Angus should stay until I have I shall send you a bag by him or by the next opportunity'. [John Munn, 7 November 1753]. And 'I have this year been disappointed of white wine so that I could not send you a compliment as I intended thereof. As I have not yet any white wine I send you by the bearer, Angus Munn, a bag containing three dozen of claret I beg you will accept of'. [John Munn, 11 March 1758]

Whatever the arrangement with Pat Ewing, Moore wrote to one of his customers at Hunterston 'It is best for me that you remit directly to Glasgow for if you pay my money to any other person to be remitted there for my account it will be thought a trouble requiring some gratification'. [John Resaid, 20 November 1757]

James Hutchison, Ayr

He was one of the more important agents - he collected money owing from over fifty customers, he was part-owner of a wherry and more than forty letters were written to him between 1750 and 1759.

By 1757 Hutchison was finding the role of agent irksome. 'The value of the bills in your hands is too considerable not to give anxiety'. [James Hutchison 26 October 1757]. Moore wrote to Andrew McCulloch, also in Ayr. 'I have no mind to send new bills to Mr Hutchison as I think it is disagreeable for him that he has any with so slow payment ... Let me beg your care in payment of these bills to Mr Simson'. [Andrew McCulloch, Ayr, 18 October 1757].

The following month Moore turned to Hector Bryce in Dunure Main for help. 'What money you receive for me now and from time to time I desire you may remit to Mr James Simson ... or, if you cannot conveniently send the money to Glasgow, I desire you'll pay it to Mr James Hutchison in Ayr, taking his receipt on account of payments made you for me'. [Hector Bryce, 24 November 1757]. However Moore's opinion of Bryce was not very high (see Chapter Thirteen).

As a result of problems with Bryce in 1758, Moore turned to William Allison 'with sundry bills to receive payment for me. Some of these are endorsed or made payable to you. As occasion may require, I desire you to assign and endorse them to Mr Allison for me'. [James Hutchison, 21 August 1758]. 'By what I have wrote to you, you will be fully acquainted with my inclination and know how to proceed in the sundry affairs whereof you have the management for me, which amounts to this that in these matters you will be pleased to do or direct for me as you would for yourself'. [William Allison, 30 March 1759]

Yet more assistance was forthcoming for Hutchison. 'I have enclosed a line to William McClure advising him to provide payment and to acquaint in like manner those in his neighbourhood'. [James Hutchison, 21 September 1759]

James Donald
Donald was another one of Moore's agents in Ayr. In December 1751 he was given 'credit for a pure cotton check and the usual abatement'. [James Donald, 31 December 1751]. The reason for this was 'I find that there are several of my customers who choose to pay money to you. It will hence I hope not be disagreeable to you that I send some of their bills to you to receive for me'. [James Donald, 12 January 1753]

Later that year Donald died. 'I was sorry to hear of the death of James Donald, whom in all my dealings with him I found to be a very honest man'. [Joseph Scott, 18 February 1754]. Moore had already written to the widow, Janet Donald, holding her responsible for outstanding debts. 'Answerable to my occasions at Glasgow I'm preparing what payments I can and for this purpose I'm applying to my friends by sending to them their accounts and drawing on them for the value. Hence it is that I herewith send you the sundry value of goods I delivered to the orders of your late husband, Mr McDonald, unaccounted for being £55.4.5'. [Janet Donald, 26 October 1753]

At first all went well. 'I see I'm obliged to Mrs Donald (who) you say has done all in her power for my interest'. [Joseph Scott, 18 February 1754]. But in August 1754 Moore sent some bills to Joseph Scott & Co in Glasgow, valued at £707 19s. 'These bills I expected they had sent you to receive accordingly and whether they be yet come to your care I know not for they write me the 18th last month that they have not received any payments. I'm surprised that no payments are made so have wrote them to know if the bills were as usual forwarded to you. If they are not I have desired they be sent you that the value be received and the sum remitted to them. If the payment fails of success I have wrote them that there is no help for directing of diligence, which it would be very disagreeable to me but the necessity must excuse'. [Janet Donald, 10 December 1754]. Her bill of £47 18s 9d had not been paid.

She was obviously experiencing difficulties, as Moore wrote 'Let Mrs Donald be as pressing as she can with Hector Bryce and Thomas Gray that they pay the balance they owe on their bills for this would leave room for other demands as well as serve to pay your account'. [Joseph Scott, 24 March 1755]. The last letter to her is dated 18 August 1755, when Moore agreed to receive one of her hogsheads of rum 'at the price you sold to James Young, which you showed me was 3/10d per gallon' towards payment of her outstanding personal debt to him.

Janine Stewart

Janet Donald was not the only woman agent with whom Moore negotiated. Janine Stewart, 'a young factor' in Girvan, was William McClure's niece, daughter of Mathew Stewart and sister of Jack Stewart (see Chapter Thirteen). The first letter to her is dated October 1751. 'Above is list of sundry sums of money owing me in Girvan, which I recommend to your care to receive the value of for me and to desire you will pay what you receive to Mr William McClure ... As opportunity offer write me account of the payments that are made to regulate my giving credit'. [Janine Stewart, 9 October 1751]

By November 1752 Moore wrote to William McClure 'I begin to be uneasy that Janine Stewart has not paid you the contents of her bill'. [7 November 1752]. 'What means Janine that she makes no partial payment either in the bills or on account of the goods she since had? I do not think that she squanders the money and so that she delays passing it is surprising'. [William McClure, 28 February 1753]

William McClure
McClure was asked to intercede over the debts owed by another woman, Jean Ross. 'If you step down to Girvan it be obliging me. Mrs Jean Ross in Girvan is owing me £7 14s 8d, for which I drew on her payable to Mr John Allan in Ballantrae but she does not it seems incline to pay him and has sent me word or Janine Stewart wrote me that she would pay the value to you. I was about writing to my doctor in Ayr to raise diligence against her. I'm pleased that this was prevented so call on her for the money. I expect she will pay you and grant her a discharge, which will be sufficient on account'. [7 November 1752] 'I see that Mrs Jean Ross has made you a partial payment of £2 on account of value of goods £7 14s 8d I delivered her order the 20th March last. You have enclosed as she desires to be given a copy of her letter and of the account. This I sent her of before and either may satisfy that her directions to me was literally observed and it is expected that she no longer will evade payment of. This is the value owing me. If you have an uncertainty let me know for any delay will cause my writing to Ayr that the utmost diligence be used'. [28 February 1753]

More intimate details are learned about Moore's system of working with his agents on the death of William McClure than during his life. 'I have received your letter of the 15th this morning giving account of your father's death. I was before told of it and am very sorry for his loss to his family and friends. I hope your sisters are recovered of their illness. As you desire me to send you a state of your father's debt I give you in manner following ... What is owing on the two bills (£143) ... may wait your convenience until you have proceeded in the settlement of your father's affairs, which I am hopeful will turn out to your satisfaction and to the satisfaction of his family and may be expected from his manner of dealings, where I wish you hearty success. I have given directions that what goods you write for to me be taken care of and sent conform with orders and I shall be always glad to deal with you.

'PS There are two bills you will find in your father's drawer belonging to me due by John Rodger and your late brother, Archibald McClure, for £51 7s and other £7 2s 10d, which I desire you will send to Mr James Hutchison in Ayr to deliver to him for me'. [Thomas McClure, 19 October 1759]

'I have wrote to Thomas McClure that he pay my draft of £42 9s 9d (his father's debt) and what is owing on the two bills as above mentioned may wait his conveniency until he has proceeded in the settlement of his father's affairs and I hope we shall end, as we began, friendly'. [James Hutchison, 19 October 1759]

John Cowan

On more than one occasion Moore had difficulties with agents. John Cowan wrote to him on 26 October 1750 'acquainting me that you had communicated my demands on my friends in Tarbert, who are at present mostly from home and that their return will be attended to mutual satisfaction. Malcolm McDugal and James Gillis write me that they offered you payment of the sums they owe me and that you refused their payments, motively you mention from the risk you apprehend in remittance. Now if credit be here given this credit should be paid at time and place in option of the creditor but to accommodate the payments you know I've mentioned Peter & John Murdoch in Glasgow, William Laing in Inverkip, John Munn in Kilfinan and have sent John Ewing and lastly I have applied to you to do me the favour of receiving for me. If in none of these methods I can succeed I do not know in what manner I can hope for success. In your receiving or remitting I never meant or do intend that you run any manner of risk, which I hope may yet reconcile you to receive for me and by the channel of John Munn or sending him what you receive to remit to Glasgow for me to be added to the sums he receives and occasionally remits to Glasgow is the best and frugalest way I can think of for having my money from Tarbert, where if my friends make payment their debt becomes discharged and thereby it is a matter of indifference to them how I direct the remittance from Tarbert. Nor do I think they will grudge that I appoint your remittance in manner most convenient to me'. [John Cowan, 7 November 1750]

Moore wrote to John Munn the following day. 'Of these (bills enclosed) are three Tarbert ones which credit I have given on the express condition of the values being paid to you for me, which is the reason why I give you the trouble of these three Tarbert debts'. [John Munn, 8 November 1750]

Two years later Moore was still trying to persuade Cowan to act properly as his agent. 'The manner hereof cannot be disagreeable to you as you can have no dislike to the confidence I repose in you. Whatever money you receive on account of these debts I desire you will remit me by the first opportunity for this in bank notes or failing such opportunity to Mr Joseph Scott, merchant in Glasgow, for my account'. [John Cowan, 11 July 1752]

'I'm favoured with yours of the 29th past acquainting me of your having received the sundry bills and that you had applied to all my debtors, who seem readily disposed to begin making some partial payments, which in your next letter I shall expect to know how far you have succeeded. Their standing so long may perhaps be in some measure injurious to them as well as to me for it will readily occur that I cannot encourage their dealing with me while these debts lie so long unpaid.' [John Cowan, 25 September 1752]

But the underlying problem continued. 'The Tarbert chaps are singular in their correspondence. I'm surprised Mr John Cowan has been so bashful in his payment for from him at least I expect some degree of punctuality. If you write him yet again it may perhaps be of some service. Let him know it is at my particular request and write him of the other payments you also expect for my account and if this fails I must try to recover payment in another manner'. [Joseph Scott, 18 February 1754]

'There is one Campbell, a merchant above the Cross, that is well acquainted with Cowan in Tarbert. I wish you could intend him to get the value or Bailie Black can oblige herein for he too knows him and probably how to prevail with him'. [James Simson, 5 September 1755]. 'I'm pleased you have sent Cowan's bill to Mr Campbell in Inverary, who I persuade myself will soon fall on a means to get the value'. [James Simson, 8 November 1755]

Perhaps Moore had found a Kintyre answer at last. 'I hope that Mr Peter Stewart of Campbeltown will succeed in the debts there'. [Alexander Morson, 18 April 1759]

John Munn, Kilfinan

For a long time Moore seemed to have complete faith in John Munn. He also attempted to help in finding a job for his son 'whom I have recommended as I think he deserves. However, I do not find that Mr Callin is disposed to take a young man. He wants rather an assistant - one who is thoroughly acquainted with business and the manner of receipt books. For the care of the cellars and the receiving and delivery of goods he is provided already with one in whom he confides. I am heartily sorry I cannot do for your son as I wished and had expected'. [John Munn, 5 September 1755]

The problems started to develop in 1759. 'I some time ago received a letter from you wherein you mentioned as if I scrupled answering your commission for goods. I know not how this has happened for I always thought your order too small. That is I should at all times send you much more goods than what you wrote for and shall be always ready to do so while I deal and when it suits your conveniency'. [John Munn, 15 January 1759]

'I have been looking over my Kerry accounts and I find that several sums of money are owing to me, which should be paid. I am the more anxious about these as my occasions for money in Glasgow are hence become more pressing, having dependence on the remittance from your part. Some of the people have wrote to my son that their money is ready to be paid you upon notice or calling, for though I do not readily give into this yet let all occasion pray be removed and on your receipt of

DEFORCEMENT AT OTTER FERRY: A STORY OF JOHN MUNN

Precognition taken before Mr John Campbell of Otter, one of His Majesty's Justices of the Peace in Argyllshire, with respect to a deforcement of the king's officers at the Ferry of Otter on the 12th April last and their seizure being carried off at one o'clock in the morning. Otter, 26 May 1750

'Dougal Livestone, one of the boatmen on board the king's boat presently stationed at Rothesay ... declares that in the month of April last, as he thinks upon the 10th day, he was left by Daniel Campbell, surveyor of the boat, along with John Burney, one of the commissioned boatmen, to take care of a boat loaded with salt, which Daniel Campbell had seized upon the 7 April last. But while Daniel Campbell was searching through the Kerry for brandy, ... Dougal Livestone and John Burney were deforced and turned out of said boat, after being beat by a number of people in disguise (but know none of them about that time of night) and carried off the said boat and salt. And further declares that upon said 12 April one Dugald Munn in Auchgoyle in Kerry, a smuggler, came to him and told him he believed he might get a piece of money if he let the boat and cargo go. To which the deponent answered did he believe him to be such a villain ...

'Archibald Black, change keeper at the Ferry of Otter, aged about sixty-five years ... declares that a day or two before the boat and salt was carried away ... John McLugas, one of the crew of said boat and partly concerned in the cargo, who resides in Drum in Kerry and **John Munn** sometimes in Auchenlochan and sometimes in Kilfinan, part-owner of the boat, were with him. They proposed that the boat might be carried off, as also the cargo, to which he, the deponent, answered that he would not advise them. For it might be of greater trouble to him than they were aware of. Upon which they left him and (he) saw none of them till the boat and cargo was carried away. And further declares that he heard John McLugas was disguised in women's clothes carrying off the boat and salt ...

'John McFarlane, smith at the Ferry of Otter, aged about forty-seven years, married ... deposes that upon the 12th day of April last, as he was coming from the Muir, he heard a noise of people at the quay below his own house, which he suspected to be a mob with a design to carry off the boat and salt ... after the boat was off from the shore, one Ninian McNichol came up to the deponent (who and John McCurry, also living at the Ferry of Otter, were sitting together above his house) and desired John McCurry (as there were few hands in the boat) to go to help away with the boat. Which John McCurry absolutely refused and declares (as he heard) that McNichol was part-owner of the boat ...

'John McCurry at the Ferry of Otter, aged about forty-four years, married, ... deposes that, after the boat and salt was off from the shore, one Ninian McNichol in Portponlag came to him ... and begged he would go aboard, as there were too few hands to carry her away, which he absolutely refused. Upon which Ninian, who was part-owner of the boat, went away ...

'John Burney, one of the commissioned boatmen on board the king's boat presently stationed at Rothesay ... deposes that ... he was left ... with Dougal Liveston ... to take care of a boat loaded with salt, which Daniel Campbell seized ,,, But while Daniel Campbell was searching through Kerry ... (they) were deforced and turned out of said boat ... but know none of them but one **John Munn** in Auchgoyle in Kerry, a smuggler ... And further declares that, ere he was turned out of said boat, he said to **John Munn** that he know him and that he would report him. And either **Munn** or one of his gang replied if he should be hanged he would carry off the boat and cargo, which they instantly did, as also one of the king's swords ...

'John Sharp, one of the boatmen on board the king's boat stationed at Rothesay ... deposes that ... while he was at Silvercraigs alongst with the king's boat and the salt boat that was deforced ... at the Ferry of Otter, **John Munn**, sometime in Kilfinan and now prisoner on board the king's boat at Rothesay, told him that he and the other hand with him should be hearty while they had the salt boat. For he would assure them that they would not have her long. Upon which he asked the said **Munn** what was his concern. He said that part of the boat and cargo belonged to him'.

'We beg leave to acquaint your Honours that Daniel Campbell by virtue of a warrant from Mr Campbell of Otter apprehended **John Munn**, one of the principal people concerned in deforcing his men of the boat loaded with salt, but by some accident or rather neglect of Alexander James, extra boatman in Daniel Campbell's boat, he made his escape during the time that the said Daniel Campbell was waiting on the justices to have him committed to prison'. [Collector at Port Glasgow to the Board, 19 July 1750]

Note: For comments on the other Cowal people involved in this deforcement see Chapter Eleven this letter let me beg that you will give notice to all and receive from them what monies you can so as that the same be remitted to Glasgow for me'. [John Munn, 31 January 1759]. Moore's suspicions were correct. 'I believe there were some who said or wrote to me that their money was in readiness or at a call to be paid you. However I knew that these kinds of say-so are not payments, which are the only thing necessary. And I assure you I never had any thought but that if you engaged or promised to do anything in a friendly way that you would act in every respect agreeable with such good faith ... and as I still rely on your management for me I have to desire the favour of your continuing your care in all instances where your care is wanted for me. For it grudges me very much to see so considerable sums which you have the account of remain outstanding at a time that my occasions are in so much want of payment of these sums'. [John Munn, 30 March 1759]

'I lately had a letter from Mr Alexander Morson at the Old Bank in Glasgow advising me that you had paid him £265 15s 3d on my account. This sum exactly corresponds with the account of receivings, which you sent to me in your last letter. But I am so surprised at the smallness of the sum and it's so much less than what I expected you would have been enabled to remit for me that I think it convenient to write this letter by post to you to desire if possible you may make another remittance answerable to my occasions at Glasgow. My son will be about taking his passage to Scotland in eight or ten days. But if in the meantime you can prevail on my customers to make you payments for the above purpose their compliance at this time will be very seasonable and in a particular manner I shall think obliging me'. [John Munn, 8 May 1759]

The Cowal smugglers are described in the next chapter but the insert includes a case in which John Munn himself was involved.

John Allan
Allan was a merchant in his own right (see Chapter Two). His goods tended to be landed at Peel so that there was then the problem of transferring them to Ballantrae. 'Charles Lennox, the bearer of your letter of the 9th inst in Liverpool, came here and left it for me. I had no doubt but that he would take the contents you directed so without more ado I caused the casks to be put to water, as I imagined he would require

them to be dispatched the day after he came to me. On telling him what you wrote me he said he would not take the whole but a small part ... I desired he would let me know the quantity. This he took a day to consider of and following that told me it was necessary I kept his brother out of the way, that he might not see or know what was to be shipped for you, because he was one of his owners. This I did not well understand and told him my directions were to deliver him a certain quantity of goods on your account or if he did not agree to receive the whole I would agree to give him some. He seemed to receive or consented to take thirty casks. He asked me if you had ordered any goods for himself. I told him it was not mentioned in your letter but that if you designed any for him that you would give it him of the goods which you had ordered for yourself. He grew very angry that his name for credit on his own account was not mentioned in your letter and for this reason told me he would not agree to take from me any kind of goods for you. I hoped he would not persist in his resolution to disappoint you and bid him call again to let me know. This he declined so I do not expect any good of him. He does not appear to be a distinct man in his own way of business'. [John Allan, 29 May 1755]

John Dickie, Loans

'I've been speaking to William Dickie about the other debts owing me in Loans. He tells me that all the persons concerned are able and very willing and telling him that I intended to send their accounts to you to receive value of for me. He has assured me that payment will be punctually made and that you would accordingly remit the same to my order. Relying hereon I have above given you list of the sundry debts owing me in Loans to be paid you ... let me beg your diligence to the end that no delay may attend the payments, which would prove of great inconvenience to me. Your favour herein will greatly oblige, sir, your most humble servant'. [John Dickie, 22 January 1752]

Moore must have been satisfied with the arrangement because he sent further bills on 8 November 1752 totalling £157 17s 10d, on 7 January 1753 two separate sums of £69 5s 4d and £151 11s 1d for goods delivered on 22 December 1752 and 4 January 1753 by Archibald McClure, Malcolm Fisher and William Dickie, who was to give the letter to his brother, on 12 January 1753 £45 16s 9d for goods delivered on 12

January by Andrew Auld and Alexander McDowall and on 8 March 1753 £66 14s 10d for goods delivered by William Dickie.

Further information about the Dickies is included in the tailpiece to this chapter while Moore's customers are considered in the next chapter and the wherry masters in Chapter Thirteen.

THE STORY OF WILLIAM & JOHN DICKIE, LOANS

The collector at Ayr went to inspect the 'Temple', a folly near Troon Point, which he believed could be converted into a customs post. 'The whole arable and pasture ground round the Temple be in the possession, by lease, of three of the most notorious smugglers there, viz. William and John Dickie and James Vallance, and who have constantly sixteen boats of their own for bringing goods out of vessels consigned for themselves and partners at the Troon and for taking ashore goods out of ships that touches there from many foreign parts in their way to Irvine and Port Glasgow, about a dozen of which boats we saw hauled up on the beach when we were there last Monday. After they land the goods we are well-informed that about five hundred horses have often been got thither in an hour's warning to carry them away to different places of the country by means of one John Law, who lives in a small hut contiguous to the Point and has it for his business to appraise the smugglers of every arrival and who in consideration of that service give him a certain number of casks of spirits out of each cargo, according to the quantity run, besides other emoluments such as paying the rent of his house and grazing two cows kept by him ... Notwithstanding the proposed guard to be kept in or near to the Temple, as the officers will have no means to get on board vessels lying off it and after goods shall be taken out of them and put into boats by which they will be landed in many by-holes and inlets on both sides of the Troon Point, particularly in the night time, when the officers we fear will not be able to answer your Honours laudable intention of suppressing the smuggling trade in this district without the assistance of a ship well-manned and armed with an experienced commander on this coast, superior in force to the smuggling vessels, who of late have been observed to carry several guns and swivels with twenty men on board each of them by which they deter the cutters and wherries in the king's service from boarding them, an instance of which happened near this place last month. A wherry in the service of the excise, David Carlile commander, presently stationed at Loch Ryan, descried two smuggling vessels who after having the assurance of hailing him and he suspecting no ill they fired at both his vessel and boat and left several shot in them before he could get clear of them. Afterwards they run cargoes where they pleased in that masterly manner which we humbly think may be prevented if your Honours approve of having such a vessel chiefly stationed at Troon Point and to extend her cruise as often as possible to the north-east as far as Irvine Bay and to the southward no further than Cullean Bay in this precinct'.
[Collector at Ayr to the Board, 22 April 1767]

contd.

In October the collector went back to the Temple where his party were 'accosted by Dickie and Vallance, described in our former letter ... who swore that no officers belonging to the King should get possession of that Temple while their tack subsisted off the land that surrounded it, being pasture ground, chiefly for sheep, and rented by them ... of which lease about seven years are to run before the heir be of age. But this threatening whereby to continue their illicit trade ... we hope they (the heritor's tutors) will over-rule as we believe these tacksmen of the grasses are ill-founded in law to pretend an obstruction to and from that house'. [Collector at Ayr to the Board, 22 October 1767]

In March 1777 information was received that the *Liberty* of Hastings was landing her cargo near Troon Point. She was commanded by Henry Hanks of Folkestone and her present cargo was believed to be from France. However, she had only managed to land fifty casks of spirits because of a north-west wind and a high sea. This weather was also preventing her from getting off the coast. Without military back-up the surveyor, Gordon, 'durst not do anything' so he sent two officers to Largs to hire a boat and go to the Cumbraes for a revenue vessel to be ordered to Troon. The only vessel at Millport was the *Nancy* at anchor but with no crew.

In the meantime the customs officers continued to watch until night, when the wind dropped and the smugglers landed more of the cargo on the rocks at Troon, using ten or twelve boats, the property of the locals. One of the Irvine tidesmen saw the smugglers from Loans or their servants carrying muskets to the landing place. As a result, when the surveyor ordered the customs officers to go along the road to Loans, the Irvine men went home. The remaining Ayr officers tried to stop the carts in an avenue at Loans. The smugglers had guns loaded with slug shot and balls. The customs officers were so close that they could identify the smugglers. James Dickie from Troon was cursing the carriers and telling them to turn about and face the officers. When the first gun was fired the voice of Hanks the master was heard. The customs officer in charge called a retreat.

'There is no stroke that could be half so sever upon the smugglers as the seizure of the boats at Troon, for without them they could not get the cargoes landed'. The Board agreed to this proposal so the collector instructed Captain Hamilton that the boats should be secured by scuttling or otherwise taken into Rothesay, Irvine or Ayr. Another suggestion was that the port of Hastings should stop the *Liberty* and that one of the revenue boats should bring her to Scotland for condemnation.

CHAPTER ELEVEN: THE CUSTOMERS

'The illegal trade carried on by almost the whole inhabitants of the parish of Dundonald, a part of which is Troon Point, and with great propriety may be called a freeport for their pernicious trade against the government and by which many of them, as well as several in this town, appear to have suddenly enriched themselves ... we wish to see them obliged to make restitution of the money they have robbed the crown of these several years past and their illegal trade checked'. [Collector at Ayr to the Board, 22 April 1767]

The information about George Moore's customers in Scotland comes not only from the letters to the customers themselves, or to the agents responsible for collecting the debts, but also from letters to James Simson at the Old Bank in Glasgow, others owed money by Moore (including Joseph Scott in Glasgow) and those responsible for raising ultimate diligence for recovery of old debts. Attempts have been made to identify these individuals in birth, marriage and death records, on tombstones, in other contempory local records and through the help of modern local historians.

Perhaps most significant of all are the cross-references in the custom house letter-books - the quotation at the head of this chapter comes from the letters quoted in the tailpiece to Chapter Ten. As a result this chapter is based on such 'sightings'. In other words instead of looking from the inside of the letter-book outwards, which is the theme for most of this book, it looks from the outside in, identifying in Moore's letters the people mentioned in the custom house records.

The Cowal Smugglers

'The seizure makers cannot depend on any assistance in Cowal so are obliged to take their party with them to support them in the execution of their office. And there is no such thing as making a seizure in Cowal unless the officers are well supported'. [Collector at Campbeltown to the Board, 13 February 1757]

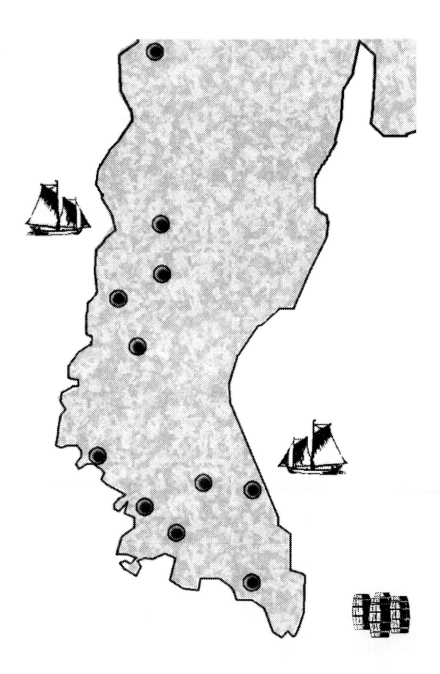

Figure 14: The Cowal Smugglers

Each dot on the map indicates previous areas of comparatively dense settlement (pre clearance), where George Moore's customers lived. Some of these places, often now either under Forestry Commission plantations or mere piles of stones, have been identified with the help of local experts. Although both Moore and the custom house letter-books tend to refer to this area as Kerry, the more familiar term Cowal has been used by the author.

What George Moore said about his Cowal 'friends'
Archibald Black: paid his debts
John Black: 'I received a letter from John Black in Corra of a prior date to your letter and in his he mentions he had paid you though your letter contradicts it. So if he is disappointed he must blame himself'. [John Munn, 26 December 1754]
Barnaby Boyle: 'Tell Bar Boyle that he forgets his promise' [John Munn, 7 January 1753]
Hugh McComehy: 'There is one McFarlane who was concerned with Hugh McConaghie in the bill £270 8s 9½d ... the balance herein owing me is £112 11s 0½d. This balance I compounded with McFarlane when I was last in Greenock. I agreed to receive and he to pay 5s in the pound, which comes to £28 3s. I desire you will receive the same from McFarlane'. [John Munn, 9 November 1751]
John McCurry: 'John McCurrie paid you £6 5s 4d per your last account, which sum answered with the value of his bill 3rd September'. [John Munn, 11 March 1758]
John McLachlane: a wherry master
Robert McLachlan: sent Moore £9 6s 2d in November 1750
Ninian McNichol: wherry master. 'Ninian McNickle's balance £3 13s 8d on his bill in you £6 13s 3d I'm not quite clear about for I find you only paid me £3 and on what footing the remainder rested I forget. You'll put me in mind thereof'. [John Munn, 7 July 1752]
Dugald Munn: received £2 3s 7½d in September 1751.

The same year the collector at Port Glasgow reported to the Board of Customs that 'Archibald Lamont of Lamont, Esquire, in Cowal has set forth to us that he is willing to do all in his power to suppress the smuggling in that part of the country and for that purpose he prays your Honourable Board will be pleased to grant him a deputation empowering him to seize uncustomed and prohibited goods and also that your Honours will be pleased to grant another, the like deputation, to Alexander Lamont, his factor'. [27 September 1757]

Yet in November 1750 Moore wrote 'I'm very much obliged to the Laird of Lamont, who has given his help towards my having justice in the divers debts (Alexander Jameson, Alexander Kerr, Inverin, Robert McLachlan and Malcolm Douglas)'. [John Munn, 8 November 1750]. And 'I hope that Laird of Lamont has prevailed with John Shearer (to pay what he owed) and every difficulty is removed'. [John Munn, 11 February 1751]. Despite this Shearer had not paid any of the debt until he produced £5 in December 1753. 'What with denial and what with delay he makes the demand of that debt a very disagreeable one. For the remainder he now puts off till May next and then ... he will have further excuse for delay. I shall be guided herein by your direction - delay until then or cause him to be pushed hard as you think fittest'. [John Munn, 14 January 1754]

Another smuggle recorded in the Port Glasgow letter-books has been included here as it is possible to identify several of Moore's contacts.

A Deforcement at Auchinshelloch
This deforcement happened at the same time as the deforcement at Otter Ferry described in Chapter Ten.

Precognition taken before Hugh McBryde of Baidland, present provost of the burgh of Rothesay and one of His Majesty's Justices of the Peace for the Shire of Bute, with respect to a deforcement of the king's officers in Argyllshire and their seizure being carried off. Rothesay 19 May 1750

'Alexander Jamieson, one of the boatmen on board the king's boat presently stationed at Rothesay ... depones that in the month of April last and as (he) thinks upon the 11th day he was sent by Daniel Campbell, surveyor of said boat, along with Daniel Tosh and other of the boatmen to search for uncustomed and prohibited goods in the part of Argyllshire called Kerry.

'And in their said search he declares that they found in a cottar's house in Auchinshelloch, possessed by **John Black**, twelve casks of spirits, that after tasting were found to consist of rum and brandy, which the declarent seized in the king's name. After which a number of people, both men and women, came upon him, when he was by himself, having sent Tosh to Mr Campbell, who was searching some other places of the country, to inform him of this seizure. And took him and tied both his hands and feet and carried off the seized spirits and left him lying there sore bruised, until he was rescued by the people of the house after the seizure was gone.

'He declares further that some of the people concerned in carrying off the spirits and using him in this unmerciful manner were known to him. Particularly Isobel Hunter, spouse to Nincone Stewart, smith in Mecknock, Mary Black, daughter to **Archibald Black** at the Ferry of Otter, who was disguised in a man's coat and bonnet, and appeared to be their leaders. Janet Lamont, spouse to **Barnaby Boyle** at Mecknock, ----- - Hunter, spouse to **Robert McLauchan**, all Mecknock, Isobel McLachlan, widow of James McCrae, all Mecknock, Margaret McCrae, her daughter, Margaret Blair at Mecknock, Elizabeth Blair, her daughter, and several others.

'What men were present were not concerned in tying the declarent nor did he see them carry off the spirits. But declares that he observed that the following persons were in the crowd with the women, when they came to attack him, viz **Hugh McComehy**, miller at Mecknock, Colin Smith in Glendaruel, who came along with the women. He saw also four men who he was told belonged to Arran but does not know their names. There was also one Archibald Baxter, who came to the declarent before the women came, and who lives at Auchiork ...

'Daniel Tosh, another of the boatmen on board said boat, solemnly declares the same with Alexander Jamieson as to their being sent upon the search and making the seizure and as to his leaving Jamieson with it and going off to acquaint Mr Campbell. But declares he tasted only one of the casks before he went away and found it to be rum. That he heard one of the Arran men, named Patrick McAlaster, own he had been there but denied his name, though the declarent knows it'.

The King's Men Known by Moore
Captain Campbell
It is believed that this is Captain Colin Campbell, who was in charge of a Greenock revenue cruiser (see Chapter Five).

'James Fisher I hear is a hand on board Captain Campbell's cutter. I've wrote a line enclosed to Captain Campbell to acquaint him of Fisher's debt and hoping he will so manage with Fisher as to prevent the expense of diligence. Direct or do herein as you think best to procure payment, the grounds of Fisher's debt being his two missive letters ... whereon I delivered his orders ... on account whereof was my draft on him ... the 7th July'. [James Hutchison, 7 November 1752]

'I have wrote to my doctor in Ayr to cause diligence to be used against him for recovery of my money but before anything this way be done I thought it best to advise you hereof to the end if any method on a peacable way can be used whereby the payment or security for the payment can be claimed this I recommend to you to do or direct as I prefer this method and I am hopeful therein to meet what favour you can do me'. [Captain Campbell of the cutter, 7 November 1752]

'James Fisher has been for some time in Ayr. I hope you have made use of the opportunity to receive or secure what he owes me'. [James Hutchison, 27 February 1753]

Captain Crawford
Andrew Crawford was commander of the Cumbraes wherry. He advised Moore on how to proceed over the seizure of Lawrence Rigg's wherry (see Chapter Thirteen) and appears in the next extract.

'There is an old bill of Carnachan's in your hands ... He's with Captain Crawford in the king's boat of Port Glasgow. Is there any way of coming at him?' [James Simson, 13 July 1757]. 'Anthony McCarnachan with Captain Crawford is just now with me and has paid £1 7s 6d (balance £6) in part of his bill. The remainder Captain Crawford has promised to see paid in three equal payments, half yearly from this date'. [James Simson, 27 September 1757]

In August 1758 the £6 was still owing. 'Captain Crawford ... promised payment. Whether he will be so good as his word let him be tried'. [James Simson, 21 August 1758]. 'I have only Captain Crawford's promise by word of mouth that he would pay Carnachan's balance due me and I believed Captain Crawford to be a man of his word. This confidence prevented my arresting Carnachan when I had the opportunity, which would have held him to payment or obliged him to give security'. [James Simson, 6 October 1758]. 'Captain Crawford's silence or delay of payment is a kind of proof that I was too complaisant in only taking his word for the payment of Carnachan's debt. He never comes to the Isle so that I have no hopes of seeing him here'. [James Simson, 19 December 1758]. 'Captain Crawford takes an unfair advantage for I have no writing under his hand to enforce his promise. So the recourse against Carnachan rests on his bill. Is he not to be met with sometimes at Greenock?' [James Simson, 17 February 1759]. The end of the story is not known.

Gilbert Gray

'In obedience to the reference of the 14th July last on the enclosed letter of Mr Duncan Forbes Paterson to your Honourable Board in regard to Ronald McAllister and Duncan Wilson, boatmen on board the Cumbraes wherry commanded by Mr Andrew Crawford, their carrying ashore from the *Three Brothers* of Ayr seized by Mr Crawford in June last **Gilbert Gray** a smuggler and part owner of said vessel and that without the knowledge or consent of Crawford. We beg leave to acquaint your Honours that we have had the parties before us and in the presence of Messrs Paterson and Crawford have examined them and others of the boatmen as to this matter and it appears that **Gray** was carried ashore as Mr Paterson has represented. How far the boatmen are culpable for carrying on shore **Gray** we humbly beg leave to submit to your Honourable Board and we only observe that we cannot learn what induced them thereto, their only excuse being that they had no particular directions from Mr Crawford with respect to **Gray** and that he stepped into the boat along with another person, not a smuggler, whom they were carrying ashore by Mr Crawford's directions, who was then on board, which we suppose was the case. We farther beg leave to inform your Honours that the reason for our being so long in making enquiry into this affair is that till now we have not had an opportunity to have all the persons before us together the one or the other of them being constantly out in their respective vessels'. [Collector at Port Glasgow to the Board, 26 November 1757]

'**Gib Gray** is backward, very backward, in his payment. Send him word that you will be obliged to use diligence on his bill if he continues to delay'. [Samuel Cuthbert, 29 July 1754]

David Galloway
Galloway's name appears frequently throughout the Ayr custom house letter-books, mainly in the context of tobacco and salt.

The main problems related to his fishery salt account. 'David Galloway went to England about the end of August having settled his account as the case then stood by taking credit for 25 bushels 18 lbs of salt 'as seized by the officers at Stranraer'. As our accounts were still untransmitted when he returned, he was informed of the Board's determination of September 11th and he wrote several weeks ago to Stranraer but has yet received no answer. If we receive none next week his account must be sent in as it stands'. [Ayr letters, 24 February 1759]

'Our fishery salt accounts for the year ended April 5th last year being all finished, as far as we are concerned, would have been sent you together with the abstract by the carrier who set out this day for Edinburgh had not David Galloway entreated for a further delay in order that he may get his salt at Stranraer put into joint custody and bonded there. And as he represented that he had already written thrice to his agent, but received no answer and proposed to send an express for the greater and more certain dispatch we consented to his request, apprehending that he would again apply to the commissioners for leave to alter his account and thereby occasion additional trouble to both you and ourselves'. [Ayr letters 8 March 1759]

To James Ross, Stranraer. 'By direction of Mr George Gardiner I send you the enclosed account executed by Mr Galloway for the salt neglected to be put under joint custody at your port at April 5th 1758 and for re-delivery of which the commissioners gave an order the 11th September last and this account you will be pleased to insert in your annual account current for the year ended 5th April last and to transmit it to Mr Gardiner with others which it seems he expects from you. At the same time you will still keep possession of the salt until Mr Galloway shall have paid the charges and given security for it. You see he swears in the account to the identity of the salt'. [Ayr letters 20 March 1759]

To Richard Swainston, customs solicitor, Edinburgh. 'Agreeable to your letter ... I this day served David Galloway, merchant in Ayr, with two writs of subpoena therein mentioned by delivering them to himself between one and two o'clock in the afternoon'. [Ayr letters, 26 October 1759]

Galloway's financial problems are reflected in Moore's letter-book (see tailpiece to this chapter).

James McFie
Although he does not appear in the Moore letter-book, James McFie of Ayr also had problems with his salt accounts. This related to salt that he had sold to people in the Stranraer district, including according to a list dated 14 February 1758, James McCaul & Co, Andrew Dremen, **Andrew McMaster**, Thomas Nasmith, William Clugston, John McCracken for **James McBride**, Charles Agnew, William Caldwell for **Alexander Kerr**, Samuel Neilson and Thomas Beggs. Those highlighted do appear in the Moore letters to the Stranraer area.

John McClure and Robert Allison
'Description of four servants to notorious smugglers in the parish of Dundonald and county of Ayr against whom the sheriff issued warrants for their being concerned in a plot to waylay and murder Mr Gordon, surveyor of the customs at Ayr ... and who have since left their mutual service and cannot be found in the county to tell who were the persons who engaged them to fire ...

'1. Mathew Reid, servant to Robert Fulton in Correath. 27 years of age. Tall stature. Black complexion with his own hair tied and was born in the parish of Symington

'2. William Strachan servant to David Dunlop in Scullochmiln. 20 years of age. Middle stature. Black complexion with his own short dark coloured hair and was born in the parish of Monktown

'3. **James Gray** servant to **James Vallance** in Loans. 20 years of age middle stature black complexion with his own black hair and was born in the parish of Monkton

'4. David Hunter, servant to **Robert Allison** in Correath and working at Willowston. 20 years of age, low stature, brown complexion, pitted with small pox, wearing his own red hair and was born in the parish of Prestwick' [Collector at Ayr to the Board, 23 April 1767]

Seventy-five people were examined and their declarations taken. As a result of this the collector believed that the attempted murder had been committed by the four servants described above, especially as they had absconded. 'We are told they went onboard a sloop or cutter after her cargo was run at Troon Point and are gone with her to France or Ireland, no doubt at the desire of their masters and others concerned in the plot to defeat the discovery of their crimes, which we wish were published in the newspapers in a concise manner and the names and designations of the four fugitives inset therein with a reward for giving an account where they are ...

'Whatever the consequence of such an advertisement it will, we apprehend, at least have some effect of terror amongst the lawless band they left behind them in the parish of Dundonald and that the officers of the revenue may travel amongst them and do their duty with greater safety than at present'.

Currently Mathew Hay and John McClure, merchant in Ayr, were in gaol for planning the murder. 'For many reasons we could wish them to be tried at Edinburgh or in the meantime carried thither from the tolbooth here, where they have a continued rioting in drinking and feasting by uninterrupted visits of their fellow smugglers from every corner of the country so they are scarcely looked upon as prisoners or persons that have been guilty of a crime in the eyes of many, part of whom, if the trials are held here, may happen to be in their jury and in consequence we fear will be the acquitting of them and the officers situation thereby rendered impossible in point of doing their duty'.

While it is unclear whether or not John McClure was one of the several John McClures referred to in the Moore letters there are definite sightings of James Vallance (see the tailpiece to Chapter Ten) and Robert Allison. Again the identity of James Gray is not so certain.

'I've also sent to Joseph Scott & Co all the bills due me in your neighbourhood, namely Adam Bryan's, James Reid's, John Cousen's, Robert Gardner's, **James Vallance**'s, John Boyd's and Neil McMillan's ... whom I desire you may acquaint that they may be accordingly provided to make due payments'. [John Dickie, Loans, 1 September 1755]

On 7 December 1751 William Dickie delivered goods worth £84 15s 9d to Robert Allison. [Robert Allison & William Allison, Correath, 22 January 1752]

James McClure

In presence of Alexander Montgomerie of Coilsfield Esq, collector, and Hugh Campbell, comptroller of the customs at Ayr, the persons aforenamed were examined upon the information of Robert McNab and David Loggie, late tidesmen at Ayr. 8 September 1757

'James Mill, tidewaiter, ... in relation to the cask of spirits said to have been sold by him two years ago to **James McClure** in Knockrawer declares that about that time he was with Alexander Ross and Robert McNab, tidesmen, to prosecute an information given to David Loggie, that they found an anker of brandy in the house of **McClure** but that it was not full, that they agreed by the persuasion of Robert McNab not to seize the same and that he was informed afterwards by the sergeant who was with them that Alexander Ross and Robert McNab sold the spirits to

McClure for 20 shillings, of which he declares he never received one farthing.

'**James McClure** in Knockrawer to the collector of Ayr,
'As for the claim you have against James Mill, of selling off that anker of spirits to me, upon oath I cannot make him guilty for according to the above I really and clearly think he never got money from me, but I wish their answers be as clear. Sir, I am your servant, **James McClure**.

'I beg your excuse for I am in disorder, being under the physick, which Dr Nimmo can make you sensible of, being so these fourteen days now.'

'This is to certify that **James McClure** in Knockraer is in a bad state of health and not capable of coming to Ayr. John Nimmo'.
According to the comments of the collector 'With relation to the cask of spirits which James Mill is said to have sold without being condemned, we refer your Honours to his own declaration and to a letter from **James McClure** to whom that cask was sold, and who being confined by indisposition could not come to town to be examined in person, as is certified by Mr John Nimmo, his surgeon, at the foot of his letter. And although we would by no means excuse Mill's conduct in that matter, yet we presume he is the least culpable of the three concerned, as he was then but a young unexperienced officer and might therefore be more easily drawn aside from his duty by his seniors Ross and McNab'. [Collector at Ayr to the Board, 30 September 1757]

James McClure was well known to Moore. 'I'm a little surprised I have not yet received advice from Mr James Hutchison in Ayr of your having paid the value of your three bills £36, £36 and £37 due me as I had expected that the value of them would by this time have been remitted for me to Glasgow where I want it'. Having added the value of his account for the preceding month 'I have this day drawn on you two bills, namely one for £85 at one month and the other for £90 9s at two months, payable to Mr Hutchison'. [James McClure, 17 December 1757]

William Allison was also responsible for collecting as much of the debt as possible from **James McClure**. 'I am satisfied that you agree with (**McClure**'s proposal). Could any security be obtained this appearance of getting the value at the seasons agreed on would give great satisfaction but really considering **McClure**'s rank and circumstances in life it is scarcely to be expected that he can obtain sufficient security and it is better to be without than having a nominal one only so that if no better terms can be obtained in my mind it is best to close with the conditions of his own proposal. For I am apprehensive that if he is pursued to the utmost his other creditors will pursue in the same manner and compel him to make defences ... which might have bad consequences by having his debts secreted, which are perhaps the most valuable part of his effects. If in your treating with him you could obtain an assignment of his fourth part in Murphy's brig whereby the sale and produce might be rendered this seems more eligible than attaching at Cork, which is a foreign process. If the brig should happen to touch here the matter would be familiar'. [William Allison, 30 March 1759]

Moore also held **McClure** responsible for the debts of Will Pollock who 'is a cancer about Glasgow and **James McClure** of Knockraer is the fittest person to assist the getting the balance due on the bill for as I remember **James McClure** recommended this Pollock and on the recommendation and **McClure**'s credit the goods were delivered'. [William Allison, 30 March 1759]

There are subtly different spellings of Knockraer both in Moore's letter-book and in the custom house letters. It has not been identified with certainty today.

William Peacock, Ayr

The previous enquiry was not the end of accusations about Mill. 'This day I, **William Peacock**, merchant in Ayr, having an information where James Mill, tidewaiter, hath received several times bribes and fees from the sailors and letting pass several times, as can be proven, quantities of teas and brandy by the persons undermentioned viz John Tod and Daniel Murchie, Thomas Potter, **James Mitchell** and James Tod, and several others if required and further, as can be likewise proven, that the said James Mill went on board of the *Nancy* brig and drunk a bottle or wine or two, making the agreement with John Tod and Daniel Murchie, when he would not accept less than five pounds sterling, which they would not agree to but ... paid James Mill three pounds sterling in Mrs Douglas's back room. So, as some of the above-mentioned witnesses is going to sail, I desire the favour of your Honours to put this in execution as soon as possible'. [25 July 1758]

'Your Honours will receive enclosed **William Peacock**'s information against James Mill, tidewaiter, together with sundry declarations taken by us thereupon ...

'Your Honours will be pleased to observe that these officers (James Mill and Alexander Ross) both deny the charge imputing it wholly to the malevolence of the informer and his partners but we beg leave to observe that though this be indeed the case as to James Mill it appears otherwise as to Ross. He is not named in the information nor was it without great difficulty that the fact was discovered against him at the examination of Tod, Murchie and **Mitchell**, who betrayed great unwillingness to name him, though he appears by their own account to have been more culpable in every respect than Mill ...

'With relation to Mill we are humbly of opinion the proof is exceptionable. For 1st it is known that the declarants are equally interested with the informer in the issue of his information, being his partners in the smuggling trade and equally incited to resentment against Mill for his diligence and fidelity in sundry instances wherein they have been concerned and particularly in seizing ten ankers of spirits belonging to **Peacock** and them, which were found lately in a gentleman's house in Ayr. They were the only persons who could say ought against him and had probably concerted previously how and what to declare in order to obtain the gratification of their malice against him

'This is now probable 2ndly from their forwardness in offering their testimony against him and their unwillingness at the same time to make any discovery against Ross. They all came to the custom house at the bare desire of **Peacock** and one of them was so keen as to leave a sick bed and come in a chair. This reason as well as the former renders their testimony suspicious nor could it be admitted in any court of law, though their characters were ever so fair, but would be rejected though for the smallest trifle from a presumption of their being prepossessed and partially interested in the issue of the question or affected to the party and indeed this is well known to be the case not only with Mr **Peacock** and the witnesses but of all the low smugglers in and about Ayr, several of whom have threatened Mill with destruction for his diligence and firmness in the service of the revenue upon which account

'3rdly we suspect this evidence as to Mill because we have always found him sober active and careful in discharging his duty nor has he ever that we know been the subject of a superior's report. We are willing therefore to suppose him innocent in the present case as we have known him resist temptations in others'. [Collector at Ayr to the Board, 22 August 1758]

'In obedience to your order of the 17th inst we gave in charge to John Christie, the collector's clerk, 'that upon **William Peacock** desiring from him a copy of sundry declarations for proving his information against James Mill tidesman at this port he, John Christie, instead of complying therewith upbraided and abused the informer instead of encouraging him for making discoveries for the interest of the revenue' which charge together with his answer we send enclosed to your Honours.

'As the respondent has given a full state of the case in his answer we have only to assure your Honours that it is a true and impartial one without exaggeration against the complainant or extenuation in favour of himself. He has even forborne to repeat sundry very provoking expressions used by **Peacock**, who had just before accosted the comptroller with great rudeness in the street, alleging his suspicions that Mill would be saved by our partiality and declaring his resolution to have him dismissed at whatever trouble and expense. When the comptroller, to avoid his incivility and lest he should be provoked by him and seem to discourage him as an informer, retired to his lodging, he followed him thither from the Cross, a considerable distance, endeavouring to provoke him by abusive language, calling him damned buggar and other opprobrious names, reproaching him with unfaithfulness as an officer and telling him frequently he did not deserve to eat the king's bread. The comptroller a little after, having come to the custom house and gone into a room with Mr Christie, was followed directly thither also by this **Peacock** ...

'Therefore he (**Peacock**) is no longer entitled to forbearance and we are humbly of opinion that, as his behaviour to both the comptroller and Mr Christie was very insolent and injurious and perhaps may be repeated by himself and imitated by others of the same stamp, it ought to be discouraged by some check or punishment as a security to the officers under your Honours in the discharge of their duty'. [Collector at Ayr to the Board, 23 August 1758]

The collector was instructed to make a more detailed enquiry into the complaint. '1st it is necessary to acquaint you that the fraud upon which the information proceeds appears to have been committed on the night of Sunday the 4th of July 1756, for the day following a warrant was obtained for discharging the ship *Nancy*, which warrant is recorded in our books of coasters inwards; 2ndly it is plain ... that Mill was at Girvan on the 16th of July 1756; 3rdly he was relieved on the 28th of August following by Robert McNab; 4thly he had stayed at Girvan a month and three weeks, the other tidesmen having been kept here by three tobacco ships which arrived successively ... he must therefore have gone to Girvan at least before the 10th of July 1756, that is five or six days at most after the commission of the fraud on the night of the 4th. And consequently was not present at the meeting in Mrs Douglas's, which both Tod and Murchie declare have been about fourteen days after it'. [Collector at Ayr to the Board, 1 September 1758]

'The balance due on **Mitchell** & McKennell's £115 10s 2d bill is included in the bill **Mitchell** accepted, £148 15s 2d. These two with **William Peacock** have these two years past an account in company with me. The first bill testifies this companyship and the balance due on that bill was therefore included in said bill drawn on them July 1st, which **Mitchell** accepted on behalf of the company. The last year's accounts were grounded on the missive dated 13th August 1758, signed by the parties, which I herein enclose you ... This sum is a considerable one and requires proper application to ascertain and secure. I must therefore desire of you to make use of all proper means and extend ultimate diligence to obtain payment. For my own part I'm very much surprised that **Mr Peacock** assumes to decline a partnership or thinks to evade making me restitution for I all along knew he was the person of the company most to be relied on. I hope it will prove in the end that my opinion of thinking myself very secure in dealing with said company will prove so'. [William Allison, 19 October 1759]

It should be emphasised that these are not all the references to George's Moore's contacts in the custom house letter-books but merely a sample.

DAVID GALLOWAY'S DEBTS TO GEORGE MOORE

'The £457 16s 8d bill, David Galloway's, I gave to Mr Arthur was on account of a tobacco debt due to Mr James Dunlop, as I remember some time in January next. This bill of Galloway's I thought very good at the time or I should not have given it to Mr Arthur ... at the time the tobacco payment in January falls due it is necessary that Mr Dunlop be paid, of which I have this day accordingly wrote to him and I desire you will accordingly pay for me at same time preserving recourse against Galloway for the payment of his bill. This I think had best been done by sending up his bill and protest to my friends Messrs Richard Oswald & Co, merchants in London, acquainting them with the circumstances and the necessity of securing the value, which I persuade myself they will find means to do as Mr Galloway went up to London to dispose of a cargo of leaf tobacco, which I hear safely arrived there'. [James Simson, 19 December 1758]

'Galloway's bill I must own I would not have passed it for payment if I had suspected that any delay would have attended the payment'. [James Simson, 17 February 1759]. 'I am since favoured with yours of the 2nd very much surprising me at Mr Galloway's behaviour in respect of his bill'. [James Simson, 21 February 1759]

'I am now to own receipt of your favour the 9th ult advising of some partial securities to order payment of Mr Galloway's bill. I'm sorry his circumstances are such as to render necessary so much trouble as this affair has given to you. I have received a letter from him praying some delay to which I shall return no other answer than what you have given or may think convenient to give for as you have been pleased to interfere every relative transaction must remain in that channel'. [James Simson, 21 March 1759]. 'Galloway's affairs I see continue perplexed so that only fair promises are yet obtained by his direction'. [Alexander Morson, 18 April 1759]. 'I observe your having got ... £31 10s from William Walker in part of Galloway's bill. He (Galloway) had in my son's custody some small parcel of rum, which by his order I have taken to my account, the produce thereof ... being £33 14s 3d I desire you to allow him in part payment of his bill'. [Alexander Morson, 14 May 1759]. 'I am very glad to hear that David Galloway's affairs are taking a favourable turn'. [Alexander Morson, 24 September 1759]

CHAPTER TWELVE: UTMOST DILIGENCE

'I grudge very much at Malcolm Fisher's delay of paying the remainder due on his bill in your hands, as it's the oldest debts of other bills. It is necessary diligence be used. You'll therefore please direct. I'm sorry I have occasion to write to you in this manner as it is alike disagreeable to you and me.' [Samuel Cuthbert, 3 February 1755]

George Moore considered debts owed for goods that he had delivered to customers in Scotland as a civil debt and so liable to the full process of the law for collection. Should a debt not be paid within a reasonable length of time, and yet it was clear that the person who owed the money had sufficient 'effects' to justify the cost of a law process, then utmost or ultimate diligence would be used to obtain the sums owed, or a composition of them. This diligence was applied for by a 'writer' under the often mistaken belief that the very fact the debt was in the hands of such a person would provide a sufficient threat for the money to be forthcoming. Sometimes this was effective.

The Galloway Debts

Moore's writer in Galloway was John McKie at Stranraer. 'I have just now wrote a letter to Mr Kerr with account of some bills due me and have therein mentioned the names of those debts I would that you raise diligence on for recovery of the value due me (Donaldson, Nibloe, McGaa, McBrigart, Kilpatrik and John Jameson). I have further to desire you will look over my papers in yours or Mr Kerr's hands. You will therein find a missive whereon I delivered some goods to the order of the Laird of Shenan. A balance hereon is still owing me and it grudges me in looking over my books to see that it remains unpaid. It is a long time since but I hope it is not yet out of his remembrance nor do I think he will rest the delay of payment arising from an accident, whatever that did happen to the wine, as he is well acquainted that my demand for the payment is founded on the delivery of the goods here at the then selling price with me. On finding this missive pray in my name ask the payment of the balance thereon due me. If payment is refused I hope he will not take it amiss that I direct you use the legal diligence for recovery thereof which I desire you will accordingly use or cause to be done for me'. [John McKie, 7 July 1752]

This appeared partially successful. 'Mr McKie has done with Cairgawne as I expected. For, though it's possible he got none of the effects for which his son was my debtor, it's probable the father got other of the son's effects, which I take to be the reason why he has entered in making a partial payment and giving his bill for the remainder. To this I suppose was owing Mr McKie's success or be it or not so Mr McKie has well managed this affair.

'I observe what you mention about Mr McKie's services to me and yours this last summer. I received from him £2 1s in part of Pat Nibloe's debt owing me. Nibloe still owes me £4 0s 8d. I think this was the only article that Mr McKie had account with me for in the last year and as Nibloe's debt still partly lay over I did not advert to making any mention about satisfying Mr McKie, intending this to rest until Nibloe had fully discharged his debt. Before the last year I remember Mr McKie recovered some debts for me. The sum was small. I desired him to let me know what I was to pay him for his trouble and I think he made a note thereof, which I paid him. I must own to you that I would be well content to make satisfaction to any of my friends who are so kind as to transact my manner of business for me and, if in any instance I have omitted this with respect to Mr McKie, it would give me pleasure if he let me know of it. For on every occasion I shall cheerfully satisfy any trouble I give him ... And as to Mr McKie, who continues disposed to oblige me in this way, let me with freedom direct the diligence to recover any debt owing me and let a charge be made in his bill or note of charges to satisfy himself for his trouble, which I refer to him and desire he may make as occasion from time to time may require. If herewith you and Mr McKie be satisfied our correspondence this way may increase rather than diminish'. [William Kerr, 20 November 1752]

The debt problems in the area continued. 'I'm hopeful you have had some success in getting payment for me of the value of the bills per amount in my letter of 29th July last but as I have not had any advice from you since then I cannot know the particulars. You have herein sundry bills and drafts, namely five as per account above, I have also recommended to your care. These I think are good and will be duly paid … The backward payments I now meet with from my customers about Stranraer give me the highest reason to be displeased with my dealing with them so that as they deserve no favour let me beg that for recovery of one and all my debts you will use or cause to be used ultimate diligence'. [John McKie, 4 December 1754]. And 'I'm plagued with the old debts and am forced to give you the trouble of them. What can be done to recover any part of these pray try'. [John McKie, 28 August 1755]

But the times were hard and Moore was tempted to take the debt collection into his own hands. 'I'm sorry to see you have had no success in getting the value of any of the bills due me. I have accidentally met with John McDowall in this Isle and held him to secure the value of what he owes but he respectively says that he has paid you. If so it must have been following the date of your letter or if he has not paid you I expect he soon will'. [John McKie, 3 January 1756]

Robert Gibson, Kilmarnock
The methods to be applied by Gibson for collecting all or as much as possible of an old debt were set out clearly. 'The directions I formerly gave you are sufficient for all purposes of diligence or compounding of any of the debts so that in any instance you cannot be at a loss how to manage for me by supposing the case were your own and acting accordingly … I've taken notice that the first offer of bankrupt creditors is generally as much as is ever made so that to delay accepting it has no good effect. However, of this (McMurtrie of Girvan who offered Gibson security for two-thirds of the debt he owed Moore) and the other debts I entirely submit myself to your management for me and persuade myself you will act with your care'. [Robert Gibson, 20 August 1757]

This was reinforced. 'I have received some intimations from other persons owing me that you are proceeding in diligence for recovery of their debts but as I have given those to your management I shall no way interfere with your transacting for me, as you have power to conclude the discharge by receiving full payment or by compromising the debt in whatever instances the occasions require'. [Robert Gibson, 10 March 1759]

And again. 'Robert Hendrie is poor and his neighbours all along told me so. To this is owing my not raising any process against him but it grudged me that from year to year no partial payment was made or that he showed no disposition to lessen the debt. Be the motive of his delay what it will, I am satisfied that you accept of the £5 in composition of his debt, if on treating with him you cannot bring him to better terms'. [Robert Gibson, 12 July 1759]

Another of the debts that Gibson was chasing was the sum owed by John Orr. 'One would expect that by John Orr's defences he is in condition to pay what he owes me and forgets how much I have indulged him by postponing any diligence to distress him ... If my oath on this occasion be necessary and is insisted on I would that you apply for commission to have the same taken here in this town before two reputable merchants or in what other manner the judge of the court thinks fitting to appoint'. [Robert Gibson 10 March 1759]. 'I should think by the manner of John Orr's defence that he has got into payable circumstances and is set on to evade justice rather than to make use of his old plea to me, which was that he was not able. I shall readily declare to the justness of the debt whenever the commission is taken out'. [Robert Gibson, 12 July 1759]. Moore was to make his disposition before Kelly, Callin or Mylrea. 'Mr Mylrea is gone to Ireland for the recovery of his health and Mr Callin is now in Scotland so that it was lucky the commission was directed to any one of those gentlemen's authority, which has been this day accordingly done and is herein returned. I observe that Orr's defences are much in the spirit of litigation. One would think he does not want subject to pay his debts'. [Robert Gibson, 8 September 1759]

John Innes
One of Moore's agents in Fairlie, John Ewing, had given Innes bills 'of sundry debts owing me in his neighbourhood, payment whereof or any part is only to be expected from using ultimate diligence, which you are designing for me and I hope will prove of service'. Moore had added to these Alexander Hendrie, near Fairlie, and David Wilson, who formerly lived at Largs 'and now I think is a tailor at Irvine, where

Robert Wilson lives. In your acting for me pray do herein as you think fit. I shall be therewith pleased for in one shape or other I would be very content these debts were extinguished but nothing can be expected until diligence is begun and wherever you think it will procure payment I desire you will there pursue'. [John Innes, 7 July 1752]

The case of Hugh Clark

This is the oldest debt for which information is available. In May and July 1739 goods valued at £43 10s 1½d were delivered to Hugh Clark. A bill to this value on him was drawn on 4 September payable to Robert Boyd and £29 of this sum was paid. In September 1739 further goods valued at £47 14s 1d were delivered. Moore drew a bill for £28 9s payable to William Somervail junior (see tailpiece to Chapter Nine). The draft was returned unpaid. It was given to Clark on 15 July 1740 but no money was forthcoming. Moore wrote to Clark on 8 November 1740 and when in Scotland during the summer of 1741 he tried, unsuccessfully, to get some money from him. In November 1741 Moore sent the two bills to Zachary Gimmel, writer in Irvine, to raise diligence. They lay in his hands until June 1743 'When he told me he did not expect to get any payment on the bills and therefore returned them'. In 1751 Moore referred the problem to John Innes. 'Following what I now write, if any doubt now remains with you in behalf of Mr Clark be pleased to acquaint me for it is my desire that he receive satisfaction, if any injury be done him, and if no injury be done him his suspicion or complaint will subside'. [John Innes, 5 April 1751]

There is no explanation of a breach with Innes but this certainly occurred. 'My stay in Irvine was shorter than I intended so that I missed seeing you there to take up sundry bills I left with you in July 1752 and 1753 ... These I desire you will please give to Robert Montgomerie's wife, who I expect will be here to see her husband on his arrival from Cette in ten days or about a fortnight ... What charges you have been at let me know and I shall order your payment or Mrs Montgomerie may pay the same for me'. [John Innes, 24 July 1754]

Samuel Cuthbert, Ayr

Cuthbert appears to have worked in close conjunction with James Simson at the Old Bank. 'Mr Cuthbert was so hurried the time I was in

Ayr that he delayed settling my account, which please get from him'.
[James Simson, 5 September 1755]. 'When I was in Scotland John Boyd
near Loans gave me as cash a Maryland bill, Anthony McCulloch on
Messrs Dunlop & Christie dated 8th August at sixty days sight £20. I told
Boyd I had some doubts about the bill but he assured me that when it
became due it would be paid so I presented it to wait its fate, which is Mr
James Simson has returned it protested and debited my account for the
value thereof with charges. I therefore am under the necessity to return it
you to effectuate the recourse whereby payment thereof and all charges
may be made. I hope you will find means to obtain without further
expense or diligence, which direct if necessary'. [Samuel Cuthbert, 23
September 1754]. By February 1755 Cuthbert had received £20 5s from
Boyd.

The Highland Debts

During the earlier period of the letter-book John Cowan was
Moore's agent in Tarbert (see Chapter Ten). Long before this, Moore
had problems with customers in the Highlands who owed him large sums
of money. At first he turned to Hector McLean, writer in Edinburgh, and
by late 1751 the debts owed by the Laird of Largie and William Boyd
were either paid or in the process of being paid (although Boyd's debt
was not finally discharged until 1755).

John Marshall, Inverary

In July 1752 Moore wrote to John Marshall, writer in Inverary. 'I
have debts owing me in Tarbert that require the intervention of your care
to render the payments effectual ... I desire you will direct to cause such
further diligence be used'. [John Marshall, 11 July 1752]. At first there
was progress. 'I am glad Mr Marshall has got the money of the principal
bill from John Campbell. As to the interest which Campbell says I
promised not to charge it is neither likely nor true. It's probable at the
time of renewing his bill I charged no interest for the time preceding nor
would I have charged any interest had the payment been made without
such delay but by this delaying and forcing me to direct diligence also
forces me to demand and expect interest and every other local demand I
can make or have to charge him with. Of this acquaint Mr Marshall and
let him act accordingly'. [John Munn, 7 February 1753]

Moore wrote to John Marshall on 26 June and 8 November 1753. 'It would be very agreeable to me to know your sentiments and proceedings whereby occasionally I might govern myself'. James Stevenson, brother to Archibald McAlister's relict, had written directly to Moore 'Proposing the payment of one third on compromise of that debt. At this distance it seems best for me to accept the proposal yet better terms may be had from circumstances I know not of'. [John Marshall, 8 November 1753]

At last there was a letter from John Marshall, dated 5 January 1754. Stevenson's proposal had been accepted, payments had been received from Alexander Campbell, Richard McAlert and Ronald McDonald of Ronachan. Other debts were still owing but 'It is at some satisfaction you explain that as soon as the herring fishing is over something will be done with some of them'. [John Marshall, 18 February 1754]

Marshall had also reported that John McAlister of Ard Patrick had given him the bill Charles Fisher owed Moore 'for some good may now be expected. No Irish though is very able to pay'. In February 1754 McAlister wrote from Ard Patrick 'importing your transaction with Charles Fisher and that you had received from him in cattle £23 6s 8d in part payment of a debt he owed me and Mr Kelly. Your giving this sum or any part of it to Mr Marshall in Inverary I suppose was with design that it be remitted to my agent in Glasgow, who is Mr James Simson ... as Mr Simson has not to this day acquainted me of any such remittance I must desire the favour of you to cause that my proportion of said sum be remitted ... as Mr Marshall nor any other person in Inverary manages any business of any kind for me but what I give in particular commission'. [John McAlister, Ard Patrick, 6 September 1758]

'I have examined into what accounts I have had with Mr Marshall ... wherein is stated every particular sum that he acquainted me he had received ... but he at no time that I remember mentioned anything about Fisher's debt or that he had received any money from you on account thereof. So that whatever sum you received I hope you will so far transact as render the payment thereof either to Mr John Munn ... (or) Mr Morson'. [John McAlister, Ronachan, 7 February 1759]

Problems were developing with Marshall. 'In July 1755 I had the pleasure of seeing you in Inverary, at which time you settled with me ... per account of particulars, which you promised to send me. To this day I have not received it. Above is account of the principal sums due on the sundry bills in your hands, which implies restitution to be made in a way suitable to the occasion, which you formerly thought as I did a very pressing one. The delay which has attended the recovery of said debts is extremely disagreeable to me, as deaths and insolvencies may affect and prevent the payments. You will hence I persuade myself not take amiss that I require to have payment of whatever sums you have received since July 1755, which I desire you will remit to Mr Alexander Morson ... or pay the value to Mr Lachlan Campbell, writer in Inverary, and that you will give up and deliver to said Mr Campbell whatever bills or vouchers of debts are in your hands belonging to me, having nominated and constituted said Mr Campbell to transact and manage all business of this kind for me'. [John Marshall, 25 September 1759]

As Moore explained in a letter of the same date to Lachlan Campbell, 'It is very disagreeable to be thus kept ignorant by Mr Marshall and the sums are of too considerable amount not to raise any anxiety to wish and direct all diligence to extinguish these debts and bring the settlement of them to a conclusion ... I thereby nominate, constitute and appoint you with full power to discharge and act for me in reference to said debts as if I myself were actually present. And I hereby confirm and ratify every act or thing you may do or cause to be done touching the premises, giving you hereby full liberty to compromise any of said debts and giving your discretional power to act herein as the occasion may require. In consequence whereof may I desire the favour of you to transact and manage these matters for me and previous to your entering into any expensive process respecting any of the said debtors that you will make or cause make enquiry into their respective circumstances so that you may act with the appearance at least of success and when you become engaged let it be done to the conclusion with vigour'. [Lachlan Campbell, 25 September 1759]

John Woddrop, Edinburgh
'The last account I received relative to the debt owing me by the representative of the late McLachlane of Castle Lachlan is contained in

the letter you were pleased to write me the 13th June 1752 and since then I have not heard if you obtained a decreet, as you expected, or what success you have since then had in getting payment of the debt owing me. By this may be hoped that all difficulties are removed and that you have obtained payment for me which it will be very acceptable to receive advise of and that you have remitted the value to Messrs Oswalds in Glasgow where I expect to be some time next month'. [John Woddrop, 4 May 1754]

In 1755 James Campbell in Inverary sent Woddrop papers relating to a process he had raised for Moore, which was suspended. Now Moore wanted the matter to be under the direction of James Simson in Glasgow, who was to nominate someone in Edinburgh to take over the papers. 'By which means I may expect now and then to hear something of what is doing herein. My own agent for highland debts is Hector McLean, writer in Edinburgh, whose name did not occur to me at Inverary'. [James Simson, 8 November 1755]

Nothing happened. 'My highland debts with Mr Woddrop will become desperate by the delay. If he did not like it or if it was not of his way to pursue it, it had been obliging to return it'. [James Simson, 6 October 1758]. 'If the highland debt I sent to Mr John Woddrop be so circumstanced as that I have not the smallest probability of success, he's surely right not to have any expense incurred and therefore I desire he may return the papers concerning that debt ... however such was not the opinion of Mr James Campbell, in Inverary, for he told me the value was recoverable by proper application'. [James Simson, 19 December 1758]

'Your seeing Mr Woddrop as you expected in Edinburgh may probably have prevailed on him to be disburthened of those papers, which unluckily I entrusted him with. For had they been with Mr McLean I believe by this time he would have secured the value'. [James Simson, 17 February 1759]. The solution was not straightforward. 'I'm surprised at Mr Woddrop that he will not give himself the trouble to return my papers, which are the foundation and whereon depends the recovery of a debt that he has slighted'. [Alexander Morson, 18 April 1759]. At last the papers were forwarded to Hector McLean.

Hector McLean, Edinburgh

'When Mr James Campbell ... gave me those papers I think he told me that however the gentleman who was become concerned might litigate the process it was his opinion that in the end it would go against him and that he would be held answerable to pay the principal sum due and all damages and for this in any future occasion would give his assistance. The principal sum on the bill which is dated November 1748 is £55 6s 4d but whereof remains unpaid £42 4s 11½d ... I do not know Mr Woddrop's expense as he never wrote to me a line since I sent him the papers. I am obliged to your letting me know that you have prepared matters for the recovery of said debt and that you are pursuing the necessary steps which you have hopes of rendering effectual'. [Hector McLean, 22 September 1759]. 'Hector McLean ... has hopes of succeeding notwithstanding some blunders which have been made'. [Alexander Morson, 24 September 1759]

Three of the Debtors

Only three of the debtors have been selected for further mention, as they each illustrate a different problem.

James Limont, Ayr

'There are I observe three of your bills in the hands of Mr James Hutchison due me, namely £46 8s 6d, £23 2s and £14 12s 5d, none of which have I yet received advise is paid. I own I did not expect that you would be so backward in your payments ... I find you have since had further goods from me by different opportunities (valued at £4 2s 9d) ... the opportunities whereby these goods were sent went safe done. It may hence be expected that you will duly pay. Until some payments are made you must excuse my giving any fresh credit'. [James Limont, 17 December 1757]. Moore waited but no payments were received. Then he instructed William Allison to raise letters of inhibition against James Limont. He explained to James's brother, David. 'As you cannot but know that I am greatly distressed by backwardness of payments of the sundry debts or sums of money which are owing to me so that necessity compels me to use that kind of diligence to recover my money, which my occasions require for the support of my trade. By what you write it might be expected that your brother had paid to Mr Allison on the first of January or thereby some money in part payment, as you hint this and that the remainder would be settled for in summer. But I have received a letter from Mr Allison of the 24th last month at which time I find that he had not received any money ... so that the management for recovery of your brother's debts due me must remain with Mr Allison'. [David Limont, 30 March 1759]

Moore was hopeful of restitution. 'I understand his house or real effects are become responsible for the sum he owes me. If so I may look on my debt as entitled to a preferable right in respect of other creditors. I refer to you whether it's best to extend this preference or accept the £20 yearly payment he offers to give security for until the debt is extinguished without interest. But I think the composition or this agreement should begin with a partial payment of £20 ... As to James Limont or William Samson's saying that I would not accept payment when they could conveniently spare it is a condition that I would not make with him nor never did any person for that would imply no payment at all. I probably told them that I would not use diligence at the exact day of payment but I never mentioned or intended to say that I would not use diligence when their delay of payment rendered diligence necessary'. [William Allison, 30 March 1759]

The house and effects could not have produced any money. 'As to James Limont's proposal of compromising his debt and giving security for payment of £50 in six years I think I formerly mentioned or desired my son to acquaint you that I agreed to any compromise you or he thought proper ... for delays are frequently attended with inconveniences and the stock seldom grows better'. [William Allison, 19 October 1759]. For once there seemed to be a satisfactory solution. 'The assignment yours covered relating Limont's draft I have this day signed before Mr J Kelly, merchant and F Taylor, cooper, in this town who have subscribed the same ... It gives me pleasure that you have ended this compromise and that the security you have received of John Crighton, clothier in Newton-upon-Ayr is sufficient in all appearance'. [William Allison, 19 October 1759]

Pat Douglas, Ayr

As Douglas was a surgeon in Ayr, he was very conscious of his public image. This meant that he did not want to be linked in any way with bills drawn on him from the Isle of Man. 'In answer to your postscript in your letter of the 5th last month, by which I find you incline I would at any time draw on you at some few days sight payable in Edinburgh or in London rather than sending up your accounts ... I have this day drawn on you at 30 days sight payable to Mr William Snell & Co merchants or order at their house in London'. [Pat Douglas, 18 January 1752]

No payment was made in London. 'In stating your account to regulate my drawing on you I concluded it would not be disagreeable to you to have all preceding articles inserted and that our account to this day be closed ... I have this day drawn on you to Mr James Simson ... to which please give due honour'. [Pat Douglas, 7 November 1752]

Still no money was forthcoming. 'I have this long respited drawing in you for contents of what as above you owe me, intending to accommodate your inclination of having no drafts appear. But in this time I had occasion to expect that you would remit to Glasgow answerable to discharge my demand'. [Pat Douglas, 6 April 1754]. 'Dr Pat Douglas gave me to expect he would have remitted you some money. But observing he has delayed is the reason of my draft, you'll please let him know is come to your hand. If he pleases, his missive or answer may serve for acceptance ... For he does not like an Isleman draft on him appear to be known. But the payment and acceptance one way or other is alike necessary'. [James Simson, 10 April 1754]

Parts of the following letter are also quoted in Chapter Nine (problems with debts) and Chapter Thirteen (relandings). 'About this time (his last order) I received two letters from you which I refer to. One is dated 2nd February 1753 in which are these words 'I have paid your draft to James Simson, Glasgow and finding that my concern in this way has been something to me in my other business I am therefore inclined to cause one to do the (public business) of it and though I am still to be the person you are to get the payment of yet it is to be in another's name and you are to direct it to him (William Boyle, a carrier in Ayr)'. The other letter is dated 3rd March 1753 in which are these words: 'As it will be disadvantage to let the filled casks lie on hand I beg you will dispose of them to any you have an opportunity of and what I wrote for may be newly filled afterwards. In so doing you will very much oblige etc'. These letters I refer to ... It would give me great concern to have a dispute with you for the recovery of my just demands. I'm rather willing to hope that on your recollection of what relates this transaction you will be pleased to wave the objection and order that payment of my draft to Mr Simson be remitted him'. [Pat Douglas, 8 October 1755]

Douglas refused to pay his draft. 'It surprises me not a little that the objection you now make did not occur to you at the time we stated accounts in Ayr July 1753, when ... in consideration of your loss (see Chapter Thirteen) I agreed to deduct off your account £2 3s 10d. For the further balance owing me, £106. You then actually promised it should be remitted to Glasgow for me, at same time telling me that money was scarce and that if I would put off fixing on a particular time for the payment it should nevertheless be remitted to Glasgow ... In April 1754 I drew on you £132 2s 6d to Mr Simson of which you only remitted him £20'. And 'I am in hopes he will not longer delay the acceptance of his bill. If he consents thereto and requires some further time for the payment I am satisfied it be to his liking. If he refuses acceptance I must be under the necessity of pursuing him, which I purpose doing at you commissary court if you do not disapprove it'. [James Simson, 8 November 1755]

'I'm surprised you have so long permitted to be unpaid the balance on your account with William Boyle, for which I've been obliged to raise diligence against you to recover the sum owing me, namely £20. As Boyle is with you herein concerned and having the opportunity of meeting him in this place I was inclined to pursue him for the payment or to oblige him to secure the payment'. [Pat Douglas, 18 November 1757] 'I observe that Dr Douglas and William Boyle design litigating to the utmost. However, they may or may not join in solemning it. For me it remains not to suffer myself to be imposed on'. [James Simson, 29 March 1758]. 'Dr Douglas's debt I left the process as you directed in Ayr. I recommend that the affair might be brought to issue as soon as possible'. [James Simson, 21 August 1758]

The next part of the story comes from a series of letters to James Hutchison (see Chapter Ten). 'I hope Mr Ferguson will not delay in diligence against Dr Douglas and am obliged to your reminding him of it'. [4 November 1758]. 'Dr Douglas by one delay or other I see avails himself and prevents his making me the restitution he owes me. I was in hopes Mr Ferguson would not have been so indulgent to him. I believe no one with more effect can bring him to payment'. [1 May 1759]. 'I have heard not one word of my process against Doctor Douglas'. [21 September 1759]. 'I am glad you have got Mr James Ferguson to work and hopeful when your court sits down that he will exert himself to bring this litigation dispute to a conclusion'. [19 October 1759]

Neil McKelvie, Campbeltown

There have been previous examples of trying to pay off debts with goods - Janet Donald with rum and Charles Fisher with cattle. In September 1758 Neil McKelvie sent Moore three hogsheads containing dried ling fish 'which as you desire I shall dispose of to the best advantage and apply the proceeds in payment of the draft you owe me'. [Neil McKelvie, 19 September 1758]

'I held up the price at sixteen shillings a hundred weight and at this price I have at last concluded the sales ... the neat produce £12 14s 7d (after charges of coopers, porterage and commission) I have placed in part payment of your £18 bill formerly ... the balance hereon, being £5 5s 5d, I hope you will not now delay remitting ... I have wrote to Mr Morson to send yours and Mr Eachran's to his friend at Campbeltown to pursue the recovery of payment but I hope you will fall on some method to pay the value and prevent the unnecessary expense of diligence'. [Neil McKelvie, 17 February 1759]

Having dealt with the customers and the (non)payment of their debts, the next chapter considers the wherries which transported the goods to the customers.

THE STORY OF THREE HIGHLAND DEBTS

'I very well remember there was an account of charges due to Mr Woddrop and since it was incurred that every year as often as I have been in Glasgow I called at your office to pay it. This account you now send me, being £8 13s 10d, to which you add interest £2 15 1½d and further have a demand of fifteen guineas for conducting my claims on Ardwell, Auchandown and McLachlane and having these debts made good to me. I have objections to these two last articles, which I think are of weight. Interest on my sum becomes due on failure or delay of payment. In this case I constantly called every year I was in Scotland or sent to your office for this account ... and received for answer that the account was mislaid and therefore that you could not tell me what the sum was so that I cannot think myself in any relative aspect blamable ...

'The debt of Ardwell's I remember I obtained security for by a disposition on a real security. This I myself transacted at Edinburgh with the assistance of the late Mr John Bogle, writer there. When the subject came to be made liable to the different creditors according to their ranking some one's appearance for me was necessary. Hence I applied to you or Mr Joseph Scott or to Mr John Woddrop, writer in Edinburgh, under your recommendation to transact for me. I do not apprehend there was any manner of intricacy in the process it ... Of this debt a partial payment was made in 1745. Some time thereafter on my coming to Scotland ... Mr Hercules Lindsay introduced me to Lord Gallaway, with whom I compromised the remainder due me by Ardwell. This was in the year 1747 when Lord Gallaway gave me his bill for £200 payable 1st August following and I abated £80 9s 5d of the amount due me and on this I granted a full discharge to Ardwell. This conclusion of Ardwell's debt was solely my own act, as was the means of obtaining the original security.

'Auchandown's debt was managed by Mr Woddrop and the payment rendered effectual by means thereof. To him also was the process recommended which was instituted against Mr Lachlane in or about the year 1750. This affair lay over until June 1754 when being in the Highlands and having an opportunity of Mr McLachlane's son being willing to conclude so long-winded an affair I compromised the debt with him and made him a considerable abatement on his payment whereon I granted a full discharge.

'These circumstances I mention to show that my interposition was used in making good two of said debts due me. I must own to you that I freely made use of your friendly offices in recommending the process to an agent at Edinburgh but I cannot say that I ever expected that you would demand or make charge of any sum by way of gratuity ... as I thought of your acting in such an instance as I myself would do and have several times done in singular ones. Nay, I have appeared with all assistance I could possibly give in endeavouring to recover debts in this Isle due gentlemen with whom I have had no other correspondence than what occasion of the receipt of their debts rendered necessary. But I never once thought myself entitled to make a charge for my trouble nor does such a charge seem covered by the usage of any of my acquaintances ... a charge should have been mutual and should have been made in the first instance. But as you made no charge on the settlement of our account current in July ... I believed that you intended to make no charge. In like manner your settlement of my account current in June 1749, paying me the balance ... which (charge) had it been made in the first instance would have prevented my giving you any manner of trouble in either of the following instances. Corresponding with this is my opinion that in any future occasions I may have to recover a debt by means of an agent in Edinburgh, through the recommendation of any friends, I would not think myself liable to any pecuniary restitution or gratuity for such my friends conduct.

'In my way of thinking any agreement for said charge receives no support from the commission I charged on your consignment to me of five pieces brandy by the *John* of Glasgow from Bordeaux in 1743 and on six hundred pieces ... (in) 1754. The charge I made was agreeable with the common practice of every merchant here ... Accordingly had any scruple remained with you with respect of this charge it would have been kind to have made some mention of it to me ... when you had leisure of conversing with me, which every year since gave opportunity for ...

'But that I may not appear either backward in discharging what I owe I have herein sent a draft on Mr James Simson £8 13s 10½d ... in respect of said interest and the article you charge for trouble, if you please I shall submit to whatever is practice of Glasgow and be determined by the opinion of merchants there so that if you oppose I shall name a person to arbitrate for me. I cannot conclude without mentioning that if my business at Glasgow under your direction was not agreeable to you it was not unlucky that I was told by several my friends there that you were by degrees withdrawing from business, which interfered with my inclination and prevented my continuing it for otherwise I see I might have gone too great lengths'. [Alexander Oswald, 26 December 1758]

CHAPTER THIRTEEN: THE SMUGGLING WHERRIES

'Mr Duncan Forbes Paterson, commander of His Majesty's tender the *Glencairn*, has informed us that on the 28th ult he had sent a party of his crew to Largs, who, having fell in with a boat with upwards of ninety ankers of spirits on board from the Isle of Man, went immediately on board her in order to secure her ... but were no sooner in possession of her than a great number of people in a tumultuous manner that gathered on the shore beat them with stones and sticks most barbarously and deforced them of all except thirty-four ankers. The crew can depone to several of the deforcers, particularly one Bailie **Hugh Morris** in the Largs, who they say was very active himself and encouraged others to be so. Mr Paterson likewise acquaints us that three of the people deforced were put under a surgeon'. [Collector at Port Glasgow to the Board, 16 April 1758]

George Moore was careful not to be too closely connected with the smuggling wherries, which transported his goods to the Scottish customers. This was the most exposed and dangerous part of his trade - direct identification as a supplier of smuggled goods was to be avoided at all costs. However, on more than one occasion Moore provided the funds necessary for the building of wherries. 'I'm surprised John Mair has not paid his bill. Yet he laid out my money in the building of a boat. Surely he should be compelled to make me satisfaction'. [John McKie, 6 March 1755]. There are no further details available about this wherry.

The *Lilly* Wherry

'I've undertaken for some people in Scotland to build a wherry here. For this purpose the bearer, Henry Calvin, goes over to Dublin on purpose to engage carpenters to come here. If he agrees them, he will have to provide several materials in Dublin to take with him. He has give me a memorandum of about the value they will cost, £72'. [Thomas Finlay & Robert Patrick, 24 July 1752]. Calvin must have been successful in persuading the carpenters to go to the isle of Man because by November Moore was able to report that the wherry had been built 'by persons skilled this way' and that 'she's allowed to be a very strong, well-built boat'. [William McClure, 7 November 1752]

He was now ready for his capital outlay to be reimbursed. In this instance William McClure and James Young had agreed to be responsible for five-sixths and one sixth of the money advanced, respectively. This time Moore was able to report 'My draft on the owners of the new wherry, which is accepted by one of them, I have forwarded to Glasgow' [William McClure, 12 January 1753] and 'By the payment you mention about the Lilly I make no doubt the full value is in Glasgow'. [William McClure, 28 February 1753]

There are very few references to the wherry during the next few months. On 12 January Moore reported to James Hutchison that he 'could not prevail on the crew of the new wherry to take any of your goods' and on 27 February 1753 'Your goods per Henry Calvin are <u>again</u> relanded and lodged with me'. 'I wrote to you yesterday by your son, who took his passage with Calvin's'. [William McClure, 28 February 1753]. 'I asked for the twenty herrings you wrote having sent by Calvin but he says he did not receive them so refused me. PS Since writing the above I have hopes to prevail with Henry Calvin to take freight for you'. [John Allan, Ballantrae, 12 March 1753]. 'I've just now been speaking to Calvin about the wherry *Lilly*. He has promised me he will return here directly to serve the freight'. [William McClure, 20 October 1753]. 'On your settlement of the wherry *Lilly*'s accounts I would be obliged to your reserving Henry Calvin's freight in your hands to be paid me'. [James Young, 10 April 1754]

Perhaps because he was disappointed that his investment had not been more productive in April 1755 William McClure attempted to sell the wherry to John Callin. 'On your writing me that you had sold the wherry to Mr Callin, I told Calvin thereof and he gave his consent. So the wherry was unrigged to wait his return, at which time Mr Callin told me that he had been treating with you and had offered money for her. The bargain he says was not closed but if you agreed to his offer you promised to write him thereof to Donaghadee, which letter you did not write him. It seems he was acting for Thomas Orr and others in Old Kirk, to whom he has wrote what lengths he went to purchase and to receive further directions he's been every day expecting and are not come to hand. How am I to do therein?'. [William McClure, 16 April 1755]

Presumably the sale fell through. 'When I last saw Mr William McClure he desired me to dispose of the *Lilly* wherry on behalf of the owners or to set her to freight as I could find best to do and to manage in all respects for their interest. In consequence of this I have been trying to sell her but I have not succeeded. It grudges me not a little to see her in the harbour here going to ruin. To prevent this and to make her of some use I am minded to repair her and let her to freight, which I have a prospect to of for the ensuing reason. If you disapprove of my acting herein in consequence of what William McClure bid me in his own and behalf of the rest of the owners I desire you will acquaint me by the first opportunity or I shall pursue his said directions in the best way for the interest of all concerned. And if the wherry meet no accident except it will be to their advantage ... I design four Manx hands and two Scots for the wherry, which are partly engaged but it must be concluded as occasion serves'. [James Young, 6 September 1755]. This wherry is not clearly identified again.

The *Robert* Wherry
This wherry was seized off the coast of Scotland. The story is told from Moore's letters, which suggest that the voyage was not quite as innocent as he had suggested, the Port Glasgow custom house letter-books and the exchequer court records in Edinburgh.

'My son Phil is concerned in a wherry that was lately seized at Ayr by Mr Picken, who acts under Captain Paterson. She was taken on her first trip but had not a drop of goods on board and was intending to take some anchors and cable for Captain Pat Montgomerie of the *Peggy*, refitting here for Virginia and under charter for Ayr. The Captain (Lawrence Rigg) is just now here. He tells me there are two people who have sworn that there were goods landed at the Troon out of the wherry, which to me seems far stretched for the boat arrived there in the night and sailed off before day. This may or may not be true. As the event is doubtful on a trial I cannot tell what to say. Captain Crawford tells me that I cannot be under better direction than yours and that he will correspond with you on the subject. I have a letter from Mr Arthur in

Crawfordsdyke. He has recommended my applying to you - the letter is enclosed. Phil has wrote to one Hector Bryce near Ayr to claim the boat in order to stand trial but Bryce is a very unfit person (see Chapter Ten). I shall therefore request you to direct herein in whatever manner you think best by claiming or by purchasing in a frugal way. For Phil would not like the wherry real lost. In case of purchase or other expense let Mr Simson pay it for me'. [Colin Dunlop, 28 September 1757]

The official version is contained in a letter from the collector at Port Glasgow to the Board. 'In obedience to the reference on the enclosed petition of Philip Moore, son of George Moore merchant in Peeltown Isle of Man, in regard to a wherry seized by John Picken, boatman at Cumbrae, in a boat belonging to the *Glencairn* tender, we beg leave to acquaint your Honourable Board that the wherry mentioned by the petitioner was brought in here by some of the *Glencairn*'s people and secured in the harbour by them as a seizure made by John Picken and that some days after John Picken came and acquainted us that the wherry had on the night between the second and third of last month run a cargo of spirits from the Isle of Man. And on that account she is returned by him for condemnation as in return of seizure No 477 this day transmitted to your Honourable Board'. [18 October 1757]

According to the Exchequer Court records, the wherry 'burthen about fourteen tons, about half wore, with her furniture (except boat) as per inventory, about one third wore' was appraised at £50. The trial started on Wednesday, 7 December 1757. 'Lawrence Rigg, master of the within wherry at the time of the seizure thereof, comes and claims the property of the same with the furniture within mentioned to belong to him'. At the first court he pleaded several legal technicalities; at the second and third courts the jurors did not turn up and at the fourth court the jurors attended and brought a verdict in favour of Lawrence Rigg, i.e. that the ship was not within the limits of a port of Great Britain.

'The wherry I some time ago wrote to you of is cleared at the exchequer in Edinburgh so the master of her, Lawrence Rigg, intends to Scotland to receive her from the custom house of Port Glasgow. On this subject Mr McMiln in Greenock is wrote by Mr Robert Arthur, who also writes a letter to his agent at Edinburgh, to Mr Wilson, in case there is appearance for recovery of damages to pursue for restitution. Whatever charges have attended or may attend pray desire Mr James Simson at the bank to pay and debit my account accordingly'. [Colin Dunlop, 14 March 1758]

Two letters from Moore dated 18 October 1757 give a significantly different picture. 'The enclosed is my letter relating to the cargo of Lawrence Rigg's wherry to which I refer you. The bill therein mentioned £228 7s 3d is enclosed herein as it seems best to send it to you to receive acceptances'. [John Dickie, 18 October 1757]. 'You have annexed the particulars of the goods by Lawrence Rigg, including the goods lost you directed to be proportioned to the sundry accounts. These accounts are stated in terms of your missive to my son ... which let me pray you will punctually pay and accordingly give notice to the persons concerned'. [John Dickie, James Allison & Co, 18 October 1757]

This was not the end of the story. 'I received your letter of the 21st last month complaining of an overcharge in the cargo by Rigg's wherry. You'll please observe that agreeable with the request of the concerned my son made up an account of average of the goods that were lost after landing and proportioned it on the goods saved. In this on average the casks saved were computed at 10 gallons and what remained of the number of gallons delivered here is as charged in the account of loss, which was, as above, £50 2s, proportioned on the goods saved. This proportioned you have above where you will see that seven tens is charged as if containing no more than 55 gallons and twenty-nine tens as if containing no more than 200 gallons rum, which number of gallons added with the number of gallons charged to the respective accounts exactly makes the number of gallons here. You'll take notice that had the respective accounts been charged with the number of gallons less than 10 gallons in each cask the proportion of the number of gallons of the casks last received have been greater so that either way the accounts it charged would have been the same. What is charged to the sundry accounts corresponding with my draft on you and James Milne and corresponding with my draft on Messrs John Dickie, John Stewart & Co is the exact account of that cargo at the current price delivered here. As my son has bore a sufficient share of loss in the wherry to accommodate that adventure, it is hoped neither you or any other concerned will grudge paying their respective shares of the bills drawn and accordingly I desire you will acquaint all concerned that no further delay may attend the payments'. [James Allison, 20 December 1757]

The *Robert* was by no means the only wherry seized. 'I have received the letter of the 3rd last month which you and others concerned in the unfortunate cargo by Alexander Kerr wrote to me of your desire to claim the wherry on trial in Ireland. I can't say what success will attend but by what I have heard on this subject it may be expected claims of this kind have of late been very frequent and the process has turned out in favour of the claimant. Kerr I'm told is in Ireland, where I wish he would let me know how I can be of service to him ... I'm concerned at the misfortunes which have happened to your wherries, which will lay you under the necessity of falling on some new scheme to correspond here'. [John Munn, 14 January 1754]

Relandings

In early 1753 there were several relandings in Peel of goods shipped on wherries for the Ayrshire coast. The situation at the time is described in a letter to John Allan at Ballantrae. 'The terms were so changed and the hazard so increased by Captain Campbell's strict watch there'. [John Allan, 12 March 1753]

Following the relandings the goods were stored in Moore's cellars (see Figure 15). John McClure of Alloway, on behalf of Thomas McClure (in theory) and James Campbell, freighted a boat to attempt another landing. The other goods taken on board were for Archibald Kennedy, Pat Douglas and William McCormick. In the meantime, Moore advised John Dickie in Loans 'I think it would be best way for you ... to look towards the Carrick shore, where there is not so strict a lookout as in yours, or towards the Fairlie where a wherry may be had to go down to or one of your own wherries'. [John Dickie 8 March 1753]

The subsequent events are described as follows. 'The boat (freighted by John McClure) belongs to some part of the north of Ireland. They proceeded but the wind shifting to the northward they put back and near to the shore of this Isle unexpectedly they met a barge, which is taken to be the one belonging to Donaghadee. Poor McClure was forced to bring to and forced to part with the cargo. He has entered a protest on his return to this Isle and I have advised his going to Donaghadee to enter his claim for the goods, under the favour of your directions and assistance, to which I recommend him. Following this he may consult the persons concerned with him so that everything necessary for recovery of the goods may be done. Your favour herein will singularly oblige'. [Andrew Agnew, Drogheda, 19 April 1753].

There is no further comment about the fate of the boat but several of the customers objected to the payments for the goods that had been lost. 'What Thomas McClure owes me I think he should be made to pay. He's able and should be made willing. His objection I think is merely frivolous. Some goods of his were returned and with his orders were lodged in my cellar. Some short time following John McClure demanded these goods for him and they were delivered to McClure. At the time these goods were landed it was understood that when the hurry or appearance of danger at home was a little over that they were to be forwarded by the first convenient opportunity and John McClure coming directly from Ayr for to freight a boat seemed a good opportunity whereby to forward Thomas McClure's goods, even though he had given no verbal directions to John McClure about them. Had no accident happened Thomas McClure had been well-pleased that they were forwarded by John McClure or by any other opportunity. You'll enquire herein and do what can be done to recover what is owing me'. [James Hutchison, 1 September 1755]

'From the circumstance of your goods being relanded and lodged with me and my disposing of part of them in care of John McClure, which he promised to deliver in the terms of your direction. I do not at all think myself answerable for the consequence nor did imagine that I was to be a loser or gainer in the safe carriage or miscarriage of the part of your goods given into McClure's care and only acted intentionally for the best for your account ... that account was founded on the sundry value of goods which from time to time I delivered your order by the safe carriage or miscarriage whereof you are satisfied I had no concern in as I could not be a loser or benifitter by either. Nor with any accident that followed my delivery of them wherein originally my demand on you was founded following said delivery. If any part of your goods were relanded

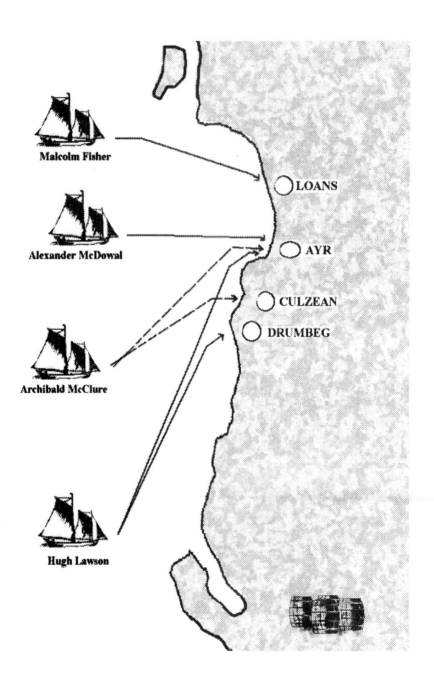

Malcolm Fisher

Alexander McDowal

LOANS

AYR

CULZEAN

DRUMBEG

Archibald McClure

Hugh Lawson

Figure 15: The 1753 Relandings

In November 1750 James Black relanded in Cowal some goods which had been returned to the Isle of Man by Ritchie Black. 'You need not have been under the least doubt of my delivering the goods … on the directions of the persons therein concerned without regard to the receipt I gave them, by which I acknowledged receiving them on account of the persons concerned, whose letters to me for the same are therefore sufficient. What goods of said parcels were wrote for were delivered accordingly, the bearers paying the porterage in and out of my cellars'. [John Munn, 8 November 1750]. This relanding was successful. Not so the attempt by John McClure to reland the goods for the customers listed below.

Customer	Location	Order	Master
John Dickie	Loans	?	Malcolm Fisher
William Samson	Ayr	2 casks white, 2 casks red wine & small casks of tea	Alexander McDowal
James Campbell	Ayr	2 casks brandy & 4 casks rum	Archibald McClure
Pat Douglas	Ayr	10 tens, 4 fives of rum, 1 bag of wine marked 'W'	Hugh Lawson
Archibald Kennedy	Culzean	2 hogsheads wine	Archibald McClure
Thomas McClure	Drumbeg	2 tens of brandy & 2 tens of rum	Hugh Lawson
William McClure	Drumbeg	?	Hugh Lawson
William McCormick	Ayr	2 casks of brandy & 4 casks of rum	Archibald McClure

with me or from the appearance of a then present danger lodged with me it was at your suit and risk and for your account as they might have been with any other indefinite period'. [Pat Douglas, 8 October 1755]

Other Problems

There were several other problems that might affect a wherry crossing. The weather might mean that they could not leave the Island, the crew might be pressed into the navy, they could be wrecked or the goods might be lost on land. Although the problems occurred everywhere the majority of these examples come from the letters to William McClure.

'The cargo per Calvin the 12th last month is still here. You would no doubt hear of his having sundry times attempted but was put back. I've lately spoken to him, as the weather seems favourable, but he declined proceeding. I did not think proper to press him much for fear of accidents'. [William McClure, 11 November 1751]

'I esteem greatly the dread of pressing here has of late prevented all intercourse with you, which I make no doubt is attended with good effect that you have thereby an opportunity of disposing of your goods in a very advantageous way. Radcliff is the only boatman that has adventured to the Heads but Charles will not stir yet'. [William McClure, 16 April 1755]

'She (Janine Stewart) wrote to me for some goods by Hugh Campbell and lucky it is for her, as well as me, that I did not deliver them. You will too soon hear of poor Hugh Campbell's fate'. [William McClure, 28 February 1753]. The hint of yet another loss at sea comes in three letters to William McClure. 'It is high time for me to expect that your son Archibald's account be paid or at least the greatest part' [4 December 1754]. 'Your late son's being concerned in the first two articles is the reason the some more give you the trouble of endeavouring to get the payment of it for me accommodated.' [21 August 1758] 'There remains in your hands I observe the particulars of what John Rodger and your late son owed me for advances I made at their request for the wherry repairs, which I'm surprised has been so long unpaid being mostly paid out of my pocket'. [21 September 1759]

And again condolences with the suggestion of a sting in the tail. 'I'm very sorry for the accident that has happened to your son on his voyage homewards. I've received from you no account of what payments have been made for me but I rely that whatever they amount to that you have or will immediately remit the same'. [James Ewing, 11 February 1752]

'I'm sorry I have no opportunity of sending you a cask of your favourite rum. Not a boatman here will engage to deliver it within three miles of Fulwood. The boatmen, if they can get it safely lodged on shore, wait the carriers bringing it from them. To avoid any further risk I had some thoughts of sending an anker or two at your risk but having no orders I've declined'. [Alexander Porterfield, 31 December 1751]

Jack Stewart's Ticket

Jack Stewart's ticket covered his wages while he was a seaman on the *Amazon* man of war. This vessel was due in Plymouth on 23 June 1752, when it was expected that the crew would be paid off. 'He tells me that nine months wages have been paid the crew and expected that nine months of his wages were in like manner paid ... his father, who lives in Girvan, was my reason to interfere herein and to give you the trouble of managing this matter'. [William Snell, 16 August 1751]

Since leaving the navy, Jack Stewart had become involved in a wherry with William Shaw. 'You must be very sensible that the willingness I saw in you and Mrs Stewart to encourage his dealing was the motive that led me to join your inclination and to give him credit for the goods'. [Mathew Stewart, 7 November 1752]. The wherry was seized. 'I find some casks your son had from me in the returned goods from Ireland, which by your appointment I shall secure for my own behoof'. [Mathew Stewart, 26 October 1752]

Originally Moore thought that he could apply the proceeds of the ticket to Mathew Stewart's account. 'When you gave me his ticket he (Jack) was not at home but on his speaking to me he told me that he had assigned it in trust and that whatever was received thereon was for his account and that he would not allow it to yours. Your being unwell when I was last in Girvan prevented my speaking to you on this subject but

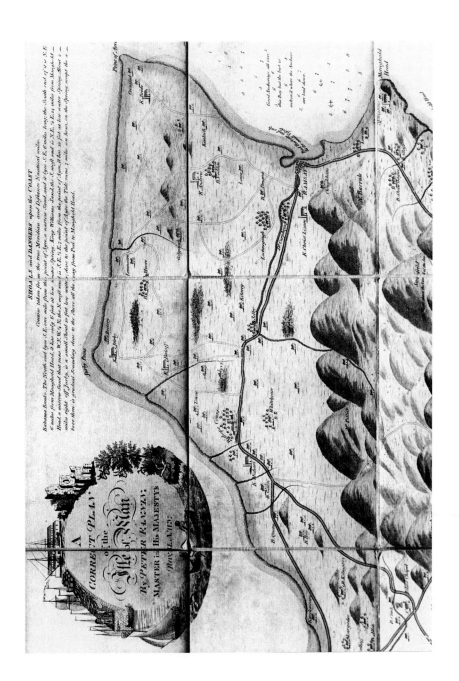

Figure 16: Jurby Point and the Point of Ayr: Wherry Losses

'You have doubtless before this heard of the accident which happened to poor (Anthony?) Kennedy going to Scotland. He was put back and forced to run on shore near Lammore, which is between Jurby Point and the Point of Ayr, where he lost his life. The cargo floated out of the boat and about three-quarters parts of it were broken up. For preservation of these I sent a man on purpose and since then have sent two men to put hoops on the casks that were beat off with the violence of the waves as I know you know I would direct everything in my power to prevent further loss. The coopers I sent down tell that it's a very insufficient house where the casks were forced to be lodged and as the people on that shore are the reverse of being relied on in respect to their probity I have directed the coopers to hire two boats to carry up to this town what remains of the cargo. The number of casks is between eighty and ninety which are saved. You'll please write to me what the concerned will direct about it necessary therein. On the other side I have sent you the list of what I shipped and I think there was about one tun more shipped here on Kennedy's boat. I think it is the best way that the loss be on a general average in equal proportions'. [John Resaid, 15 November 1754]

There were other dangerous parts of the coast. 'What was in Hore's boat shared his fate near Langlass Point. I've given directions to Phil to wait on Mr McDowal of Logan, on whose ground the wreck of the Skerries boat was stranded, and to see what he could in favour of Mr Griffin. Since then I've wrote a letter to Mr McDowal in the same strain to give all the assistance I can to your friend. Mr Hamilton since he last came from Ireland told me he had applied to the Laird of Logan. I referred to this in aid and am hopeful of success from the joint application'. [John Onge, Hayestown, 8 June 1757]

'In November last I sold to John Hore eight half chests of bohea, value £108 17s British. The misfortune of his loss has prevented the payment of this sum which he had agreed to in three or four months following my delivery of it. I have now wrote to his wife, acquainting her of my demand, which I am hopeful she will direct or cause be put in the speediest way of payment. I've been speaking to Mr Callin on this subject and I beg you'll speak for me to John Hore's widow so that by joint means I may be paid and I desire you will return her answer so soon as you can'. [Thomas Grumley, Rush, 8 June 1757] after my return home I wrote you thereof in my first letter at a time when I expected that your son and you would accommodate this matter on faith, that what he told me further on this matter was true is very much the reason that he's so much in my debt, which otherwise would not have happened'. [26 October 1752]

Jack Stewart was killed and there was a hold-up over payment of the ticket in London. Moore still hoped to be reimbursed some of the money owing by the Stewarts. 'William Shaw is now here with the wherry but he says that your son some time before the accident of his death made to him a disposition of his part in Belfast so that in respects of the wherry I cannot avail or thereby extinguish any part of your son's debt ... If herein I must come to be a sufferer I shall think it very hard'. [Mathew Stewart 7 November 1752]

Having received a letter from Stewart in November 1752 'I waited an opportunity of seeing Shaw to secure the wherry or the part of her that belonged to your late son. This offered. Shaw and the wherry, or the part, were here. All I could do with Shaw was in an amicable way for the half the wherry on my allowing half of the expenses for her repairs. His demand acceded the value of the wherry so I durst not venture to attach her, as the court must allow if Shaw would come to swear to and in this event I should not be paid for what my attorney's bill would come to. Another objection also occurred to me how far I might be liable if I intermeddled with your son's effects without administering in our spiritual courts. However, I was well inclined to secure the wherry for part of the debt I durst not venture. The cure seemed worse than the decease. So Shaw went as he came unmolested. I'm thinking that if administration be taken out in Scotland some good may arise. How else can any money owing your son be got. In some debts must be owing him which without administration must be lost or never paid?' [Mathew Stewart, 28 February 1753]. It was early 1754 before James Hutchison received the ticket from Snell and was able to pass it on to Mathew Stewart.

Having considered Moore's smuggling friends, it is now time to look at the more domestic aspects of the letters.

THE STORY OF MALCOLM FISHER, MASTER OF THE JENNY & GRIZZY OF AYR

To the collector and comptroller, Ayr Custom House.

'We have received your letter of the 15th inst enclosing a copy of the report of Malcolm Fisher, master of the ship *Jenny & Grizzy* of Ayr, from Cette in France with thirty-four hogsheads of brandy; twenty-six hogsheads of wine; two boxes of brimstone; three small casks of wine and nine boxes wine in flasks or bottles pretending to be bound for Ireland and to call at the Isle of Man for orders, at which place it appears by his report that he landed seventy-seven pieces and nineteen hogsheads of brandy before he came to Ayr, signifying that from the suspicious circumstances attending this vessel and that a part of the cargo either had or was intended to have been run, that you have stopped her until an enquiry shall be made with respect thereto. We approve of your keeping your hands upon the ship until you shall have made the most particular enquiry as to bulk having been broke or part of the cargo smuggled on the coast or the hiring of boats for that purpose and who are the proprietors of the cargo. In the doing which it is to be recommended to all the officers to give their most effectual assistance'. Signed: M Cardonnel, Basil Cochrane (see Chapter Seventeen), A Legrand [18 September 1764]

On 3 October 1764 the collector reported that from talking to the crew of the *Jenny & Grizzy* 'There is the greatest reason to believe the cargo was designed to be run but that the master had no opportunity as several of the king's cruisers were plying along the shore, upon which the vessel stood close in to the bay of Ayr and a gale of wind coming on was obliged to take to the harbour'.

To Captain Colin Campbell of the Prince of Wales sloop or in his absence to Captain Galley or Barker at the custom house, Greenock

'By last post we had a letter from the solicitor directing us to apply to you with respect to the ship *Jenny & Grizzy*, Malcolm Fisher master, which vessel came into this harbour on the 13th ult from Cette in France with wine and spirits but last from Peeltown in the Isle of Man and desiring that you might inform us how the wind and weather stood upon the 12th of September, the day of their departure from Peeltown, and upon the 13th when she arrived at Ayr and whether if the wind was favourable from Peeltown to Douglas, where she pretended to be bound. The master gives out that on the 12th he was forced off the Isle of Man by a violent gale of wind and that he could not make Douglas. For if this should prove false it would go far in proving a fraud was the intention and as you was on the coast at that time you will be so good as describe the proper course according to the weather then was from Peeltown to Douglas and from the former to Ayr to all which we beg an answer as soon as possible that the same may be laid before Mr Charters'. [Custom House Ayr, 10 October 1764]

A letter of the same date to Samuel Charters, the Board's solicitor, reported on progress, or rather the lack of it, adding in the investigation into the *Jenny & Grizzy* 'It is merely impossible to make anything of the sailors or any other persons on this coast for they are all too concerned in that villainous trade of smuggling'.

The last letter in this sequence is from the collector to the Board, dated 17 November 1764. 'In obedience to your Honours orders of the 29th we have secured in a warehouse the thirty-four hogsheads brandy, twenty-six hogsheads and one half hogshead wine, one containing syrup, and two boxes for the duties, which were imported in the *Jenny & Grizzy* from Cette in France, as the merchant proprietor (**James Young**) refused to enter and pay the duty for the said goods. Enclosed your Honours will please receive the return of seizure for the prohibited goods imported in this ship'.

It is possible to trace some of Malcolm Fisher's subsequent voyages from the 'Account of the Money received by James Logie, collector, for the Royal Hospital at Greenwich commencing 17 January 1765 to March 1774':

20 September 1765 master of the *Jenny & Grizzy* for Dublin; 3 August 1767 the *Jenny & Grizzy* for Bergen; 14 January 1768 the *Jenny & Grizzy* for the bounty white herring fishing; 26 September 1768 the *Jenny & Grizzy* for Roscoff; 4 May 1769 the *Jenny & Grizzy* for Belfast; 13 October 1769 the *Jenny & Grizzy* for Gothenburgh; 29 June 1772 master of the *Hutchison* of Ayr for Dublin; 4 August 1772 the *Hutchison* for Bergen; 17 September 1773 master of the *Jenny* on the fishing.

Malcolm Fisher also appears in the Ayr Port Books between 1774 and 1776 as master of the *Royal Oak* of Ayr, a 45 ton brig, carrying deals, limestone etc to London, Dublin, Bergen, Larne and Memel. Between 1777 amd 1778 he was master of the *Mary* of Inverary, a 24 ton brig carrying coal (personal communication from Eric Graham).

THE FAMILY AND FRIENDS

THE MOORE FAMILY

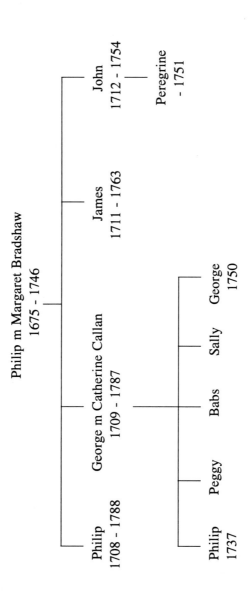

Philip m Margaret Bradshaw
1675 - 1746

Philip
1708 - 1788

George m Catherine Callan
1709 - 1787

James
1711 - 1763

John
1712 - 1754

Peregrine
- 1751

Philip
1737

Peggy

Babs

Sally

George
1750

Note: It has been difficult to distinguish the relative ages of George Moore's children from the letter-book

CHAPTER FOURTEEN: THE FAMILY

'When you return bring with you for me a small parcel of Moore's worm powder made up for a child of four years old and another parcel for a child of between one and two years'. [Daniel Mylrea, London, 15 August 1751]. These worm powders were for George Moore's children Sally and George respectively.

All the information about George Moore's family contained in this chapter has been extracted from the letter-book. Comments about his wife Katty, the daughter of Patrick Callan of Chancery Lane, Dublin, are found in Figure 17. The remainder of the chapter deals with his children Phil, Peggy, Bab, Sally and George, with his brother, James - there is little personal information about his other brother, Phil, in the letter-book, and with his brother-in-law, John Onge of Dublin. The tailpiece gives an insight into a family dispute.

Phil

Moore's son Phil was at school in Glasgow at the beginning of the letter-book. As there were clearly problems about his attention to his studies and as he appeared to have a strong inclination to become a merchant, Moore took him away from the College and, having trained him, set him up in business in partnership with John Callin, as the junior member of John Callin & Co.

Schooling in Glasgow

'I received a letter from Phil of the 8th past wherein he says he is to leave Mrs Robertson in two days, which he is very sorry for. May I desire the favour of sending to speak with Phil to know his reason for being sorry to return to Mr Lindsay's. If it be a sufficient one, it must be removed. However I would not that Mr Lindsay knew of Phil's writing any such thing to me. Pray do herein as you would were the affair yours or as you think I would do were I in Glasgow'. [Peter & John Murdoch, 9

November 1750]. The problem appeared to be short-term. 'I'm obliged to your mention of my son and pleased he's satisfied with being at Mr Lindsay's'. [Peter & John Murdoch, 17 January 1751]

'I should sooner have owned your letter of the 5th ult mentioning your receipt of the £20 note and that Phil was become Mr Purdie's own scholar and entirely under his eye. What adds to the pleasure is that he is applying pretty well to his books. You take notice that he wants some clothes, which you intend in a plain way for him. This I think necessary and what is so may suffice while he is at school. But let him have no wants against the inclemency of the weather in a cleanly way. This I need not now have mentioned as I think I spoke to you to this purpose and I make no doubt you will accordingly direct'. [Hercules Lindsay, 7 January 1751]

The clothing problem continued. 'I wrote to Phil to acquaint him of his aunt's death in Dublin and as all my family is in mourning on this occasion I desire he might also be in mourning. For this let a dark grey cloth be provided him'. [Hercules Lindsay, 5 April 1751]

In September 1751, as he was about to enter Glasgow College, Moore wrote a letter to his son. 'The time of your entering the College is very nigh and as it is the effect of your own inclination I expect you have used proper diligence to prepare yourself. The means for your improvement you must see that I am very careful to consult. Nothing is wanting the usefulness of a good education. This is what makes the distinction in mankind. To please me, your friends and in the end to please yourself is now in your power by duly attending your studies. If you neglect this opportunity I shall tell you what will be the consequence. You have another brother and may have more. When the time comes that education is necessary I shall give him the same means of education that I now give you and if he makes better use of his time than you do whoever is most deserving you may be sure will be distinguished for having exerted his capacity. A greater esteem and in every other respect greater will follow. If you apply to your studies I'm extremely well satisfied. If you do not apply to your studies I've desired Mr Lindsay to give a true account of it. For it would be very trifling that you enter the college for the appearance of education only and that thus I throw away my money to no purpose.

'Your Mama gives her blessing your sisters their love'. [Philip Moore, Glasgow, 24 September 1751]

The parallel letter to Lindsay is also quoted. 'I'm very sorry Phil is so negligent as to give himself little or no trouble about his books. His entering the College I'm afraid will not answer my design. He will have more leisure than at school and give less attention. If the bent of his inclination be against learning to try to force will in my mind be a fruitless attempt. However the experiment will be made. I've wrote him to the purpose you desired. Pray have a diligent eye to him and give me a true state of his progress. The alternative will be I must make him well acquainted with figures and book keeping, which from the prejudice he has taken will perhaps suit his inclination, which is certainly necessary to follow. If he has any taste for French I would be satisfied he were tried'. [Hercules Lindsay, 24 September 1751]

Phil's excursion to Alexander Porterfield was discussed in Chapter Nine. This is the rest of the letter to his headmaster. 'I do this to give Phil this instance of my having confidence in him and to try his diligence ... Pray have an eye to Phil and direct in such manner that the notes be securely preserved for I would be very angry with the misapplication of one of them'. [Hercules Lindsay, 12 October 1751]

It appeared that with pressure from both his father and Lindsay Phil was improving. 'I need not mention how much pleasure it gave me to know that you have got my son in a good way. Let me entreat the continuance of your favour that nothing may intervene to direct his studies. As you desired me, I have wrote him of the pleasure this change has given me and have sent him two twenty shilling notes as a token of my satisfaction. I've sent him another note for his horse hire and diligence in delivering the bank notes I sent to his care for Mr Alexander Porterfield, who has wrote me a letter acknowledging his receipt of them.

'The whole family are pressing to see Phil here next summer and as his paying us this visit may I expect be done without prejudice to his education they have got me on their side. My being at Glasgow will be in about June as is usual with me. I intend that he come with me and stay six weeks or two months and that he be accompanied with some discreet young man, who is to be his tutor to assist his reading while he thus stays here. If you approve hereof let me know and on what terms such a tutor may be had'. [Hercules Lindsay, 27 December 1751]

'I've got my son with me from Glasgow. He has a young man who assists his reading. On examining into him I find it will be very hazardous to lose sight of him so that I'm minded to keep him here and not let him return to Glasgow, where amusement has taken more of his time than study'. [John Onge, 24 July, 1752]

'My son's coming to this place is attended with the circumstance that he's more inclinable to be a merchant than ever. This notion has so long been grafted in him that I'm satisfied it is the reason he has given so small application to his studies. On examining the lad I find he has little acquaintance with the rules of grammar. It is vain to contend against the streams of his inclination so that I am minded that he stay with me here and return no more to College. His desk let be delivered to Mr Robert Finlay, to whom I have wrote about forwarding it here. Therein let be put whatever books or small matters he left behind him, whereof cause an inventory be made and sent me'. [Hercules Lindsay, 28 July 1752]

The Merchant
'I have taken Phil to assist me in my business. He is very willing and in a little time will I hope be of service to me'. [John Onge, 15 January 1753]

There have been several references to Phil's activities in trade throughout this book. The following letters describe how his father attempted to pave the way for him.

'Some considerations have led him (John Callin) to withdraw his partnership with Mr John Kelly of this town, which is dissolved with respect to any new transactions or engagements in trade. In consequence whereof I have on behalf of my son joined Mr Callin in trade, to support which a fund is established ... for their mutual account share and share alike in equal proportion, to continue for seven years. For my son I have agreed with Mr Callin that Mr Robert Arthur merchant in Crawfordsdyke be concerned with them on a fourth part in the tobacco trade only'. [Claud Johnson & Son, 14 April 1755]. And 'My son as to trade is in his infancy so that it may be some time before he will correspond with you. I'm also for myself very much obliged to you as you appear disposed to contract a friendship with me. I'm equally disposed to make a beginning, which may create or serve a mutual confidence'. [Claud Johnson & Son, 4 June 1755]

Phil's Visits to Ireland

There is a suggestion that Phil made regular, independent, visits to Ireland. 'Phil often thinks of you and longs for the season of going to Hayestown'. [John Onge, 15 January 1753]. 'I'm extremely surprised what avocations have interfered with my son Philip's design of returning home, as I directed him. The apology he makes does not answer the purpose. He knows in what instances I wait him and there are others that he knows not of, alike pressing. I therefore have to desire you will be so kind as to hasten his coming here by the first opportunity of a boat from Rush to this Island, which give me leave to expect in a day or two following your receipt hereof, as the frequency of boats will admit'. [John Onge, 20 October 1754]

This letter was not sent to Phil. 'I have several times wrote to hasten your return home but in vain so that I begin to see your own inclination is uppermost and if this continues I write this to assure you that it will thwart my inclination and be productive of effects disagreeable to you so that your own choice shall determine'. [Phil, 28 October 1754]. Instead 'I have the pleasure to acquaint you that Phil is just now arrived. I was quite tired for want of him for I find it is not in my power to go through the business with the application that it requires'. [John Onge, 28 October 1754]

Peggy and Bab

Moore's two older daughters, Peggy and Bab, do not develop as characters from the letter-book. As a result, they are not separated but treated as a unit. 'Peggy is very well. Bab got a cold three months ago, she has not yet recovered of'. [John Onge, 23 March 1752]. And 'Peggy and Bab went to Castletown last week and are to stay there a week longer'. [John Onge, 15 January 1753]

By the beginning of the letter-book Peggy was based on the Isle of Man but Bab was still being educated in Dublin. 'Bab will be in Dublin I suppose before this letter comes to hand. I quite forgot speaking to you about her being paid her allowance quarterly as usual, which I desire the favour of you to pay it. Direct the first quarter's allowance, being five pounds Irish, on the 2nd day of August to be continued from that time quarterly while she stays in Dublin. Mrs Weekes is also to be paid her account half yearly so that one payment from you is desired, which will be about the 1st of November next'. [John Onge, 23 May 1753]

'I left Bab at Haystown in her maid's care. I suppose she will incline to stay there a few days till she has recovered her black eye. Should it happen that her quarterly allowance falls short to furnish her with what you think necessary for her this also supply as you think convenient and charge her account. Peggy is too much hurried and concerned to think of writing now to you or Bab so she must be excused'. [Mrs Weekes, 23 May 1753]. 'Bab I find likes well being in Dublin and am obliged to your care of her'. [John Onge, 6 September 1753]

However, the stay was not long. 'The opportunity now offers whereon Peggy purposes her passage to Dublin and she is in great spirits getting ready. The wind is very favourable and in a day or two I hope she will have the pleasure of seeing you. Bab's being at Mrs Weekes will be at an end on Peggy's arrival in Dublin, as it is best they be together until they return home ... Peggy has desired to see her uncle in Cavan and we have consented. This will take up a great deal of their time'. [John Onge, 25 March 1754]

Both the girls were married in 1757, Peggy to John Quayle and Bab to Charles Kelly. 'It gives us all great joy that you approved of the match and I'm very much mistaken if Bab has not got a careful diligent young man, who is extremely fond of her, which I think is a very lucky circumstance'. [John Onge, 8 June 1757]. Both the couples went to England that year. 'Charles Kelly proposes going to London some time this summer. I am obliged to your readiness to introduce a correspondence to favour his occasions'. [Richard Oswald & Co, 31 May 1757]. 'The comptroller and Peggy are gone to London where Charles Kelly's business has also called him'. [John Onge, 29 August 1757]. 'The comptroller and Peggy are returned from England highly pleased with their jaunt'. [John Onge, 6 October 1757]

Finally, 'Bab grew so pale. It was so unhealthy at Douglas that we were willing to have her here until her time comes, which is expected in the next month'. [John Onge, 26 March 1759]

Sally

The youngest sister, Sally, was sent to Mrs Haughton in Liverpool for her education. There she made friends with Nancy Kelly and Miss Dunbar. She was given permission by her parents to visit Preston for Christmas 1757. 'Sally's stay at Preston shows that she is well pleased with being there'. [Haliday & Dunbar, 25 January 1758]. Despite this, and the fact that she was given permission again, she did not return to Preston the following Christmas. 'Going there or staying in Liverpool was at her own choice'. [Robert Kennish, 7 February 1759]

Sally progressed well. 'I'm very glad to hear from Sally and that she is beginning to grow up. My wife is very much obliged for your civilities to her and hopes she'll so behave as to continue to be a favourite with you, which will always give great her great pleasure'. [Robert Kennish, 31 May 1757]. She appears to have been Moore's favourite. 'The crate of earthenware is become more acceptable from Sally's choice and pray tell her that her Dada likes them better than any that ever came form Liverpool'. [Mrs Christian, Liverpool, 5 January 1758]

Sally's health was cause for great worry. 'I am favoured with yours of the 22nd and the 14th inst mentioning that Sally was well and had been so. A very different account we had of her health, which motively made me write some time ago for her return home, but being now satisfied in that particular my thoughts of her coming here subside'. [Haliday & Dunbar, 29 August 1758]

'My wife and I are very much obliged to the account you give us of Sally and it's a pleasure to us to hear that she's improving ... perhaps she thoughts of coming here this summer sufficiently entertain her. Miss Haughton's coming over with Sally is hoped for and that Nancy Kelly will get leave to be of the company'. [Robert Kennish, 7 February 1759]. 'My wife intends sending for her to see her in May and says that if her school fellow, who she thinks is Miss Dunbar, is not well and that a trip to this Isle may be thought any way to contribute to her health, she has a most hearty invitation to come with Sally to stay three weeks or a month and my wife will send a servant to accompany their coming and return'. [Haliday & Dunbar, 5 April 1759]. 'This I hope will be handed to you by Mr Kelly, who my wife has prevailed on to go to Liverpool to accompany Sally's return, which I suppose will be with the first opportunity'. [Mrs Haughton, 4 May 1759]. 'Sally landed on Saturday morning in good health' [Haliday & Dunbar, 28 May 1759]

'My wife is extremely well satisfied that you have been very obliging and indulgent with Sally all the while she has been with you, which she desires me to acknowledge. But her constitution is weak for on the slightest occasion she is subject to catch cold. It's a great loss to her and I regret her being from school but the means of health is a more prevailing argument for without this all accomplishments become insipid. She is now in a regular way with the pills and santry and within these few days a change is become perceptible and I hope will continue for really so delicate or tender a constitution as she has had is unfit to be from home with. So soon as her health seems confirmed it's intended that she return to your care. Sally's compliments to you will be in her own letter, which she says she's to write'. [Mrs Haughton, 6 July 1759]

'She's certainly a sick little mortal and has the appearance of health here rather I believe than in any other place, which will be a great argument for her staying'. [Robert Kennish, 22 December 1759]. 'If Sally was anywhere to go from home we surely would prefer her going to Liverpool, where she has been so kindly used to any other place. But she's so tender a mortal and her health is so delicate away that her mother has no thoughts of letting her go anywhere from home. Bathing we find is very necessary for her and nowhere can she be better accommodated with fresh or salt water. However I am very much obliged to your concern for her'. [Robert Kennish, 5 February 1760]

George Junior

'George is this day taken ill and we think it is the small pox so that our best manner of nursing is providing'. [John Onge, 26 October 1755]. He recovered and in 1757 went to school in Douglas, staying with his sister and her husband. But Moore had other ambitions for his education.

'I am at this time looking out for a school to which to send my son and namesake for education. He's between seven and eight years old and preferring that he go to such a school wherein his education may be finished, I am much inclined to have his tuition under the care of Mr James Burgh, who keeps an academy at Nevington Green, Middlesex. May I beg the favour of you to make enquiry about Mr Burgh's character and if it prove agreeable I would be further obliged to your enquiring and letting me know if he would take into his care a child of that age and on what terms for his boarding and schooling. Reading and Latin are the first objects and as the boy grows up other exercises will be necessary'. [Richard Oswald & Co, 21 February 1758]. 'I am well pleased with the character you give of Mr Burgh's academy'. [Richard Oswald & Co, 29 March 1758]

'I have not heard from George or how he does since I left him at your house. However I concluded that he's well as I have not heard to the contrary. But the satisfaction will be convinced by the pleasure of a letter from you, which I desire you will favour me with. I want to know your opinion of him, what progress he makes and if he minds his books. Dancing I suppose he is begun. French will be his next study when you think it time to direct'. [Mr Burgh, 4 August 1758]. 'I am very much obliged to your manner of writing about George. I've since then had a letter from Mr Burgh about him, giving me a favourable account of him'. [Richard Oswald & Co, 8 September 1758].

'I have not a word of my son George or about him. When you have an opportunity pray speak to Mr Burgh that he may direct the youngster to write any kind of letter himself, or by any other means, so that now and then we may have the pleasure of knowing that the boy is well. For I have but one letter since he went to school'. [Richard Oswald & Co, 5 April 1759]

240

Figure 17: Peeltown: George Moore's wife, Katty

George Moore's wife, Katty, is mentioned frequently in the letter-book, usually in terms of sending her love or compliments. The majority of these quotations come from letters to John Onge in Dublin. They produce a somewhat gloomy commentary on Katty's health.

'Katty is nigh her time which would give me great pleasure were she not in a very weak state of health. She is become timorous, very timorous, but I'm hopeful in a few days the occasions for her fears will be well over'. [9 October 1750]. 'Mrs Moore was brought to bed with child the eighth of last month. The child was named after her and lived about a fortnight. She has a been very weak and recovers slowly'. [16 October 1751]

'Katty is in her worst way and indifferently well'. [23 March 1752]. 'My wife has been extremely ill, much more than I thought her ... (the illness) must have carried her off had not Dr Mun from the north of Ireland been providentially here and to him is owing that she's now alive and with hopes of recovery. We think her out of danger'. [23 May 1753]. 'I have the pleasure to tell you that Katty has so recruited in the country that she is perfectly recovered. She has walked to town'. [6 September 1753]

This did not last long. 'Kath is but in a very indifferent state of health'. [25 March 1754]. However, 'I have the pleasure to tell you that Katty is so well recovered that she was this day in Church so all our fears are removed'. [20 October 1754]. 'She's now so well as to be able to go into the country. This day she was at the youngest, nursing there'. [28 October 1754]. 'The last addition to my family is your godson and namesake He's at nurse in the country with all appearance of health'. [James Moore, Cavan, 28 October 1754]

The last comment about Katty relates to a gift she sent to Ireland. 'By the first opportunity Mrs Moore hath sent your lady a bit of samphire and as soon as the samphire season comes in shall send some more, which will be now in a short time'. [Roger Hall, Newry, 8 March 1758].

James

There is very little domestic information about Moore's elder brother, Phil. However, his younger brother, James, appears throughout the letters.

'The motives which have determined your leaving off keeping school are doubtless prevailing and the consideration for which you have disposed seems a valuable one. Foreign to the purposes does any engagement or situation in life turn if the circumstances cease to be agreeable or require a disagreeable attendance, which I have often thought with respect to yours. And if you found that this at last became insupportable the alternative you have chosen is laudable. I'm quite of your opinion that while we are in security it's our duty to act under the social principles therefore not be idle spectators so that your preferment or advancement has my hearty warmest wishes. But sorry I am no further can I go to give you assistance. I've been several ways thinking if it was in my view or compass of my power all against my inclination the highest and the only length have I tried without prospect of success or doing you the least service. The point was by intermediating with the Attorney General and for this no other could apply to but our governor, a gentleman with whom I'm in exceeding good favour. It happens he has no (contact) with the Attorney or long correspondence with him but what results from forms in a legal way. For the attorney represents the Duke of Atholl by appointment in matters of appeals from this Isle. I was very inquisitive with our governor and found by him that he can do no manner of service. At same time I avoided explanation so that I'm sure he did not suspect the cause. At this distance from the scene of action it is difficult for me to point out a method for yours and yet I cannot help thinking the field seems fair and open to a regular chance every way inviting'. [Brother James, Cavan, 28 October 1754].

Moore continued to try and help his brother. 'I have received your letters of the 21st and 27th last month and in receipt of them I took horse to consult my friend on the measures necessary to be taken for your appointment to the vacant benefice in this Isle. On the incumbent's demise an immediate account was sent to his Grace. Five candidates there are, three of noble families in Scotland. Their names are Hume, Murray and Boyle. There is also another Thomas Murray in Dublin.

What interest these three have with his Grace I know not. Mr Murray's is supposed to come from his brother's influence with the attorney general in London. However this is I'm persuaded of that there was no engagement or promise made to any of the candidates previous to his Grace's having notice of the vacancy. It yet remained to do what could be done to serve the application I made and the conclusion is this. It is hoped and expected that the nomination will be respited until his Grace writes a letter to this Isle and receives an answer and on this rests the success of my application and hence will arise the hopes I wish. A plan of proceeding I have agreed upon and a fair field is before me. The principal condition is in case of your preferment that you will act in conjunction with his Grace's representative in this Isle and unite the distinction of civil and spiritual authority to operate for the good of the general interest of the people, which his Grace has very much at heart. And for this I have given my word and promise.

'On account of my trouble in this occasion I expect you will give me for my son, your namesake, one thousand pounds English to be laid out in a settlement for him in such manner as I think proper and if you are pleased herewith it is necessary that this sum be in readiness to wait my calling or occasion for it'. [Brother James, Duke Street, Dublin, 11 April 1755]

'My brother is chaplain to one of the regiments in America but his state of health is in so infirm a way that his going from Ireland was dispensed with and he was allowed to appoint a substitute to serve in his stead. His being now here is by advice of his physician, who thought his native air would be of benefit to him'. [Richard Oswald & Co, 22 February 1758]

Brother, Counsellor John Onge, Dublin

Onge, who was Moore's brother-in-law, appears to be the closest to a friend from the viewpoint of the letter-book. Indeed he appears far closer to Moore than his brothers Phil and James and it is from the Onge letters that so much valuable information about several topics is obtained.

'This day I had the pleasure to receive both your letters and am heartily glad to know you are well and in a good state of health for I have several times heard that you were in such a way as gave me a great deal of concern. What if you were to take a trip to this would not the sea passages think you be of some service?' [John Onge, 5 March 1755]

There are few references to George Moore's domestic problems. An exception is given in the tailpiece. But it is in the context of his garden where there is an insight into his determination to carry out his schemes at all costs (see Chapter Fifteen).

THE CASE OF THE REVEREND ANTHONY HALSAL

'In 1742 my father left lodged with Mr Halsal £380 as per recital in these words 'I do hereby acknowledge to have in my hands belonging to Mr Philip Moore senior the sum of £380 in bonds and cash for which interest is to be paid to him or order from the 30th of January 1741 as witness my hand this 31st of May 1742 (Signed) Anthony Halsal'. In my father's last will and testament bearing date the 3rd day of August 1748 there are the following words '(Item) whereas my son John Moore deceased hath left a son behind him and by the best account I can learn or get after the strictest enquiry I have cause to think he was married to the mother of the child, though not now living, I leave and bequeath to the said child named Peregrine Moore £380 British value, which is at interest on land security in Lancashire ... in the hands of the Revd Anthony Halsal of Great Crosbie. I nominate and appoint Mr Halsal and my son James Moore to be his guardians, the interest of the money to be applied towards his education and in case of his death before he shall arrive at the age of twenty-one years I do leave and bequeath the £380 equally between my three sons Philip, George and James Moore'. Thus in case of Peregrine Moore's death before the age of twenty-one years I was left by my father the third part of said £380 and so it happened that this was the only legacy left me by my father. Peregrine Moore died last year on South Carolina. The account hereof being confirmed, I wrote to Mr Halsal thereof in May last and of the circumstance of this legacy to me, desiring he would let me know the state of that affair to the end that knowing when I might expect my money I should act accordingly and requested Mr Halsal's favour herein. I repeated this request but so far it has fallen out that to the day of the date of my draft nor any time since then have I received from Mr Halsal the state of said affair, how the money is circumstanced or what time I may expect to receive my third part of said £380. On Mr Halsal's declining or delaying to give me satisfaction, I requested the circumstance or state of said affair or when I might expect to receive my legacy from my father ... My brother Philip gave me a copy of the receipt which Mr Halsal gave my father for the £380 and looking over my father's will it appeared extremely plain to me, unattended with any doubt that my third of said £380, the legacy left me by my father, is in the hands of said Mr Anthony Halsal, whose acknowledgment to be accountable to my father's order entitled me to demand the same from Mr Halsal ... let it be considered if my demand on Mr Halsal by drawing on him in terms of his receipt to my father can be held (as) ... being so peremptory and importunate that he does not think proper to comply until he is better advised ... Whether the acknowledgment Mr Halsal gave my father be a receipt ... I shall not determine. If it be a receipt to be accountable to my father's order and Mr Halsal is satisfied that my father is dead and that I am one of his sons to whom my father bequeathed ... the third part of £380, my drawing or ordering that Mr Halsal pay you for me my third part in terms of my father's will seems to me to be a demand reasonably founded and wherewith Mr Halsal's compliance may be yet expected. Let Mr Halsal be made acquainted herewith and let me receive his result. If he continues to delay to honour my draft, I can see no other alteration than that it be protested and returned me. If he honours my draft, I am satisfied to allow or acquit my share of the interest due since Peregrine Moore's death. If in any manner you think I should do pray favour me with your opinion for my government herein'. [James Crosbie, 21 November 1752]

Moore's feelings had been fanned by a letter from brother James in Cavan, forwarded to Halsal, who in turn wanted Moore to show to his brother Phil in Douglas. 'I've read over the said copy of my brother James's letter. I shall not take on me in any way to interfere with the contents. There are some expressions which to me seem the effects of warmth but be this as it will I'm persuaded it will be displeasing to my brother Phil. Now as you know the one is my elder, the other my younger brother, you perhaps will hence not disapprove that I avoid communicating the contents of said letter to my brother. If you or my brother James yet think it necessary I must desire to be done in some other way or if my brother James on recollection should choose to soften his sentiments or suppress giving offence I'm pleased that I have so far contributed that this yet may be done'. [Anthony Halsal, 12 August 1752]

In October 1752 George Moore drew a draft valued at £126 13s 4d at 30 days sight on the Revd Anthony Halsal of Great Crosbie, near Liverpool. This was dishonoured and returned to James Crosbie in Liverpool - hence the letter quoted above.

In March 1753 Philip intervened, offering George security of payment. As a result Moore dropped his idea of commencing a lawsuit against Halsal on the Island. Despite this, Perry's money was not received until 1755.

CHAPTER FIFTEEN: THE GARDEN

'The land has invited me to build a house with a good garden and it is much wished my design of improvement could be executed in a genteel taste, which perhaps would not prove more expensive than having my improvement in no taste or a bad one'. [John Onge, 9 October 1750]

The Estate

'I have lately succeeded in purchasing some lands nigh this town ... at our last courts held here I was admitted tenant and entered accordingly. The lands join to the Revd Mr Ratley, which is about a mile off, has some meadow and plenty of marl so that I have the prospect of turning farmer, as far as the occasions of the family has dependence on the country. Now the time to begin my improvements of ditching. But as I can do nothing this way without quicks and some trees for hedging rows I'm forced sending the bearer, Henry Lord, who is my country servant, to Dublin to be provided with these and some other small matters we want ... How the bearer will find an opportunity of returning I know not. What assistance you can give or direct will be wanting and I have wrote to Alexander Brown to do what he can for him'. [John Onge, 9 October 1750]

'My land improvements have of late given me enough employ and as I think fencing and ditching the first necessary I have a constant number at this work. In the fences where I join to other land I'm in deciding to run them in straight lines and in some places I have succeeded in. In part I join to the demesnes belonging to his Grace the Duke of Atholl. The present boundary is an old very insufficient copse and remarkably crooked ... I have applied to our worshipful deputy governors to have the boundary made a cass and ditch in a straight line and to give boon men to assist making the boundary with me. After some consideration they returned me answer that what I asked was reasonable

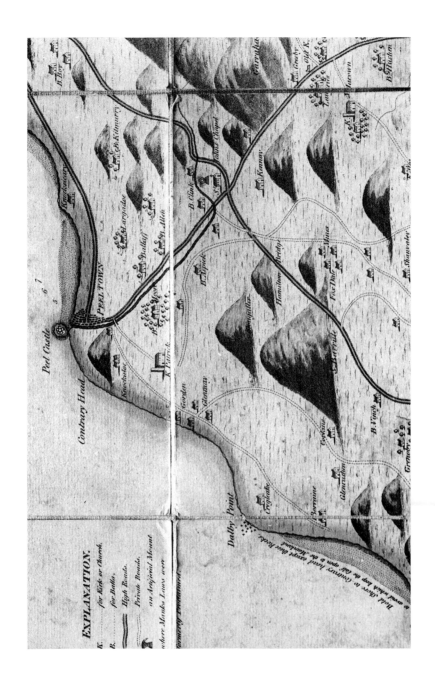

EXPLANATION.
K .... for Kirk or Church.
B .... for Baths.
_____ High Roads.
_____ Private Roads.
_____ an Artificial Mount

where Manks Laws were
formerly Proclaimed.

Peel Castle
Contrary Head

Peel Castle   5 6 7

P. PEEL TOWN

Fontenary

B. Kilmurry

Laxeydue

Spittall

St. Ann

Knockalloe

K. Patrick

Giordan

Salomaar

Teskina

Dreshak

Dalby Point

Well there is Contrary head, carrit asser that Rocke
a word which they keep in all upon it, the Manland.

B. Clark

Billas Chapel

B. Appold

Hamilton Bridge

Botiniddus

Water Mines

Fox Dale

Ash Point

B. Finch

Glenrushen

Boreviur

B. Kamen

Garrghan

The Greeby
light K.

Bloown

B. Thastar

Grenby

Shawater

Grenby

248

Figure 18: Ballamoore: The Trees

'(I'm) in mind of getting if I can a little of the seed or cones of some different kinds of foreign pine or fir trees, namely Siberia fir, Russia pine, Livonia and Prussia fir and of the cedar of Lebanon. Gardeners have shown me fir or pine trees, to which they gave said names. However that be, they are of different kinds I would be glad to have a little of or of other foreign fir and pine trees I expect may be had of the Sandemans ... what I want of these is to have a diversity in a small plantation I'm about'. [Isaac & Zachary Hope, Rotterdam, 17 January 1756]

The trees which Moore appears to have planted included ash, beech, filberts, fir, holly, hornbeam, horse chestnut, myrtle, oak, pine and spruce. 'I'm very glad your trees have throve so well this season. Mine are very far from answering my expectation. The situation and climate are against me'. [John Onge, 16 October 1751]

'On consulting my lord Duke's gardener you thought it best not to take up the young trees till March ... I thank you for this favour and desire that the young trees be sent to the care of Mr James Hutchison, merchant in Ayr, to whom I shall write in what manner to forward them me. As to the time in March the sooner it will be convenient to you to send them the better to serve the season of having them here. As I am a young planter and am very fond of trees you may imagine how much it will gratify my inclination to have some of my collection from Dunkeld'. [Humphry Harriol, London, 26 December 1754]

'I received your letter of the 11 February acquainting me that you had wrote to my Lord Duke's gardener at Dunkeld to send a horse with the young trees etc etc to Ayr and that you expect they would be there the beginning or between that and the 10th March. About that time I sent a wherry to the Mull of Galloway and a lad to go Ayr to meet the carrier, who was not arrived there the 20th March so the lad returned from Ayr. I was very angry he did not stay a few days longer'. [Major Harrison, Dunkeld, 14 April 1755]

Apart from these ornamental trees, Moore also ordered from various sources apple and pear trees producing summer and winter fruits of different sorts, dwarf red and black cherry trees and vine trees, 'I would leave have them half red and half white of the sweetest kinds from a place the hardiest of most, exposed to the inclemency of the weather'. [Peter Berail, Cette, 26 October 1754] but that they could not alter any boundaries belonging to his Grace without his consent or your direction so that however serviceable it may be or mutually to have the boundary straight by their answer I'm referred to his Grace, to whom it may be improper for me to apply or I do not know if he would like to be troubled in this or any such subject. Would you advise my applying to his Grace or keeping to the old copse'. [Governor Lindesay, Edinburgh, 1 January 1751]

'I'm obliged to your opinion about my farm. There is one circumstance attending it favourable for its improvement. In the different places I have plenty of good marl, serviceable to raise any kind of grain, so that in summer I intend to begin and every one here tells me it will answer my expectation. Hence I may have corn and grain and my dunghill will be usefully employed on the meadow ground. The new ditching I find very expensive yet I find no reason to complain of my purchase. It's subject to a prescription not to tythe.

'I'm pleased you approve of my having even marches and that you think his Grace of Atholl will not be against my proposal where I join to his demesne. For this purpose, as you mention, I have taken the liberty of writing to his Grace and put my letter under cover to Captain Daniel Mylrea, who is at London from the government (see Chapter Seventeen)'. [Governor Lindesay, Edinburgh, 21 March 1751]

'I've been this long while till his Grace the Duke of Atholl's officers made a report whether the copse or boundary in a direct line be of any prejudice to the demesne. They were at Ballamoore with me two days ago to view the ground. The governor was also there. On showing them where I proposed the boundary, they unanimously were of opinion that the boundary in a direct line was in no manner of prejudice to the demesne, which I suppose they will acquaint his Grace of, and by their report I may expect to have what I desire to me. The boundary in a direct line seems equally serviceable and of benefit and both thereby will have a much more agreeable appearance. So soon as his Grace is pleased to approve the new boundary pray communicate it, as I suppose the direction will be to Governor Cochrane. Nothing can be done about the boundary any till towards the latter end of next month. A copse with quicks on each side and a ditch on each side will prove an agreeable and serviceable boundary'. [Daniel Mylrea, London, 15 August 1751]

A report was submitted to the Duke. 'As he proposes and we are of opinion that this alteration will not be prejudicial to the demesnes and the difference in value of both parcels is quite inconsiderable, provided Mr Moore makes a sufficient open fence with a sufficient trench on both sides by his own charges allowing him for the present only the assistance of some of your Grace's boonmen'. [Insert in the letter-book, dated 13 August 1751]

Moore described his house '(it) is not a good one for it's of a very old standing. However there's a parlour, two closets ... and a room above stairs, which for the present we are very content with'. [Mr Lindesay, Edinburgh, 7 October 1751]. There are some details later in letters about the building of a new house but in the meantime Moore turned his attention to the planning of his garden and for this he decided that only the services of landscape planner Mr Stevenson of Dublin would be acceptable.

Stevenson
'To be satisfied herein (the garden plan) I would willingly follow the judgement of Mr Stevenson with whom I was at Hayestown. His opinion cannot be had unless he were on the spot. If therefore you can persuade him to come here for this purpose I would esteem it a particular favour and satisfy him with pleasure for his trouble of coming here. On Harry's return home I purpose beginning to lay out the ground for the garden so that if Mr Stevenson will consent to come here by this opportunity ... it would be most convenient ... If Mr Stevenson will not come over I must be content to work on Andrew's plan. In case Mr Stevenson does come pray give me a hint what sum I should give him or he may expect. Mr Stevenson may perhaps furnish the trees that Harry wants on equal terms with another for I would prefer having them from him'. [John Onge, 9 October 1750]

'Such an opportunity (the Murray deeds being brought to the Island - see Chapter Sixteen) would be a kind of encouragement to my friend Mr Stevenson to come over to plan for me at Ballamoore and if you come

Figure 19: Ballamoore: The Gateposts and More of the Garden

'I have begun on the garden wall which Mr Stevenson laid out for me but I cannot extend it eastward as was expected so must be content. I've got a draft of it made by Captain Murray, which is enclosed. I desire you will give or send it to Mr Stevenson that he may herewith do as he thinks proper, to be returned me as soon as possible, which pray do. For now that I'm begun I shall be anxious to have it finished'. [John Onge, 6 September 1753]

'When I was this summer in Bath I took a walk with my son to see Mr Allan's gardens. In our way we called in at a stone cutters, I think it is the second on the river from Mr Allan's but I forgot his name, to look at and cheapen some stone vases was my business and I bought and paid him for two eagles and two pomegranates, which with their pedestals he promised immediately to make up to be shipped at Bristol and forwarded to the care of Messrs Haliday & Dunbar, merchants in Liverpool, from where I have lately received a letter that mentions their not being come yet to their care. Give me leave to desire the favour of your making enquiry for my eagles and pomegranates or direct this enquiry. What intelligence you receive pray communicate by a letter to me directed to the care of Messrs Haliday & Dunbar ... Pray make my compliments to my friend Mr Henderson should any chance give me an opportunity of returning his civilities it would give me great pleasure'. [Kitto, Bath, 29 August 1758]

'I'm not surprised with the misfortune your orchard met with in your absence for I find nothing so well thrives about a farm as under the master's eyes. Lord safely brought the basket of fine apples you sent us. I had but five apples growing last year and they were stole two months before they were ripe. Next year as I'm in hopes I shall have occasion I intend setting fox traps in my garden I hope will prove some security'. [John Onge, 8 February 1752]

An attempt to trace 'Mr Stevenson' suggests that he was Robert Stevenson, who in the 1720s designed the formal gardens at Headfort House, Kells, County Meath. 'A fine hedge of Irish or Florence-court yew is all that remains of the formal garden'. He is also included in a list of eighteenth century Irish Nurserymen in Dublin, with the dates 1734 to 1757. In this his address is The Orange Tree, East Side of St Stephen's Green. He was connected with the (Royal) Dublin Society which 'provided a fee for boys taken by nurserymen to train as apprentices'. [Sources: *Lost Demesnes* and Irish Forestry - see Bibliography]

I give you a commission of engaging Mr Stevenson's coming with you. I never asked him what he would expect for coming and being with me four or five days, which I would have done had he been to have come with me. However this is to be done you'll therefore ask him about it and agree with him for me'. [Robert Murray, 15 August 1751]

'A great addition to this pleasure (Katty and the children spending some more time in the country the following summer) will be having a plan from Mr Stevenson. In short nothing will do without him and how he's to be got over here I know not. For in your absence I wrote to Mr Robert Murray to prevail on him. But I've had no answer from Mr Murray or any account of Mr Stevenson'. [John Onge, 16 October 1751]

'I'm so fond of having Stevenson over that while I've hopes he will come here I must beg you'll use your interest with him and engage him. At same time I would be content you agreed with him what he's to have for his trouble. I would willingly give him ten guineas or more if he expects it'. [John Onge, 6 November 1751]

'If Mr Stevenson will come here an opportunity presents by return of Mr Thetford ... If you can prevail on Mr Stevenson coming here pray do so for waiting him I've delayed laying out the ground about my house or whereof intend it'. [John Onge, 8 February 1752]

At last there was success. 'I've had Mr Stevenson with me this fortnight he has planned a garden, offices and the manner of planting trees I'm very fond of so I hope they'll do'. [Edward Kean, 21 March 1751]. 'He has taken a great deal of pains to mark out a plan of improvement for me and has already done some things which show he has been the director. Almost since he came here the weather has been very cold but he's so anxious that not one day has been missed. What he has laid out will take me some years to execute for my firming is not yet nigh finished and that is the first requisite to be done about a farm, next the offices however I'm quite satisfied that I'm now in an agreeable as well as useful manner of improvement'. [John Onge, 23 March 1752]

A STORY OF TWO ORDERS FROM LIVERPOOL

'I have further occasion for fruit trees and some other articles which are in your way to supply ... I desire you will send me by the first opportunity. I confide in your sending the above articles of the best kinds as you are not unacquainted how vexatious it would prove to have one's expectation in this way disappointed. The charges I shall pay you when you please to order. Should it happen that you yourself have not any of the above articles let it be sent for to where you may be furnished that I may not lose the benefit of the next season. One of the parcels of the last fruit trees you sent me were lost for not one of them budded. This I attributed to their being too long out of the ground. Pray let these trees be under ground till the wind proves fair and let a little mould be sprinkled on the roots when they are packed up'. [Daniel Clark, 28 December 1750]

This order included: 100 lbs white clover seeds; 40 lbs red clover; ½ lb onion; ½ lb Dutch turnip; 3 ozs leek; 1 oz cucumber; 4 ozs asparagus; ½ oz Gus lettuce; 3 drops selicia lettuce; 2 drop Dutch brown lettuce; 5 drops cauliflowers; 3 drops purslane; ½ oz green Savoy cabbage; ½ oz red Dutch cabbage; 3 drops thyme; ½ lb parsnip; 2 lbs ranunculas roots; 20 kinds of annual flower seed; a drop of each kind of radish seed

A copy of this list was sent to John Quayle in Castletown.

255

'I wrote some time ago to Mr Daniel Clark, seedsman in your town, to send me some garden seeds. I desire you will be pleased to cause ask him if he has sent them or intends it by the next opportunity. If not pray give the above particulars to some other seedsman to be forwarded by the next opportunity under your direction to me that I may not be disappointed of having my garden seeds this season. I desire you will send two iron garden rakes. Let the teeth of one be a little wider than the other'. [Mrs Roughsedge, Liverpool, 5 February 1755]

CHAPTER SIXTEEN: OTHER ACQUAINTANCES

'Until of late or for these two years past the most of my time has been taken up and employed in intricacies and disputes appertaining to law than which nothing on earth is more disagreeable to my bent and inclination. Yet this takes me so much from the necessary exercise of my business that I may as well be a merchant in Japan as in Britain. What determines me from biding here farewell is my remembrance of Lady Charlotte and Mr Murray. This gives me life and solace as every difficulty in what shape soever it appears I esteem'. [Sir John Stewart, 12 March 1760]

This chapter describes a selection of George Moore's other acquaintances from Sir John Stewart of Grandtully to John Allan, a merchant in Douglas.

An Influential Friend: Sir John Stewart of Grandtully, near Perth
'We were in great pain about your passage to Scotland for the night you left this it blew a terrible gale of wind and it was believed that if you tried to gain Kirkcudbright the wherry would not go in in time. For two days the wherry was driven to the eastward of this Isle and got into Derbyhaven with great difficulty on Wednesday. With great joy I received your letter, which acquainted me of your safe landing and removed all our fears. I must own to you that the opportunity of seeing you I esteem a very lucky incident wherewith I was extremely pleased and if it was agreeable to you I became obliged. But the return you have made very far exceeds any civilities that were in my power. Yesterday I received the kind letter you wrote to me the 6th December. Your having got no further then on your journey than the Gatehouse-of-Fleet is a proof of the difficulty you met with. I did not imagine there was so great a want of accommodation on a way so much frequented. I hope you proceeded on the remainder of your journey more pleasurably and expeditiously and that you safely got to Edinburgh. I thank you for your intention at Dunkeld and the share you take in my fortunes. The willingness you show to obviate the perplexities which surround me is extremely

obliging. The success I have met with in application to his Grace convinces me that his Grace's dispositions have a tendency and incline to make happy all his people so that I entertain great hopes that your intercession will prevail. Indeed as to my own concerns and for other several considerations I most heartily wish that we may have a charge of measure, peace being the most desirable condition of human life ... how little desirable or gloomy soever it is to be thus circumstanced yet there are intervals of amusement which sometimes contributes and reminds us of the most pleasurable week we have had I am sure these twelve months. I wish you may meet at Grandtully as much pleasure in the enjoyment of a friends or your acquaintances as here you favoured us. My wife and son join their most respectful compliments'. [Sir John, 7 January 1760]

'I congratulate you on your safe arrival in Edinburgh and most heartily that you have prevented and removed the malicious attempts that were calculated to hurt and throw your affairs into disorder. So ill-timed a behaviour is a proof of the intention and may such intentions for ever meet the same fate and be for ever baffled'. [Sir John, 12 March 1760]

Twenty Sheep, and Lambs
'I was very unwell when I received your letter. This has delayed my answering it as well as that I might with certainty write how I had proceeded in getting you the Loughton sheep. They are scarce. However the man I employed ... has secured and purchased twenty. They must stay with the persons from whom they are bought until I receive your directions to forward them. I wish you had mentioned it for this is a good time to remove them and I'm afraid they will daily grow poorer. You'll have no objection to their smallness for in this I dare say they will answer Lord Barnard's expectance. I'm singularly obliged to you as it gives me an opportunity of assuring you of my warmest wishes and what joy it would give me if it were in my power to do you any kind of service'. [John Murray, York, 30 November 1753]

The sheep were to be sent to the care of Joseph Dean, who was a tidesurveyor attached to the custom house in Whitehaven (he lived in Lowther Street). 'You will please take care they be forwarded to his Lordship at Raby castle'. [Joseph Dean, Whitehaven, 15 April 1754]. But no vessels bound there had called at Peel. As a result the sheep were to be forwarded to the care of David Forbes at Ramsey. 'I hope you will not find it difficult to get grass for them in a safe place while it's wanted ... there are this day seven lambs'.

This did not work out. 'The custom house there (Whitehaven) has not permitted them to be landed and the Manx boat that was purposely freighted with them to Whitehaven was forced to take them back and land them at Ramsay. They were four or five days on board and on their return almost famished to death. Mr Forbes was forced to pay the boat hire and says that four of the sheep and four of the lambs died the day after their landing at Ramsey. The remainder he has taken grass for in his neighbourhood to wait what further directions you think convenient to give about them'. [John Murray, 6 May 1754]. Nothing more is heard of the sheep.

In the meantime John Murray had left York and two letters are addressed to him at Whites Chocolate House, St James Street, London. 'I was extremely pleased with your confirmation of his Majesty's appointing you his minister to Venice. I heartily congratulate you on this accession of honour and so agreeable an employment and may all happiness herein attend you is my warmest wish. Your going to Venice will give encouragement to make some mercantile enquiries and if I can find any branch of trade inviting to an experiment I shall do so with pleasure. It may serve my design in trade and will serve my inclination of corresponding with you so that I'm doubly obliged to your favour.

'PS Before you set out if you favour me with a letter it would greatly oblige me. I want your address or how to direct a letter to avoid any error in the manner. Pray let me know'. [John Murray, 19 April 1754]

The Son of a Friend: Thomas Savage, son of Andrew Savage
Moore gave credit to Thomas Savage. 'For I believed there was no manner of risk in giving credit to Mr Andrew Savage's son. In this opinion I was confirmed for in several conversations I had with my brother Philip he told me that he had a general letter of credit from Mr Andrew Savage in favour of his son, Thomas Savage, whereon reliance might be had as on counter security. On my brother's telling me this I should at any time thereafter have given goods on credit to Mr Thomas

Savage and hence readily gave the goods which now I want the restitution of for the general letter of credit Mr Andrew Savage to my brother is dated in October 1753'. [Roger Hall, 17 May 1759].

Moore gave credit to Savage for brandy, wine and vinegar. The bill for this was dated 21 March 1758 and valued at £119 3s, payable at four months. When no money was forthcoming, Moore asked Savage when the payment would be made. In February 1759 Savage wrote to Moore 'that his brother, Mr Edward Savage, a young counsellor is going to London and will pay you ... I desire that you will enquire of Edward Savage to obtain the payment or, if you can, his security for the payment'. [Richard Oswald & Co, 15 February 1759]

'Having received a letter from my friends Messrs Richard Oswald & Co dated the 1st of this month wherein are these words: 'We have called and sent frequently to Mr Savage about his brother's debt to you but from all circumstances we are afraid they only trifle with us and therefore we herewith return you the bill that you may try what can be done with the original draft in Ireland'. [Thomas Savage, 17 May 1759 - crossed out]. The bill was forwarded to Scotland 'where appearances of success become every day less favourable'. [Richard Oswald & Co, 28 May 1759]

Next Moore turned to Roger Hall. 'I desire you will favour my applying to you to try to obtain payment for me by whatever means you think convenient or necessary and failing gentle means that you will direct a law process for recovery of the debt to obtain security which I submit to your discretionary direction and appointment'. [Roger Hall, 17 May 1759]

When Hall refused to become involved, Moore wrote to Nicholas Harrison. 'I received your letter giving me an unpromising account of Thomas Savage's debt. He is by no means bashful in his promise of payments and making appointments of days. I think it would be more candid at once to tell that he's not able to pay than to amuse with such low shift. If nothing can be done with his father, who appeared in the establishment of his dealing and credit in this town, it seems as if no restitution can be expected in any other manner and his engagement in so vague a way that I am thinkful it will be to very little purpose to commune a law process so must hope for what can be done through your mediation'. [Nicholas Harrison, 5 November 1759]

'I see that my affair with Savage is in a bad way. It vexes me when I think of my being so cheated by his father. In Mr Andrew Savage's letter which he wrote to you the 7th March, the old gentleman says that he never advised me to credit him by word or letter or any other in the Island. How consistent this is with the letter he wrote to my brother Phil in Douglas, which letter I think I sent to you with the other papers pray look into if any good can be thence formed. What debts Thomas Savage owes in this Isle I know not nor do I think it will be of any service to enquire about and of no service can it be thought to enquire about the debts which are owing to him in Ireland, where doubtless the last penny he could he has scraped'. [Nicholas Harrison, 26 March 1760]

The Oats Property, Douglas
'You may remember when I was last in Dublin I told you I had purchased from Mr Robert Murray, (Revd) Mr Thomas Murray and Miss Murray ... a concern in a holding in Douglas, consisting of a house and outhouses nigh the chapel in Douglas, formerly named Oatses, with a small garden and a seat in the chapel of Douglas for £300 Irish value'. [Edward Kean, Dublin, 7 November 1751]. 'This purchase in several respects proves convenient to me. One is I have a house and cellars in Douglas, where I was in want of both and with great difficulty such convenience can there be met with for the town is so burthened with foreigners daily flying there that no manner of room is unemployed'. [Edward Kean, 21 March 1752]

Inevitably there were problems. 'No minutes of our agreement was taken in writing but I gave Mr Murray a Portingale piece of gold, which he received in earnest. One hundred pounds was to be paid in hand and the remainder of the consideration was to be paid following the deed of sale being confirmed in our courts, according to the laws of this Isle necessary to secure my purchase ... I wrote to Mr Murray in August last on this subject, to which I've yet received no answer. So, as I gave no directions, no one has yet called on you for the money. I have now wrote to Mr Murray and acquainted him that you will pay him and his brother this hundred pounds ... taking their receipt for the same. Let therein be recited the condition viz their and their sister's sale to me ... In the receipt let be recited the £1 18s 10d I gave in earnest and the £100 you are to pay them. The rent I am entitled to from the first day of May last, which let also be inserted'. [Edward Kean, Dublin, 7 November 1751]

'I take notice of the offer that has been made you for the house etc at Douglas since my purchase thereof. The one probably was the occasion of the other for there are some who would be content I had not purchased. Be this as it will, I'm obliged to your wishing me success herein. Agreeable with your letter, I have herewith sent to Mr Edward Kean a bill of sale drawn up in the Manx way for the signing. This is to be done by you and your brother and by both your Mrs Murrays. You are also to sign for your sister, Miss Betty, in sight of her power of attorney to you ... The witnesses you know must be two persons who are to come to this Isle to acknowledge the same before our deemster for his attestation, following which the court's confirmation will in course be. This is the legal and therefore necessary method'. [Robert Murray, Dublin, 10 December 1751]

'If the sale is already signed it is to be forwarded by the bearer, Mr William Thetford. If it is not already signed I desire it may be before him as witness, in which case I've directed he get some other person as witness so that on their return to the Isle the deed may be attested and in course confirmed, when please let me know. After allowing for £100 further, I expect the bearer will pay, how you would have the payment for the remainder therein due?' [Robert Murray, 8 February 1752]

'The day after Mr Thetford left this I received together both your letters ... By yours 27th February I find I could not have used a more effectual method than by means of Mr Thetford's application, which has succeeded to my expectation ... All their friends on this side were against their selling me their holding and I think were active to influence their withdrawing from their agreement. Now all is over and I give you many thanks'. [Edward Kean, 21 March 1752]

But all was not over. 'I some time ago received the favour of your letter 8th November agreeable with my expecting you would not disapprove what your brothers in Dublin agreed for in your name - the sale of the Oats's tenement in Douglas. The recital in the sale of a pew or seat in the chapel was necessary as an appurtenance belonging to the tenement ... Your seat in the gallery never belonged to the tenement so that it could not be disposed of unless by particular agreement. A penalty is mentioned in all deeds of agreement or consignment in this Isle and the practice is such that no deed is a legal one ... unless a penalty be inserted ... The penal sum mentioned be it pence or pounds seems to me to be of equal weight. The sale can be executed no other way than by your signing it before two witnesses ... or by your signing in this Isle or by your signing before any two witnesses and acknowledging it before the Duke of Atholl, who may underwrite the same and appoint it to be recorded'. [Betty Murray, York, 5 March 1753]

'I wrote to you the 5th of March ... As I have not since received any answer I conclude you have not met with the opportunity (of signing). I have therefore to desire you will be pleased to sign ... before two witnesses in the presence of a notary public, who may attest the same. This seems to me necessary. It will establish at least an equitable conveyance and I hope our court in this Isle will confirm it on your writing to Mr William Murray in Douglas to assent therewith in your name'. [Betty Murray, 23 August 1753]

'I received the favour of your letter the 24th September and from Mr William Murray the bill of sale, wherewith I have used all my influence with our court to address it to be recorded. But this is positively refused me. The court will not allow what they have no precedent for and say no sale is legal unless it be signed before two witnesses, who must declare upon oath ... In order to have the sale conferred at the next May courts, which is necessary, I think it the best way to send from this two persons who may be witness to your signing the sale ... You'll be pleased sign before them and add the day of your signing. The sale will in this manner be established on its return by the bearers, that which you signed before is returned'. [Betty Murray, 18 February 1754]

John Allan and Thomas Mylrea
George Ainslie shipped some brandy for John Allan with a cargo for Moore. 'On any future occasion of your sending a cargo I must desire

that no goods be shipped on any other person's account, which from the last instance I find proves very inconvenient'. [George Ainslie, 18 October 1758]. In the meantime Moore accepted Ainslie's draft on Allan for £412 3s 11d. 'The brandy is sold on arrival here to Mr Thomas Mylrea and as payment was agreed on at London I told Mr Allan it would be best to give Mylrea's bill, the payment whereof would answer discharge, with his own acceptance. Accordingly Mylrea's bill for £460 dated 2nd inst at four months I shall send with Allan's bill to Messrs Knox Craghead & Co'. [George Ainslie, 17 October 1758]

This would have seemed to be a simple solution but there were problems. 'The value of your draft, £412 3s 11d will become discharged by Mylrea's payment of £47 16s 3d I have desired Messrs Knox Craghead & Co to remit to you on my account, answerable to discharge a debt between £20 and £30 which Allan owes me and my son-in-law Charles Kelly and the remainder I shall pay to Mr Allan'. [George Ainslie, 23 November 1758]. 'In a day or two Mr Mylrea had some considerable demand on Allan, which he used all means to have deducted from the value of his own note and had been done if I had been less inclined to serve Mr Ainslie. I acquainted Mr Allan by letter of the manner I had directed your applying said surplus to which I conclude he assents from his silence'. [Knox Craghead & Co, 20 December 1758]

Within weeks Allan had paid Ainslie for another cargo of brandy with a bill, which was returned protested. He then, through Moore, offered two further bills, but these were also protested. 'My taking from you those bills to replace your preceding protested bill or on account thereof will prove extremely disagreeable to Mr Ainslie and he may blame me perhaps for having any concern with bills so unmercantile. This consideration will excuse me in insisting that you no longer delay payment which that you make me I send you by the bearer on purpose to request your compliance'. [John Allan, 14 May 1759]. Allan did make partial payment, but a fortnight later and to Charles Kelly.

The more significant semi-political matters in which Moore became involved on the Island are described in the next chapter.

THE DEATH OF WILLIAM THETFORD

William Thetford was involved in George Moore's dispute with the Murrays over Oats's property. 'I find I could not have used a more effectual method than by means of Mr Thetford's application, which has succeeded to my expectation'. [Edward Kean, 21 March 1752]. His name also occurs in reference to the tea trade.

'About three weeks ago for the benefit of being in the country Mr Thetford went out of this town where seemingly he was better and his health recovered. On Sunday seven night he rode out a little and on his return complained of getting a fresh cold. Yet he was tolerably well until Thursday night last and on Friday morning I have disagreeably and am very sorry to acquaint you he departed this life. On Sunday evening he was interred.

'At his funeral there appeared one Smith who lives in Castletown. He told me that he and his parents were now in England but that he was a nigh relation of Mr Thetford's, that Mr Thetford had made some kind of a verbal will whereby Smith was his executor. At the same time Mr Fear the schoolmaster of this town told me that Mr Thetford had made a written will some time ago. Yesterday I examined into all his papers and finding no will it remains hence necessary to enter a caveat against Smith's administration and the probate of the pretended verbal will or so it appears to me until your directions hereon. I know Mr Thetford all along intended that his debts in this Isle be first paid and that if his effects should remit farther that the same be divided in proportion to the debts he owes in Ireland. As you are his heir at lieu you may herein do as you think fit. It seems necessary that you come over here or that you make out a power of attorney and substitute me to act for you herein. If a power of attorney be sent you must sign it before two witnesses, who will come here and in person swear to your signing the same, on which I think administration be had in your name. Any two persons coming here will serve this purpose or if you consider coming here I shall be well pleased and you will be extremely welcome to have a room and be with me while you are in this Isle. I cannot with certainty tell what Mr Thetford was owing in this Isle but when all matters are settled I compute there will be about £50'. [Ann Dowdall, 16 April 1753]

'Mr Cain is doing all in his power to adjust and settle your uncle's accounts. He's become heartily tired of the attendance on the spiritual courts which this affair requires for there are several demands that have a very doubtful aspect and it rests on the claimants' oaths to fix the debts. The law allows of a year wherein all claims must be made and proven so that it is impossible in less time to close the account ... all his goods have been sold at public auction, at which was bought for you his father's and mother's pictures and the book of sermons delivered to the care of the bearer, the pictures cased up. There were no sets of china or any that I thought worth directing to be bought for you. We have Mr Thetford's own picture which he gave some years in some whim with my young family that they would not permit to be set up at auction.

'I'm very sorry to hear of your mother's death and your so great loss'. [Ann Dowdall, 5 September 1753]

'All the Manx debts which have been claimed and proved are paid but as our law allows three years for the claim and proof of all foreign debts some of these may yet appear for payment whereof Cain and his bondsmen our court holds liable ... I believe there will be remaining of your uncle's effects £40 or £50 Manx ... there were a number of claimers that were not paid the demands but every farthing was paid of what was thought to be just debts, Kitty Radcliff's with the rest was paid. She spoke of a promise of a legacy but if these kind of promises had prevailed they would have extended them beyond bounds'. [Ann Dowdall, 15 March 1755]

In April 1758 he was able to tell her that £57 7s 2d Manx was ready to be claimed. This letter was forwarded to her by way of John Gordon. 'I hear that Miss Dowdall, niece of my late friend Mr Thetford, is married. I do not know the name of the gentleman to whom so cannot properly direct a letter to her, which I have occasion to write. I therefore give you the trouble of the enclosed letters for her I desire you will cause be delivered. I very heartily salute you'. [John Gordon, 10 April 1758]

CHAPTER SEVENTEEN: THE INCIPIENT POLITICIAN

'Very contrary to our hopes it's now said that our governor is to stay till March next and his friends affect to say that he's not to go at all. His Grace may doubtless in the management of his domestic affairs do as to him seemeth meet. But surely in this appointment he is well acquainted that he's forcing the superintendency of a person extremely disagreeable to many, very many, of his Manx subjects'. [John Onge, 4 October 1759]

One of the most interesting developments throughout the letter-book is the slow but sure change in the focus of Moore's interest from that of trade to that of any and every matter that affected the freedom and rights of the Manx people and of himself in particular. The following incidents are discussed as nearly as possible in chronological order.

The Dow Affair

This story was told in 'The Isle of Man in Smuggling History' and can be found in several other publications. In this section, Moore's involvement is emphasised. 'A dispute has arose with Captain George Dow, commander of a small vessel in His Majesty's service, and his Grace the Duke of Atholl's government in this Isle. Malicious aspersions are given of the inhabitants and of the merchants, which unnoticed might be attended with consequences fatal to the privileges (of the Island). I have made some kind of representation for the merchants, which you have enclosed. You have also a letter enclosed for his Grace the Duke of Atholl, which I desire you will please deliver him, to desire to know if his Grace will be pleased that the merchants of this Isle join council with his officers for the common good herein. I desire you will act as his Grace may think fit to appoint or give leave - what the merchants have to say is in this representation wherewith let be done as may be best advised. The expense hereon attending please debit my account with and I desire as to your transaction you will use justice and secrecy'. [William Snell, 1 February 1751]

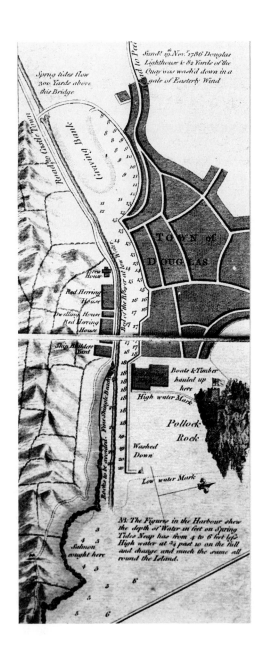

Figure 20: Douglas Bridge

'The Governor is taking some new steps which give occasion of clamour and offence. One is in supporting a scheme of building a bridge cross the harbour of Douglas, which is grieved by the merchants who are natives'. [Richard Oswald & Co, 30 November 1757]

Moore appealed to the merchants in Liverpool. 'What I wrote ... about the harbour of Douglas was to give you an idea of the inconvenience evidently appearing if a bridge is built. I thought it at this time not improper to communicate to you and the gentlemen in Liverpool, who have kindly assisted to prevent a great nuisance to shipping, how frequently their vessels and ships trading to Douglas may be exposed to damages on their coming into that harbour, which some easterly wind or south-east wind and to give spirit and add weight to the application they have made'. [Haliday & Dunbar, 30 November 1757]

'I have since then (30 November 1757) had some conversation with one of your London captains in regard of Douglas harbour and the proposed bridge there. His opinion is joined by the opinion of some other friends at the time in Douglas and sent me in writing ... which I send you that you may know the sentiments of your ship commanders'. [Haliday & Dunbar, 5 December 1757]

'His Grace the Duke of Atholl has appointed that a survey be made of the harbour of Douglas but whether this survey has been yet done I have not heard. The party for the bridge is headed by Mr Rywood, whose lands lying contiguous to the harbour on the south side give room to suspect that his private interest is his motive. The strangers in Douglas join him and as several of these were lately naturalised their being advocates of the bridge gives room to suspect that the governor of our Isle is for the bridge. The party against the bridge is the native inhabitants ... the opinion of commanders of ships may be esteemed unmoved by prejudice to a favour of either party, as the accommodating of the harbour to the conveniency of safety of ships must be their guiding principle (these have been) since added to or confirmed by the opinion of other commanders of your ships, which I sent to your mayor for the satisfaction of your corporation, by which you may receive farther knowledge of that matter'. [Haliday & Dunbar, 5 January 1758]

The bridge was built.

'This is intended by Mr Daniel Mylrea, who is going to London by direction of the government of our Isle relating to Captain Dow's affair ... if he should have occasion for any sum to £50 let him have the same ... Referring to the enclosed I have to desire your handing to his Grace of Atholl my letter ...I could not tell how to address it, as I do not know how or if there be any occasion ... His Grace of Atholl it is expected came to London some time last month. Should any accident have prevented his coming it will be prove very injurious. In this case you may open my letter to him and consult Mr Daniel Mylrea to regulate your acting for joining with him to which I discretionally refer'. [William Snell, 11 February 1751]. Mylrea only needed £27 10s.

'I presumed to write to your Grace on the subject of debate with Dow, being my proposal on behalf of some few merchants who have agreed with me to stand on half of the expense with your Grace's officers resulting from what I esteemed not unbecoming and the effect of my warmest wishes for success and protection against future insults. In what ever degree my proposal has been favoured with your Grace's approbation I submit'. [Duke of Atholl, 7 March 1751]

'I'm highly pleased his Grace took in good part my proposal of bearing one half the expenses in Dow's affair and I'm hopeful the issue will yet prove not unfavourable. Dr Wilson has been at some pains to discover his having any hand or manner of concern in the several papers which have been so industriously dispersed about the trade of our Isle, motively to engage the Duke of Atholl's disposal of it or to pave the way. Notwithstanding the Doctor's letters to his friends in this Isle he's busying himself too much in these matters. It is believed that the trade has received a very considerable stagnation from the apprehension of the Isle's being to be alienated. Yet a few among us entertain a firm belief that the apprehension is groundless and a little time will restore its usual circulation. Pity it is that no method has yet been tackled whereby the traders of the Isle might be solely occupied by its natives, which the nature of our trade argues a great deal in favour of. Herein we should follow the example of Jersey and Guernsey, where a much more extensive trade than we have is carried on without envy or noise by exercising the like caution. We in like manner would establish a reputable character. Our youth would have encouragement sufficient to stay at home and not look abroad to be employed and in a few years would be trained a sufficient number of Manxmen to carry on the trade in a way I'm sure as extensive as has hitherto been'. [Daniel Mylrea, 15 August 1751]

'Mr Mylrea is arrived. The affair with Dow by his account has a better appearance than was expected'. [William Snell, 3 September 1751]. This is the same letter that started the affair of the *Grizzy* (see Chapter Three).

Naturalisations

'I am embarrassed in an affair of a public nature in this Isle. His Grace of Atholl, by recommendation of our governor as is supposed, has granted naturalisations to sundry strangers in this Isle, and some of them papists. No instances of the kind have been these sixty years. They seem not agreeable with our laws and against the opinion of all the natives, whose peculiar privilege it is by law to have a priority in payment of debts. No instances of such favours to papists were ever granted by the lords of this Isle so that at this time they become remarkable and may subject us to the displeasure of Great Britain. What appertains to the party which I join is to act as to please the people and not to disoblige his Grace, which is a point difficult to steer in'. [Richard Oswald & Co, 2 January 1758]

Peel Harbour

'There are just now riding in this bay three Liverpool ships bound for the coast of Guinea, intended to call at Douglas to take on board part of their cargoes. They left Liverpool with a south-east wind and blowing fresh. When they came to this Island they were afraid to look into the bay or run into the harbour of Douglas so for safety came round to this part of the Isle and it's a pity to see them riding in our bay waiting their goods coming from Douglas. Had their goods been in this town they would speedily have been shipped and the ships by this time clear of the coast of Ireland with a south-east wind.

'The circumstance of the harbour here conveniently situated to the North Channel, favourable for ships coming in or going out with a east-south-east wind, has been thought sufficient encouragement for the

Figure 21: Castletown: The Case of Radcliff's Quarry

'I find it's uppermost with me to write to you about the quarry. Every step, every device has been taken to favour Radcliff and to injure me. This matter has ended in an appeal, which I handed to the governor in the Castle, accompanied by my cousin, J Moore, and Mr Callin ... He told me that he must consider of it whether or not to accept it, for he was much blamed he said for accepting my last appeal. I told him that I thought it was not his province to judge or determine the merits of an appeal and therefore he had not a negative to give to the acceptance. After a little chat I withdrew to make way for the consultation, which was immediately called. About six in the evening the receiver came to tell me that his honour would give an answer to my appeal about twelve o'clock the next day ... Mr Moore, Mr Callin and I went to the governor to tell him that I had received his answer to my appeal, which denied the relief I wanted, and therefore I was under necessity of continuing my appeal to obtain redress. He said I might do as I pleased, to which I said that I would apply further acceptance of my appeal before his Grace's commissioner of appeals at London and desired that his honour would stop Captain Radcliff's proceedings ... until I received an answer to the application ... But this ... was refused and, being denied every means of relief, I returned from Castletown very much affected. It was the 11th inst I received his honour's answer to my appeal and on the 13th inst I served Captain Radcliff with notice that I would transmit the appeal to London ... (he enclosed several papers) which I send you in order that you immediately proceed to lay these matters before his Grace's commissioner ... The occasion requires address and dispatch that so unheard of proceedings may be checked ...

'My brother Onge has been with me this fortnight past ... He was a witness of the proceedings before the inquest on the 6th inst and is intimately acquainted with what has been done. He's gone off with an opinion that in no part of His Majesty's dominions are there such instances of the oppressions of government as in this Isle and that this of mine is a shocking one contrary to law and to the spirit of laws. He said he was sure that the commissioner at London would speedily give me redress. But if the contrary ... it was his opinion immediately to apply to King and Council. For my own part you know I am an enemy to any and every degree of oppression so that the stroke being now levelled at me I may perhaps be prejudiced or too sanguine. However if you coolly look on and consider of this matter with advice and some eminent opinion and in consequence thereof I desire you do all that can be done of my obtaining justice and relief by whatever means you think best or are advised'.
[John Stevenson, at Captain Whitsin's, Dorsgate, London, 15 September 1760]

enlargement of the harbour and to render it commodious for large ships. In the proposed manner we shall have as much water in the harbour in depth as is equal to the flowing, which is as much as any harbour in this Isle can have. On a plan much more commodious than in any other harbour in this Isle, as there will be a place for the small craft separate from the large ships. To execute this £1,600 will be wanted and having tried I cannot get here advanced above £500 so that £1000 more are wanted on security of the harbour (dues) at 5 per cent interest. Could the borrowing of such a sum in Liverpool on those terms be obtained? If so it would give spirit and expedition to our intended improvement of the harbour. In which case I would require the assistance of some person from Liverpool you would recommend in respect of the intended work and communicate the same to our Governor in this Isle'. [Haliday & Dunbar, 5 January 1758]

'Captain Clements I find continues his opinion of the great utility of the intended improvement of this harbour. I some time ago wrote to the Duke of Atholl about it and am expecting to receive the favour of an answer. For this convenience is necessary and may be expected from the tendency it has to his advantage and the revenue of the port. I was telling Mr Clements that £1500 was the least sum wherewith it could be proposed to begin and as the complexion of every other part of the Isle is against and not for this improvement, or so it seems, the raising of said sum ... will go nigh to complete the work as proposed and recommended ... I am getting ready a plan of the harbour with the intended improvement which in a day or two I shall send you copy of'. [Haliday & Dunbar, 5 April 1759]

'I have lately had a letter from the Duke of Atholl about the enlargement of the harbour here. He seems to be very much for it which is a good thing and will help to bear a great variety of delay and opposition that shows against us in the Island. I hope that our design will proceed and grow up to maturity. I shall be glad to know what opinion you have of the plan which I sent you'. [Haliday & Dunbar, 18 April 1759]. 'The season of the year with some intervening obstacles will necessarily postpone the intended improvement of the harbour here'. [Haliday & Dunbar, 7 July 1759]

The Highway

'The public matters of conversation now in this Isle are the commissioners at Castletown and the affair of the highway through my lawn, pursued and defended with the utmost litigation. When I had last the honour of seeing his Grace, which was at London near two years ago, I made face to acquaint him that I was in some fears that the governor's resentment against me would descend to personal injuries. His Grace was pleased to assure me that this would not happen. The different motions and alterations which I have since then experienced make me think that his Grace's inclination in this respect is not apparent in that point of view which his Grace gave me leave to hope. There is no one thing in life I have a greater dislike to than to be at variance with the government of this Isle. But how must I behave or demean myself in instances where my honour or my property comes to be attacked? In other respects I would content myself with being silent'. [Sir John Stewart, 7 January 1760]

'I think it a very lucky circumstance that you have had the opportunity of seeing Lady Charlotte and Mr Murray at Edinburgh. His disposition of having peace and quiet established I have been favoured with many marks of and impresses me with the highest sense of gratitude. His appearance or Lady Charlotte's appearance in any affair that I solicit either from a principle of public good, however the interest of the family may be connected, or from any person's motive are become alas matters of great delicacy. Yet it is some consolation that following a storm succeeds a calm and it seems this season be patiently waited. The agreement you have made with Mr Murray, from the situation I remember of the ground, will prove extremely agreeable to his Grace and the footing you have put it on seems so eligible that no treaty can be more honourable so that I make no doubt this matter will be concluded on the first interview to the satisfaction of all parties. This, as I hope, may introduce a familiarity which may prove favourable to the intercession you generously have begun and support the languishing cause which humanity inspires'. [Sir John Stewart, 12 March 1760]

From the later letters in the letter-book it appears that George Moore is becoming more and more harassed from each and every quarter. In fact his career as a politician was only just beginning (see Figure 1). But that is the subject of another story.

APPENDIX I: THE LETTERS

Note: Sometimes the letters are addressed to 'Sir', 'Madam' or 'Brother'. Where the identity of this addressee is known, it has been included in brackets.

1750
October 8 William Rowan; **9** Thomas Finlay, (John Onge), Alexander Brown; **12** Thomas Finlay; **20** (John McCulloch), **30** John McCulloch, William Snell. **November 6** Richard Smith, William Snell, James Crosbie; **7** John Cowan; **8** John Munn; **9** Peter & John Murdoch; **10** John McCulloch; **22** Thomas Finlay, Daniel Musendine. **December 3** Richard Smith & Co, Richard Smith, Bagge, Wilson & Pike, William Snell; **10** James Crosbie, William Kerr, William McClure, William Jamieson, Pat Ewing, James Hutchison, John Ewing, William Laing, Joseph Scott, William Snell; **11** Pat Montgomerie; **27** Gerrard van Hoogmerf; **28** Daniel Clark, Mr Christain; **31** Jacob Wilkinson.
1751
January 1 George Ainslie, Peter & John Murdoch, Sir; **3** William Snell; **5** Walter McKirdie; **7** Hercules Lindsay; **14** William Snell, (John Onge), Jacob Wilkinson, William Samson, James Donald, Robert Crawford, John Harvey; **15** James Hutchison, William McClure, William Laing; **17** Peter & John Murdoch; **21** Mr Ewing or Captain Montgomerie, Joseph Scott; **22** Pat Montgomerie, Alexander Porterfield; **23** Daniel Musendine, John Mowat, John Stedman, William Snell, James Crosbie; **25** Bartian van Banken; **30** Pat Ewing. **February 1** Alexander Porterfield; **December 30** William Laing. **February 1** William Snell; **11** William Snell, John Munn, William Laing, Joseph Scott, Pat Montgomerie, open letter to the master of the *Lilly*, James Allison, Robert Crawford (2), Peter & John Murdoch, William Laing; **10** Walter McKindrie; **11** Hercules Lindsay; **20** Pat Montgomerie; **27** James Hutchison, William McClure, Robert Kerr. **March 5** Jacob Wilkinson, George Ainslie; **7** Andrew McMaster, Wal Geoghegan, Bagge, Wilson & Pike, John Black, John Stedman, John Thomson, Peter & John Murdoch, Richard & Alexander Oswald, Richard Smith, William Snell, Duke of Atholl, James Crosbie; **12** Walter Logan, Robert Montgomerie, Pat Montgomerie; **18** John Allan; **21** Walter Logan, Pat Lindesay, Sir, Peter & John Murdoch. **April 5** Walter McKirdie, (Hercules Lindsay), John Innes; **15** (Andrew McMaster). **June 8** Richard & Alexander Oswald. **July 1** Green & Stanton, Pat White, Peter Berail, John Blundell, Pat Montgomerie (2), Robert Montgomerie (2), James Reid. **August 6** Surveyor of Donaghadee, Peter & John Murdoch, George Ainslie, Armour & Stewart, Ralph Sampson, Patrick Bogle, John Mowat, Pat Ewing, David Ferguson, Alexander Porterfield, Bagge, Wilson & Pike, William White, Richard Smith & Co, Richard Smith, Sam Onge,

Alexander Brown, Robert Finlay; **15** Robert Murray, Pat Lindesay, Daniel Mylrea, Pat Montgomerie, Robert Montgomerie, Peter Berail, Pat White, John Blundell; **16** William Snell, James Crosbie; **20** John Stedman; **26** (Tyndall & Co), William Snell, James Crosbie, Green & Stanton. **September 3** Robert Montgomerie, Peter Berail, Green & Stanton, Ralph Sampson, John Blundell, John Mowat, William Snell; **4** James Crosbie; **9** John Munn; **10** Robert Finlay, Thomas Orr, Sir; **24** Smellie and Hopkirk, Philip Moore, (Archibald Gilchrist), James Young, Malcolm Fisher & John Rodger, John Allan, Peter & John Murdoch; **26** Joseph Scott & Co; **27** John Munn. **October 7** Alexander Porterfield, (Hercules Lindsay); **9** James Stewart, William Laing, John Ewing, William McClure; **12** James Hutchison, Alexander Porterfield (2), Philip Moore, James Watt, Hercules Lindsay; **14** John Mowat, Gerrard van Hoogwerf, James Cunningham; **16** Alexander Porterfield, William Kerr; **14** Robert Finlay, John Blundell, Pat White, Pat Montgomerie (2), William Snell, James Crosbie, Robert Montgomerie; **18** George Kippen & Co; **16** (John Onge). **November 6** (John Onge). **October 16** George Wilson. **November 6** Sir; **7** Robert Murray, Edward Kean, William Snell; **9** John McMunn; **11** James Wilson, (William Ferguson), John Allan, William Kerr, William McClure; **12** James Hutchison, John Ewing, Sirs, Hector McLean, Pat Lindesay, Peter & John Murdoch, Sir; **22** Robert Finlay, William Cumming junior, Alexander Porterfield, Smellie & Hopkirk, Peter Berail, Green & Stanton, John Blundell, Pat White, William Snell; **25** James Crosbie. **December 10** Robert Murray, (Edward Kean), **27** (Hercules Lindsay), Peter Berail, Green & Stanton, Robert Montgomerie; **28** Pat Montgomerie; **30** Jacob Wilkinson, Richard Smith, Richard Smith & Co, William Snell, Mrs Roughsedge, Mrs Then? James Crosbie; **31** George Kippen & Co. **January 1** Phil. **December 31** William Samson, James Donald, Alexander Porterfield. **1752**
January 6 Allan Glen; **11** Janine Stewart; **18** James Young, John McClure, Thomas McClure, Hugh Lawson, John Vass, James Limont, William Samson, John Hamilton, Pat Campbell, Hector Bryce, Joseph Scott & Co, William McClure, James Hutchison, William Kerr, Pat Douglas, James Hutchison; **22** John Dickie, Robert Allison & William Allison, James Allison, William Cuming, Robert Finlay, Peter & John Murdoch, Mathew Stewart, Janine Stewart, Madam, **23** Pat Lindesay, William Kerr; **27** John Blundell, Green, Stanton & Ford, Richard Smith, William Snell & Co, James Crosbie; **30** Smellie & Hopkirk. **February 7** William McNellie; **8** Robert Murray, Thomas Finlay & Robert Patrick, (John Onge); **28** William Snell & Co; **11** James Ewing; **20** James Hutchison; **25** John Stedman, Marcus Ezehiel, Green, Stanton & Ford, John Blundell, William Snell & Co, Claud Johnson & Son, George Ainslie. **March 21** (Attorney), (Edward Kean), Thomas Finlay &

Robert Patrick; **23** (John Onge); **16** Pat Lindesay, Peter & John Murdoch. **April 8** John Munn, Alexander Porterfield, Peter & John Murdoch; **11** James & George Piersy, William Snell & Co, Joseph Popham, Thomas Finlay & Robert Patrick, Richard Smith & Co, Barbados (2), Robert Colhoun, Robert Samson, Robert Montgomerie, James Hutchison; **15** Green, Stanton & Ford, Marcus Ezechiel; **17** Mrs Christian; **15** William Snell & Co; **17** Hercules Lindsay, Robert Montgomerie, James & George Piersy; **18** Robert Montgomerie, Thomas Finlay & Robert Patrick; **21** William Snell & Co, Samuel Crisp, Green, Stanton & Ford, Richard Smith, James Crosbie, Henry Atkin, John Mowat; **23** William Snell & Co, Philip Moore (brother). **May 18** Samuel Crisp, Aeneas Mackay & Co, Hector McLean, John Blundell, Green, Stanton & Ford, Tynall & Co, George Ainslie, Marcus Ezechiel, John Stedman; **19** Philip Moore (brother); **18** William Snell & Co; **20** James Crosbie, Peter & John Murdoch. **July 7** William Kerr, John McKie, (Jean Ross), Colin Douglas, James Donald, John Allan, Hugh Lawson, Sir, John Innes, William Laing, John Munn, Joseph Scott, James Stevenson, John Cowan, **11** John Allan, John Marshall, John Cowan, John Munn, James Hutchison; **13** Henry Atkin, John Rowe, Joseph Scott & Co, George Montgomerie; **20** Alexander Houston, Thomas Finlay & Robert Patrick, James & George Piersy, Alexander Houston; **22** Andrew Grant; **24** Robert Finlay & Robert Patrick, (John Onge); **10** David Nathan; **25** Anthony Halsal, John Arnall, Richard Smith & Co; **28** Colin Dunlop; **29** Robert Finlay; **28** (Hercules Lindsay), Marcus Ezechiel, John Stedman. **August 12** Anthony Halsal; **13** John Stedman, William Snell & Co, James Crosbie; **15** Thomas Finlay & Robert Patrick; **29** William Snell & Co. **September 16** William Snell & Co; **19** Thomas Hartley; **20** Robert Finlay, Thomas Finlay & Robert Patrick, Richard Smith & Co, John Halliday & Brothers, Robert Colhoun, Richard Smith & Co, unaddressed (West Indies), Robert Montgomerie (2); **25** John Cowan; **27** Robert Ross; **28** Thomas Finlay & Robert Patrick, Robert Montgomerie. **October 4** Colin Dunlop, George Montgomerie, Joseph Scott & Co; **10** Thomas Finlay & Robert Patrick, **13** Antony Halsal, John Hillhouse, Robert Montgomerie, Thomas Finlay & Robert Patrick; **14** David Nathan, John Blundell, Pat Montgomerie (2), Harris Crisp & Co; **15** William Kerr; **16** John Stedman, William Snell & Co, James Crosbie, John Thomson, James Simson; **18** William Kerr; **17** Agnew; **24** Thomas Finlay & Robert Patrick, James Crosbie; **26** Mathew Stewart, William Laing; **18** Robert Kerr. **November 7** William Kerr, Pat Douglas, James Allison, Thomas Gray, Mathew Stewart, William McClure, Janine Stewart, James Hutchison, Captain Campbell of the Cutter; **8** Joseph Scott, William Samson, John Dickie; **13** Abraham James Hillhouse, James Simson, Alexander Houston, William Quayle; **14** Sir; Alexander Houston, John Munn, James Warden; **20** Marcus

Ezechiel, William Kerr, Sir, Abraham James Hillhouse; 21 James Crosbie; 24 George Ainslie; 21 Peter Berail, Pat White, Andrew Stuckey & Co; 23 (Archibald Gilchrist), Captain Chisholm, Alexander Houston, Colin Dunlop, Hugh Mackay & Co, William McMunn, William Laing, Abraham James Hillhouse, William Snell & Co; 25 James Crosbie; 24 Thomas Finlay & Robert Patrick. **December 6** Alexander Houston, Thomas Finlay & Robert Patrick, John Mowat; 7 Captain Chisholm, Abraham James Hillhouse, James Crosbie; 14 Sir

1753
January 6 James Young; 7 James Hutchison, John Munn, John Dickie; 10 William Quayle; 9 Harris Crisp & Co, James Stevenson, Joseph Scott & Co; 10 William Kerr; 12 James Donald, James Hutchison, Pat Ewing; Robert Dickie, John Resaid & William Tweek; John Dickie, William McClure, Thomas Gray, William Allison & Robert Allison, William Allison, James Allison, James Logan, Hector Bryce, William Samson, James Young, James Simson; 14 Thomas Moore, William Quayle, Thomas Finlay & Robert Patrick, (John Onge), Abraham James Hillhouse; 15 Peter Flanagan; 14 Richard Smith, William Snell & Co; 15 James Crosbie; 18 Philip Moore & Sons. **February 5** Robert Colhoun, Alexander Houston; 3 James Simson; 5 Patrick Bogle & Alexander Stevenson; 8 John Glassford & Co; 7 John Munn. **March 5** David Nathan, Marcus Ezechiel, Gerrard van Hoogwerf & Son. **February 28** Patrick Ewing, Mathew Stewart, William McClure; 27 James Hutchison; 26 Joseph Scott & Co. **March 3** James Donald; 5 Betty Murray, Gerard van Hogwerf & Son, William McClure, James Hutchison; 7 Ralph Sampson, John Rowe, Harris Crisp & Co, Abraham James Hillhouse, Richard Smith & Co, Richard Smith, Cunningham & Gordon, George Ainslie; 8 Abraham James Hillhouse, William Snell & Co, James Crosbie, Phil Moore & Sons, John Dickie; 9 Thomas Finlay & Robert Patrick; 12 James Simson, John Allan; 20 Pat Ewing. **April 16** Ann Dowdall, 10 Alexander Houston, George Kippen; 14 Archibald Kennedy, William Samson, James Campbell, William McCormick, Pat Douglas, Thomas McClure; 19 Andrew Agnew, Thomas Finlay & Robert Patrick; 24 James & George Piersy, John Mowat, William Kerr, John Rowe, Abraham James Hillhouse, William Snell & Co, James Crosbie. **May 1** James Simson; 3 James Hutchison; 23 Joseph Agnew, Robert Montgomerie, Thomas Finlay & Robert Patrick, (John Onge), (Mrs Weekes); 25 Archibald Brazier, Hamilton & Kissack, James Simson. **June 4** James Crosbie. **July 20** Pat White (2), Edmund Stritch, John Blundell, David Forbes; 21 George Ainslie, John Halliday & Brothers, Harris Crisp & Co, James & George Piersey, John Rowe, Thomas Finlay & Robert Patrick, Robert Montgomerie; 23 Allan Glen, Dr Moor, John Dickie, Joseph Scott & Co, Daniel Montgomerie, John Rowe, Pat Montgomerie, James Simson, Peter &

John Murdoch, Richard Smith; **24** John Rowe, Andrew Stuckey & Co, Abraham James Hillhouse; **25** James Simson, James Crosbie, William Snell & Co; **29** Philip Moore & Sons, Hamilton & Kissack. **August 7** James & George Piersy, Robert Montgomerie, Andrew Stuckey & Co, Harris Crisp & Co, Abraham James Hillhouse, James Crosbie; **10** Dugal Richie; **14** Pat Montgomerie, Phil Moore & Sons, William Murray senior, James Simson; **23** Betty Murray, John Murray, John Munn; **24** William Laing **September 5** Abraham James Hillhouse, Joseph Scott & Co; **6** Richard Smith, William Snell & Co, James Watt; **21 August** James Crosbie, **3 September** James & George Piersey, Harris Crisp & Co, Pat White, Peter Berail, Moore & Strich, Isadore Lynch & Co, Robert Montgomerie, John Blundell; **5** James Simson, Andrew Stuckey & Co, Ann Dowdall, John Mowat, Bagge, Wilson & Riche, Abraham James Hillhouse, Joseph Scott & Co; **6** Richard Smith, Richard Smith & Co James Watt, James Crosbie, John Moore, Robert Ross, (John Onge); **21** Gab Mathie, Alexander McAuslane & Thomas Barklay; **23** Bagge Wilson & Hall, James Crosbie. **October 3** James Simson; **5** Alexander Houston; **15** James & George Piersy, Thomas Finlay & Robert Patrick, (John Onge); **16** Robert Ross, Hamilton & Kissack; **18** James Crosbie, (Mrs Roughsedge); **20** William McClure; **25** William Kerr; **26** James Logan, Hector Bryce, Malcolm Fisher, Janet Donald, James Young, Thomas Gray, William Alexander, Hugh Lawson, James Hutchison, William Allison, James Milne, John Dickie, James Simson; **30** William Murray senior; **29** Joseph Scott & Co; **30** Cunningham & Gordon, Moore & Stritch, Harris Crisp & Co, John Blundell, Pat Montgomerie, Andrew Stuckey & Co, Abraham James Hillhouse, William Snell & Co, James Crosbie, Richard Montgomerie. **November 7** John Munn; **8** Gabriel Mathie, Alexander McAuslane & John Hartley, John Marshall, James Stevenson, Pat Ewing, Robert Dickie & John Resaid, John Ewing; **26** James Watt; **30** John Murray, James Dyges Latouche, Simon Vashon; **20** William White & Co, Peter Berail; **30** Hamilton & Kissack, Thomas Finlay & Robert Patrick, Abraham James Hillhouse, Colin Dunlop. **December 4** Richard Smith, William Snell & Co, John Rowe, Abraham James Hillhouse, John Crosbie; **10** William Laing; **18** Abraham James Hillhouse (2), James Simson; **19** David Forbes, James McCulloch, Hamilton & Kissack.
1754
January 14 James Crosbie, James Simson, Dowall, Miliken & Houston, John Allan, John Munn; **16** John Dickie, Robert Dickie & Co, John Innes, John Ewing, William Laing, Alexander Houston, Peter Berail, James Hutchison, Robert Montgomerie; **17** Colin Dunlop; **29** John Quayle. **February 8** John Munn; **11** Thomas Finlay & Robert Patrick; **12** William Laing; **13** Mr Best, Roger Hall, James Simson; **18** (Betty Murray), (John Murray), John Cunningham, Joseph Scott, John Marshall; **19** James Simson, William Kerr;

20 Richard Smith, Andrew Stuckey & Co, Harris Crisp & Co, John Blundell, George Ainslie, Peter Berail, Abraham James Hillhouse, William Snell & Co, James Crosbie. **March 1** Colin Dunlop, Mr Watson, David & John Gregory, Joseph Scott; **21** Abraham James Hillhouse, Robert Montgomerie, **25** Sir, (Mrs Weekes), Hamilton & Kissack, (John Onge). **April 3** John Munn, William Laing, John Dickie, **4** John Resaid, John Dickie, Joseph Scott; **6** Archibald Kennedy, George Paterson, Pat Douglas, William Samson, James Allison, William Allison, William Orr, James Watt; **10** Malcolm Fisher, James Young, Janet Donald, Colin Dunlop, Joseph Scott, James Simson; **12** James Hutchison, Thomas Gray, James Logan, Hector Bryce; **15** Joseph Dean, David Forbes, James Simson; **17** Colin Dunlop, Joseph Scott, James Muir; **19** Janet Donald, John Murray; **23** Walter Corrie; **24** James Simson. **May 3** John Stedman, David & John Gregory, James Orr; **4** John Woddrop, Peter Berail, Cunningham & Gordon, Thomas Finlay & Robert Patrick, John Rowe, John Blundell, Harris Crisp & Co, Colin Dunlop, Abraham James Hillhouse; **6** James Crosbie, John Murray. **July 24** John McKie, John Allan, John Innes; **29** John Moure, William McClure, Samuel Cuthbert, Pat Douglas, James Simson. **August 2** George Montgomerie, James Limont, Hugh Lawson, William Samson, Archibald Kennedy, Thomas Orr, Joseph Scott; **10** Paul Bridson, James Coulter & Buchanan & Co; **13** Colin Dunlop, Joseph Agnew, Richard & Alexander Oswald; **14** John Rowe, Pat Montgomerie; **15** Moore & Stritch, David & John Gregory, George Ainslie, John Stedman, Harris Crisp & Co, Peter Berail, Abraham James Hillhouse; **20** James & George Piersy, John Rowe, Robert Montgomerie, Abraham James Hillhouse, James Simson; **21** Daniel Montgomerie, Bagge, Wilson & Hall, James Crosbie, Philip Moore (brother); **24** James Hutchison; **30** William Laing. **September 20** John Munn, John Murdoch; **21** James Simson, John Cowan, Colin Dunlop; **23** Samuel Cuthbert, William Kerr; **30** John Marshall; **26** John Johnston; **30** John Marshall. **October 1** John McGregor, James Simson, Livingston & Symson, James & George Piersy, Patricia Barclay & Francis Twiss & James Crawford, Peter Berail, Roger Hall, Abraham James Hillhouse, James Crosbie, Thomas Finlay & Robert Patrick; **20** (John Onge), **21** James Hutchison; **22** Richard Oswald & Co, James Simson; **24** Daniel Montgomerie; **26** Peter Berail, Richard Oswald & Co, James Crosbie; **28** (James Moore), Philip Moore (son), (John Onge), Thomas Finlay & Robert Patrick. **November 2** James Simson; **4** George Carmichael & Co, John Wylie & Son, Robert Montgomerie, Pat Montgomerie, John Blundell, Nickson, Moore & Stritch, Pat White, Harris Crisp & Co, Peter Berail, Cunningham & Gordon; **5** Abraham James Hillhouse, Richard Oswald & Co, James Crosbie; **12** Alexander Houston; **15** John Resaid, William Laing; **29** George Paterson; **20** Mrs Montgomerie, James Simson; **22** Phil Grumley; **20** James Hutchison. **December 4** John

McKie, William McClure, William Laing, Pat Lindesay; **5** James Limont, Andrew McCulloch, David Lamont, John McClure & Co, William Samson, James Milne, Hector Bryce, James Logan, David Mitchell, Hugh Lawson, William Orr, Thomas Gray; **9** Dugal Ritchie, John Dickie, James Simson, James Hutchison; **10** Janet Donald, James Young, Joseph Scott & Co; **12** Andrew Kerr, Mr Hamilton, Thomas Finlay & Robert Patrick; **13** James Crawford & Francis Twiss executors of John Stedman, Harris Crisp & Co, Peter Berail, Richard Oswald & Co, Abraham James Hillhouse; **17** James & John Crosbie; **26** Humphry Harriol, John Munn

1755

January 8 Thomas Finlay & Robert Patrick (2), **14** Thomas Finlay & Robert Patrick; **15** William Laing, Thomas Orr, John Alexander & John Russell; **17** John Callin. **February 3** Janet Donald, John Wyllie & Son, Joseph Scott & Co, Alexander Houston, James Simson, Samuel Cuthbert; **5** Theobald Dillon, Abraham James Hillhouse, Richard Oswald & Co, Mrs Roughsedge; **6** James & John Crosbie; **12** Thomas Finlay & Robert Patrick; **13** James Simson, Marcus Ezechiel, Philip Moore & Sons; **15** John Munn; **17** John Dickie; **27** Thomas Finlay & Robert Patrick, James Young, Janet Donald.**March 3** James Simson, Alexander Houston; **4** John Resaid, William Laing, Robert Arthur; **5** (John Onge), Pat Ewing; **6** John McKie, James McBride; **15** Alexander Houston, Ann Dowdall; **18** Alexander Houston, Robert Arthur; **20** Pat Lindesay; **22** James & George Piersy, Thomas Finlay & Robert Patrick; **24** Joseph Scott & Co, Harris Crisp & Co, Peter Berail, Theobald Dillon, Abraham James Hillhouse; **25** Richard Oswald & Co, James & John Crosbie; **27** Theobald Dillon, Abraham James Hillhouse, Thomas Finlay & Robert Patrick. **April 11** (James Moore); **14** Major Harrison, Claud Johnson & Son, Abraham James Hillhouse, James Simson; **15** James & John Crosbie; **16** James Hutchison, William McClure, James Simson; **19** (John Onge). **May 2** Sirs, Sirs, Mrs Roughsedge; **6** John Munn, John Marshall; **8** William Laing, James Hutchison; **19** John Allan; **23** Sir; **28** James Simson, Alexander Houston, Thomas Finlay & Robert Patrick; **19** John Munn. **June 2** James Simson, Pat Lindesay, Sir, James & John Crosbie, James Hutchison; **4** John Rowe, Richard Oswald & Co, Claud Johnson & Son; **5** Crosbies; **7** Colin Dunlop; **19** Thomas Finlay & Robert Patrick, **20** Peter Berail; **21** Claud Johnson & Son, Richard Oswald & Co, James & John Crosbie. **August 16** William Laing & Thomas Orr; **15** John Blundell, Peter Berail, John Rowe, Harris Crisp & Co; **18** George Ainslie, Janet Donald, Richard Oswald & Co, James & John Crosbie; **25** Claud Johnson & Son; **26** Walter Logan, John Rowe, John Murdoch; **28** John McKie, William McClure; **30** John Brown. **September 1** John Dickie, Joseph Scott & Co, Daniel Montgomerie, James Hutchison; **5** William Laing, John Marshall, Hugh Muir, Robert Gibson, John Munn, Pat

Douglas, James Simson; **6** James Young, John Wylie & Son; **22** Robert Arthur; **27** Robert Montgomerie. **October 3** Edward Kean, (John Onge), Thomas Finlay & Robert Patrick, Claud Johnson & Son; **6** James & John Crosbie; **4** Thomas Finlay & Robert Patrick; **6** Richard Oswald & Co, Harris Crisp & Co, John Blundell, Claud Johnson & Son; **8** Robert Arthur, James Simson, Pat Douglas; **9** Pat Ewing, James & George Piersy; **23** Sirs; **26** William White & Co, Thomas Finlay, (John Onge). **November 8** Abraham James Hillhouse, Peter Berail, John Woddrop, James Simson; **10** Claud Johnson & Son, Thomas Finlay & Robert Patrick, James Simson, John Crosbie. **December 1** Thomas Finlay & Robert Patrick; **24** George Ainslie, Joseph Scott & Co, Thomas Finlay & Robert Patrick, Peter Berail, Richard Oswald & Co, Claud Johnson & Son, James & John Crosbie, Isaac & Zachary Hope.

1756
January 5 Richard Oswald & Co; **3** John McKie; **7** John Wylie & Son, Pat Montgomerie, John Dickie, Robert Montgomerie; **8** William McClure, William Laing; William Laing & Thomas Orr; **17** Isaac & Zachary Hope, Richard Oswald & Co; **20** William Hyndman; **28** John Munn.

1757
May 31 George Ainslie, Richard Oswald & Co; **June 5** Haliday & Dunbar; **May 31** Robert Kennish. **June 1** Richard Oswald & Co, James Simson; **8** (John Onge), Thomas Grumley; **27** George Ainslie. **July 14** William Bowie; **13** James Simson; **14** Isaac & Zachary Hope, Francis Moore, Richard Oswald & Co, Haliday & Dunbar; **17** Hector Bryce; **18** James Hutchison; **25** Richard Oswald & Co. **August 8** George Ainslie (2), **16** Richard Oswald; **18** John Blair, James McFearran, John McKie, John Callin, David Muir, David Young, William McClure; **19** Hector Bryce, James Hutchison, William Laing, Hugh Morris, John Resaid, John Dickie; **20** Robert Gibson; **29** Richard Oswald & Co, George Ainslie, Isaac & Zachary Hope, Haliday & Dunbar, (John Onge). **September 1** James Simson; **12** Pat Montgomerie, William Laing, Haliday & Dunbar, Roger Hall; **16** James Simson; **14** John Munn; **17** William Prisk; **20** Haliday & Dunbar; **27** James Simson; **28** Colin Dunlop. **October 1** George Ainslie, Knox & Craghead; **3** Richard Oswald & Co, Lane & Booth, George Kippen & Son, John Rowe; **6** Roger Hall, John Onge, Richard Oswald & Co; **7** George Ainslie, Haliday & Dunbar; **18** Andrew McCulloch & David McClure, John Dickie, James Allison & Co, William Orr & David Rowan, John Dickie, James Young & William Dickie, James Young; Andrew McCulloch, James Simson; **26** Isaac & Zachary Hope, George Ainslie, Richard Oswald & Co, James Hutchison. **November 1** Thomas Taylor, John Russel for Peter Craig; **2** John Allan, **3** Livingston & Symson Richard Oswald & Co; **4** Robert Kennish; **16** Robert Colhoun; **18** Pat Douglas,

James Simson; **19** William Laing; **20** Robert Morris, John Resaid; **24** Hector Bryce; **28** Haliday & Dunbar; **30** Haliday & Dunbar, Richard Oswald & Co. **December 5** Richard Oswald & Co, Haliday & Dunbar; **10** George Ainslie, Richard Oswald & Co; **15** Hugh Paterson; **17** Ross, Black & Christian, James Limont, James McClure, James Logan, Hector Bryce, Thomas Gray, James Hutchison; **20** James Allison, James Simson; **26** George Murdoch; (No date Mr Marquise)
1758
January 2 George Murdoch, Livingston & Symson, George Ainslie, Richard Oswald & Co, James Simson; **5** Haliday & Dunbar, Knox & Craghead, George Ainslie, Mrs Christian, Robert Kennish, John Allan; **6** George Ainslie, Knox, Craghead & Co, James Simson; **11** William Laing, William Alexander; **16** Robert Kennish; **24** George Ainslie, Knox Craghead & Co, James Simson; **25** Richard Oswald & Co, Haliday & Dunbar; **27** Hugh Paterson, Robert Gibson; **31** James Paton & Co. **February 14** John McKie, **20** James Hutchison, James Limont, William Orr, James McClure, James Simson, William Samson; **21** Richard Oswald & Co; **22** Richard Oswald & Co, Haliday & Dunbar, William Skole; **23** Hugh Kerr, William Laing; **20** James Simson. **March 9** Charles Dalrymple; **10** Daniel MacIntyre, Daniel Campbell, William Langwill, Duncan Ballantine & Daniel Currie; **11** George Ainslie; **10** Knox Craghead & Co; **11** Haliday & Dunbar; John Munn; **14** Colin Dunlop; **17** Haliday & Dunbar; **18** (John Onge); **29** Hugh Connor; **31** William Quayle & Sons **29** Peter Berail, George Ainslie, Livingston & Symson, Cunningham & Gordon, James Simson, Richard Oswald & Co. **April 3** Abraham Demetrius; **4** Robert Kennish, Haliday & Dunbar; **7** James Simson, Mrs Kerr; **10** Ann Dowdall, John Gordon; **11** William Tiar; **13** John Thomson; **16** Cunningham & Gordon, Captain Robert Hogart; **22** Archibald Malcolm, John Kneen; **24** Archibald Malcolm, Roger Hall. **March 8** Roger Hall. **June 8** John Jolie; **18** Hugh Connor. **August 4** (James Burgh), Richard Oswald & Co; **12** George Ainslie, Peter Berail, Richard Oswald & Co; **21** Mathew Stewart, Thomas Craig, David Muir, William McClure, James Simson, William Allison, William Laing, John Dickie, Hugh Paterson, Robert Gibson, William McJennett & John Watt, Hector Bryce, James Hutchison; **25** James Simson, John Allan, John McKie; **29** David Forbes, John Allan, Kitto, Haliday & Dunbar, Frances Lascells, Roger Hall; **31** Pat Boyd, Robert Arthur. **September 1** Andrew Buchanan & Son, David Leggat, Haliday & Dunbar; **6** William Alexander, John Hamilton, John McAlister, Andrew McMaster; **8** Isaac & Zachary Hope, James Crisp & Jacob Emery, **5** Livingston & Symson; **8** George Ainslie, Richard Oswald & Co, Haliday & Dunbar; **21** Robert Paygan; **18** Colin Dunlop; **19** Peter Berail, George Ainslie; **15** Blundell & Walther, Richard Oswald & Co; **19** Haliday & Dunbar, Neil McKelvie, James

Simson, McClure & McCree; **27** Roger Hall, John Onge; **23** George Ainslie; **25** Richard Oswald & Co, Haliday & Dunbar; **27** Robert Gibson. **October 4** Richard Arthur, Thomas Orr, William Alexander; **6** John Allan, David Rowan, James Simson; **7** Colin Dunlop; **9** John Allan; **17** George Ainslie; **18** George Ainslie, Knox Craghead & Co, Henry Hardwar; **19** Richard Oswald & Co; **23** George Ainslie, Scott & McFarlane, Richard Oswald & Co, Haliday & Dunbar, James Oats; **25** Paul Bridson & Son. **November 1** Paul Bridson & Son, William Laing, Robert Morris, Thomas Savage; **2** Hector Bryce; **4** William Allison, William McClure, James Hutchison, William Laing & Thomas Orr, William Hyndman; **3** John Munn; **8** Pat Boyd; **13** John Maine; **14** Major Harrison, David Galloway, Robert Arthur, James Crisp, Peter Berail; **21** James Simson, Ebenezer Munro; **23** Knox Craghead & Co, George Ainslie (2), Robert Kennish; **24** John Maine; **26** Richard Oswald & Co; **29** Isaac & Zachary Hope, Cunningham & Gordon, Livingston & Symson. **December 2** William Smith, Robert McKirdye & Co. **November 30** Peter Berail, George Ainslie, Richard Oswald & Co, Robert Gibson, Thomas Savage, Roger Hall. **December 2** Ross Moore; **4** Richard Oswald & Co, George Ainslie, Ebenezer Munro; **8** Thomas Savage; **9** Thomas Savage, Richard Oswald & Co; **18** Philip Moore & Sons, Abraham Vianna, James McClure; **19** Daniel McIntyre & Co, James Dunlop, Colin Dunlop, Hector McLean, James Simson, James Hutchison; **20** Knox Craghead & Co, George Ainslie, Richard Harris & Co, Richard Oswald & Co; **26** Ebenezer Munro, James Simson, Hugh Clarkson, Thomas Stevenson & Sons, Robert Arthur, Alexander Oswald; **30** William McClure, James McFadzen, Hector Bryce (2), Thomas Gray, Andrew McCulloch, James Logan, James Young, James Hutchison.

1759
January 6 William Laing & Thomas Orr. **December 30** Robert Morris, John Munn, John Resaid, James Milne. **January 15** John Munn; **30** Robert Arthur; **23** Colin Dunlop & Alexander Houston, James Simson, Alexander Morson, William Laing; **30** David Mitchell; **31** John Munn. **February 1** Richard Oswald & Co, Knox Craghead & Co; **2** George Ainslie; **3** Richard Oswald & Co; **7** Robert Kennish, Haliday & Dunbar, John McAlister; **8** Robert Donald & Son; **14** John Allan, Peter Berail; **15** Robert Herries & Co, David & John Gregorie, Richard Oswald & Co; **17** Sir; James Simson, Alexander Morson; **21** Colin Dunlop, James Simson, Alexander Morson. **March 1** John Allan, Knox Craghead & Co, George Ainslie; **2** Haliday & Dunbar, James Gildart; **8** David Forbes; **10** Mr Strachan, Robert Gibson; **12** William Allison, James Simson, Haliday & Dunbar; **17** James Simson; **19** John Allan, Knox Craghead & Co, James Simson, Pat Montgomerie, Alexander Morson; **20** Isaac & Zachary Hope, Livingston & Symson, Richard Oswald & Co; **21** Robert

Arthur, Alexander Morson, James Simson; **25** James Simson; **26** John Allan, (John Onge), Philip Grumley, **28** Philip Moore & Sons; **30** John Munn, William Allison, David Limont. **April 2** Haliday & Dunbar, George Ainslie; **4** Knox Craghead & Co, Philip Moore & Sons, Roger Hall; **5** Richard Oswald & Co, Haliday & Dunbar; **9** Richard Oswald & Co, Haliday & Dunbar; **14** Robert Kennish; **16** Richard Hall, Knox Craghead and Co; **18** Alexander Morson, Colin Dunlop, Robert Herries & Co, Richard Oswald & Co, Hugh Clarkson, Thomas Stevenson & Sons, Haliday & Dunbar; **19** George Strachan, David Forbes; **20** Robert Kennish, Charles Kelly, George Strachan; **18** Pat Montgomerie; **23** Pat Montgomerie, Alexander Morson, James Simson Brown & Co; **16** Thomas Rumbold & Co; **30** Hamilton Gordon. **May 1** Hector Bryce, James Hutchison; **4** Mrs Haughton, Robert Kennish; **7** George Strachan; **8** John Munn, David Galloway; **14** John Allan, George Strachan, Alexander Morson, David Galloway; **16** George Strachan; **17** Thomas Savage, Roger Hall; **18** Roger Hall; **21** John Allan; **25** George Strachan; **26** Robert Herries & Co, Thomas Rumbold, Knox Craghead & Co, George Ainslie; **28** Richard Oswald & Co, Haliday & Dunbar; **29** David Forbes; **30** Alexander Morson, James Hutchison, Robert Gibson, Pat Montgomerie; **31** James Simson & Co, George Strachan, Charles Kelly. **June 4** John Quayle; **6** John Quayle, George Ainslie, Richard Oswald & Co; **25** George Ainslie, Knox Craghead & Co. **July 3** William Wattleworth; **6** Mrs Haughton; **7** Robert Kennish, Haliday & Dunbar; **12** Robert Gibson, Alexander Morson, James Simson; **16** Thomas Savage, Nicholas Harrison; **18** Lascelles & Maxwell, Ross, Black & Christian; **19** John Callin; **27** John McClure & McCree, Andrew McCulloch; **30** Nicholas Harrison. **August 1** William Allison; **3** Alexander Morson. **September 5** John Callin; **6** Charles Kelly; **5** Alexander Morson; **6** John Kelly; **8** Robert Gibson; **15** Hector Bryce; **20** Richard Walter, William Allison; **21** William McClure, James Hutchison; **22** John Murdoch, Hector McLean; **24** John Quayle, Alexander Morson, James Hutchison; **25** Lachlan Campbell, John Marshall. **October 3** John Resaid, Robert Morris, William Laing; **9** Alexander Morson; **16** Robert Patrick & Co; **4** John Onge; **16** Roger Hall; **19** William Allison, James Hutchison, Thomas McClure; **23** James Hutchison. **November 5** Nicholas Harrison. **December 3** Neil Beaton; **12** John Jolie; **19** Charles Fleetwood; **22** Robert Kennish.
1760
January 7 Sir John Stewart. **February 5** Robert Kennish. **March 12** Sir John Stewart, **16** Sir John Stewart, **2** George Ainslie, Knox Craghead & Co; **26** Richard Harrison; **May 3** Charles Kelly; **20** Robert Black. **July 3** Phil (son), **14** Thomas Arthur. **September 15** John Stevenson, John Tauberman; **19** William Allison; **22** Frank Moore.

APPENDIX II: THE FRIENDS

<u>Note</u>: This includes the people to whom George Moore addressed his letters

Andrew Agnew, Drogheda
Joseph Agnew, Glasgow
George Ainslie, Bordeaux
William Alexander, Greenock
William Alexander, Kilmarnock
John Allan, Ballantrae
John Allan, Douglas
James Allison, Correath
Robert Allison & William Allison,
   Cudain
William Allison, Correath
Armour & Stewart, London
John Arnall, Rotterdam
Robert Arthur, Crawfordsdyke
Thomas Arthur, Douglas
Duke of Atholl
Henry Atkin, Boston
Attorney, Dublin
Messrs Bagge, Wilson & Pike,
   Gothenburg (later Bagge,
   Wilson & Hall)
Bartian van Banken, Rotterdam
Neil Beaton, Fort William
Peter Berail, Cette
Mr Best, Ireland?
John Black, Bordeaux
Robert Black, Douglas
John Blair, Gagbory
John Blundell, Alicante
Blundell & Walther, Alicante
Patrick Bogle, Glasgow

Patrick Bogle & Alexander
   Stevenson, Glasgow
William Bowie, Ayr
Pat Boyd, Dublin
Alexander Brazier, Dublin
Paul Bridson, Douglas
Alexander Brown, Dublin
John Brown, Ayr
Hector Bryce, Dunure Main
Andrew Buchanan & Son, Glasgow
James Burgh, Nevington Green
John Callin, (Peel, Rush, Glasgow)
Captain Campbell of the cutter
James Campbell, Ayr
Lachlan Campbell, Inverary
George Carmichael & Co, Glasgow
Captain Chisholm, Port Glasgow
Mr Christian, London
Mrs Christian, Liverpool
Daniel Clark, Liverpool
Hugh Clarkson, Barbados
Robert Colhoun, St Christophers
Hugh Connor, Douglas
Walter Corrie, Glasgow
James Coulter & Buchanan & Co,
   Glasgow
John Cowan, Tarbert
Knox Craghead & Co, London
Thomas Craig, Girvan
Robert Crawford, Irvine
Harris Crisp & Co, Barcelona

James Crisp & Jacob Emery,
    Barcelona
Samuel Crisp, London
James Crosbie, Liverpool
James & John Crosbie, Liverpool
John Crosbie, Liverpool
William Cumming Jun, Edinburgh
Cunningham & Gordon, Lisbon
James Cunningham, Saltcoats
Samuel Cuthbert, Ayr
Charles Dalrymple, Grangefield
Joseph Dean, Whitehaven
Abraham Demetrius, London
John Dickie, Loans
John Dickie, James Allison & Co,
    Loans
Robert Dickie, John Resaid,
William Tweek, Camp Hunterston
Robert Dickie & John Resaid,
    Hunterston
Theobald Dillon, Rotterdam
James Donald, Ayr
Janet Donald, Ayr
Robert Donald & Son,
    Greenock
Pat Douglas, Ayr
Dowall, Miliken & Houston,
    Glasgow
Ann Dowdall, Belfast
Colin Dunlop, Glasgow
James Dunlop, Glasgow
James Ewing, Fairlie
John Ewing, Fairlie
Pat Ewing, Fairlie
Marcus Ezechiel, Rotterdam

David Ferguson, Ballantrae
William Ferguson, Ballantrae
Robert Finlay, Glasgow
Thomas Finlay, Dublin
Thomas Finlay & Robert Patrick,
    Dublin
Malcolm Fisher, Ayr
Peter Flanagan, Rostrevor
Charles Fleetwood, Dublin
David Forbes, Ramsey
David Galloway, Ayr
Wal Geoghan, Rochelle
Robert Gibson, Kilmarnock
Archibald Gilchrist, Glasgow
James Gildart, Liverpool
John Glassford & Co, Glasgow
Allan Glen, Irvine
Hamilton Gordon, Dublin
John Gordon, Belfast
Andrew Grant, Douglas
Thomas Gray, Auchnish
Green & Stanton (& Ford),
    Barcelona
David & John Gregory, Campvere
Thomas Grumley, Rush
Halliday & Dunbar, Liverpool
Richard Hall, Falmouth
Roger Hall, Newry
John Halliday & Brothers, Antigua
Revd Anthony Halsal, Great
    Crosbie, Liverpool
Hamilton & Kissack, Dublin
Mr Hamilton, Dublin
John Hamilton, Ayr
Henry Hardwar, Liverpool

Humphry Harriol, London
Major Harrison, Dunkeld
Nicholas Harrison, Co Down
Thomas Hartley, Whitehaven
John Harvey, Irvine
Mrs Haughton, Liverpool
Richard Herries & Co, Barcelona
Abraham James Hillhouse, London
John Hillhouse, Antigua
Captain Robert Hogarth, Lisbon
Gerrard van Hoogmerf, Rochelle
Isaac & Zachary Hope, Rotterdam
Alexander Houston, Glasgow
James Hutchison, Ayr
William Hyndman, Greenock
John Innes, Irvine
William Jamieson, Ayr
Claud Johnson & Son, London
John Johnston, Narrow Water
John Jolie, Douglas and Dublin
Edward Kean, Dublin
Charles Kelly, Douglas
John Kelly, Peel
Archibald Kennedy, Culzean
Robert Kennish, Liverpool
Andrew Kerr, Wigtown
Hugh Kerr, Old Kirk
Mrs Kerr, Newfield
Robert Kerr, Kilmarnock
William Kerr, Stranraer
George Kippen & Co, Glasgow
Kitto, Bath
John Kneen, Ramsey
William Laing, Inverkip

William Laing & Thomas Orr,
    Inverkip
Lane & Booth, London
Lascelles & Maxwell, London
James Dyges Latouche, Dublin
Hugh Lawson, Newton of Ayr
David Leggat, Glenluce
David Limont, Ayr
James Limont, Ayr
Hercules Lindsay, Glasgow
Pat Lindesay, Edinburgh
Livingston & Symson, Rotterdam
James Logan, Barnhill
Walter Logan, Doston
Isadore Lynch & Co London
John McAlister, Ard Patrick &
    Ronachan
James McBride, Glenluce
McClure & McCree, Ayr
James McClure, Knockraer
John McClure, Ayr
Thomas McClure, Ayr
Thomas McClure, Drumbeg
William McClure, Drumbeg
William McCormick, Ayr
Andrew McCulloch, Ayr
Andrew McCulloch, David Limont
    & David McClure & Co,
    Ayr
Andrew McCulloch & David
    McClure, Ayr
James McCulloch, (Kirkcudbright?)
John McCulloch, Kirkcudbright
James McFadzen, Beachhead of
    Ayr

James McFearran, Kirkmaiden
John McGregor, Dublin
David MacIntyre, Daniel Campbell,
William Langwill, Duncan
Ballantine & Daniel Currie,
Campbeltown
Daniel McIntyre & Co
William McJennett & John Watt,
Ballig
Aeneas Mackay & Co, Boston (later
Hugh Mackay & Co)
Neil McKelvie, Campbeltown
John McKie, Stranraer
Walter McKirdie, Glasgow
Hector McLean, Edinburgh
Andrew McMaster, Sandmiln
William McMunn, Greenock
William McNellie, Ballantrae
John Maine, Liverpool
Archibald Malcolm, Douglas
John Marshall, Inverary
Gab Mathie, Alexander McAuslane
& Thomas Barklay,
Greenock
James Milne, Correath, Largs
David Mitchell, Ayr
Mrs Montgomerie, Irvine
Daniel Montgomerie, Glasgow
Dr George Montgomerie, Glasgow
Pat(rick) Montgomerie, Irvine
Richard Montgomerie, Glasgow
Robert Montgomerie, Irvine
Dr Moor, Kilmarnock
Moore & Stritch, Vinaros
Francis Moore, Dublin

James Moore, Cavan
John Moore, Liverpool
Phil Moore, Glasgow, etc
Phil Moore & Sons, Douglas
Ross Moore, Carlingford
Thomas Moore, Douglas
Hugh Morris, Largs
Robert Morris, Largs
Alexander Morson, Glasgow
John Moure, Girvan
John Mowat, Campvere
David Muir, Girvan
Hugh Muir, Glenside
James Muir, Glasgow
John Munn, Kilfinan
Ebenezer Munro, Glasgow
George Murdoch, Glasgow
John Murdoch, Glasgow
Peter and John Murdoch, Glasgow
Betty Murray, York
John Murray, York & London
Robert Murray, Dublin
William Murray, Sen, Douglas
Daniel Musendine, Belfast
Daniel Mylrea, London
David Nathan, Rotterdam
Nickson, Moore & Stritch,
Valencia
James Oats, Douglas
John Onge, Hayestown
Samuel Onge, Dublin
James Orr, Campvere
Thomas Orr, Inverkip
Thomas Orr, John Alexander &
John Russell, Inverkip

William Orr, Ayr
William Orr & David Rowan, Ayr
Alexander Oswald, Glasgow
Richard & Alexander Oswald,
  Glasgow
Richard Oswald & Co, London
George Paterson, Kilmarnock
Hugh Paterson, Irvine
James Paton & Co, Largs
Robert Patrick & Co, Dublin
Robert Paygan, Ramsey
James & George Piersy, Cork
Joseph Popham, Cork
Alexander Porterfield, Glasgow
William Prisk, Liverpool
John Quayle, Castletown
William Quayle, Douglas
James Reid, Gibraltar
John Resaid, Hunterston
Ross, Black & Christian, Douglas
Jean Ross, Girvan
Robert Ross, Rostrevor
Mrs Roughsedge, Liverpool
David Rowan, Ayr
William Rowan, Dublin
John Rowe, Boston
Thomas Rumbold & Co, Liverpool
John Russell for Peter Craig, Old
  Kirk
Ralph Sampson, St Eustatius
William Samson, Ayr
Thomas Savage, Portaferry
Scott & McFarlane, Gothenburg
Joseph Scott & Co, Glasgow
Simson, Brown & Co, Glasgow

James Simson, Glasgow
William Skole, Ballwally
Smellie & Hopkirk, Glasgow
Richard Smith, London
Richard Smith & Co Barbados
William Smith, Robert McKirdie &
  Co, Largs
William Snell & Co London
John Stedman, Rotterdam
James Stevenson, Tarbert
John Stevenson, Dorsgate, London
Thomas Stevenson & Sons,
  Barbados
Janine Stewart, Girvan
Sir John Stewart, Edinburgh &
  Grandtully
Mathew Stewart, Girvan
George Strachan, Ramsay
Edmund Stritch, Vinaros
Andrew Stuckey & Co, Rotterdam
Surveyor of Customs. Donaghadee
John Tauberman, Castletown
Thomas Taylor, Crawfordsdyke
Mrs Then?, Liverpool
John Thomson, Douglas
William Tiar, Douglas
Tyndall & Co, Bristol
Simon Vashon, Douglas
John Vass, Ayr
Abraham Vianna, Douglas
Revd Richard Walter, Portsmouth
James Warden, Greenock
Mr Watson, Glasgow
James Watt, Greenock, Ballig and
  Kirkwill

William Wattleworth, Ramsay
Mrs Weekes, Dublin
Pat White, Benicalro
William White & Co, Dublin
George Wilson, Dublin
James Wilson, Greenock
John Woddrop, Edinburgh
John Wylie & Son, Kilmarnock
David Young, Girvan
James Young, Ayr
James Young, Malcolm Fisher &
    John Rodgers, Ayr
James Young, Ayr and William
    Dickie, Loans

BIBLIOGRAPHY

Primary Sources
<u>Manx Documents</u> (reproduced by Courtesy of Manx National Heritage)
The Letter-book of George Moore, 1750 to 1760, Bridge House Papers
MS 501 C (MIC 68)
Ingates 1750 to 1755
<u>Custom House Letter-books etc</u>
CE51 (Dumfries) 1/3; CE60 (Port Glasgow & Greenock) 1/1, 1/2, 1/3,
1/4, 1/5, 1/6; CE71 (Irvine) 1/1, 1/2; CE76 (Ayr) 1/1, 1/2, 1/3, 1/4, 1/5,
1/6, 1/7, 1/8, 1/9, 1/10, 2/2; CE82 (Campbeltown) 1/3
A Continuation of the Collection of Such Statues relating to His
Majesty's Customs, and duties upon Salt, as have passed since the last
Collection of the Statutes, printed in the year 1744, to this present year
1754, inclusive. Edinburgh 1754.
<u>Exchequer Court Records, Edinburgh</u>
E368/6 Roll No 1694 (Lawrence Rigg and the *Robert* wherry
<u>Municipal Archives Rotterdam</u>
ONA 2748/135; ONA 2752/727 (John Mowat)
<u>Gentleman's Magazine</u>
1755, 1757, 1758

Secondary Sources
Anon. *Banking in Glasgow During the Olden Times.* Glasgow. Past &
Present 1862
Burness, Lawrence R *A Scottish Genealogist's Glossary.* Scottish
Association of Family History Societies 1991. ISBN 0-947-659-84-6
Devine, T M. *The Tobacco Lords. A Study of the Tobacco Merchants of
Glasgow and their Trading Activities c1740-1790.* John Donald
Publishers Ltd. 1975
McCrackin, Eileen *18th Century Irish Nurserymen* Irish Forestry Spring
1967
McKerlie, P H *History of the Lands and Their Owners in Galloway.*
Paisley: Alexander Gardner 1906. Facsimile Reprint Heritage Books Inc
1992 ISBN 1-55613-580-7
Malins, Edward & the Knight of Glin *Lost Demesnes* Irish Landscape
Gardening 1660-1845
Pares, Richard *War and Trade in the West Indies 1739-1763.* Oxford
1936

Scottish Association of Family History Societies. *The Parishes, Registers and Registrars of Scotland*. ISBN 1-874722-05-6

Scottish History Society. *A List of Persons concerned in the Rebellion. Transmitted to the commissioners of Excise by the several supervisors in Scotland in obedience to a General Letter of the 7th May 1746 and a Supplementary List with Evidences to Prove the Same.* Edinburgh 1890

Scottish History Society. Ed. William Mackay. *The Letter-book of Bailie John Steuart of Inverness 1715-1752.* Edinburgh 1915

Vyse, Charles *A New Geographical Grammar, containing a Comprehensive System of Modern Geography, after a new and curious method.* London 1779

Wolters' Woordenboeken. *Nederlands-Engels.* Groningen 1986

Woods Hole Oceanographic Institution *Marine Fouling and its Prevention.* United States Naval Institute, Annapolis, Maryland 1952

Further Reading

Craine, David *A Manx Merchant of the Eighteenth Century.* Isle Man Natural History & Antiquarian Society Proceedings Vol IV No IV March 1740 to March 1742

Graham, Eric J *The Shipping Trade of Ayrshire 1689-1791.* Ayrshire Monographs No 8 Ayrshire Archaeological & Natural History Society Sept 1991

MacGregor, David Merchant *Sailing Ships 1775-1815. Sovereignty of Sail.* Conway Maritime Press Ltd 1985 ISBN 0-85177-323-0

Mathieson, Neil *Sir George Moore & His Sons, Being Some Account of the Moores of Ballamoore during the second half of the Eighteenth Century.* Isle of Man Natural History & Antiquarian Society Proceedings Vol V No II April 1946 to March 1950

Slack, Stuart *Harbour Bridges at Douglas 1757-1937.* Isle of Man Natural History & Antiquarian Society Proceedings

Wilkins, Frances *The Isle of Man in Smuggling History.* Wyre Forest Press 1992 ISBN 1-897725-00-0

Wilkins, Frances *Strathclyde's Smuggling Story.* Wyre Forest Press 1992 ISBN 1-897725-02-7

Wilkins, Frances *Dumfries & Galloway's Smuggling Story.* Wyre Forest Press 1993 ISBN 1-897725-03-5

Wilkins, Frances, *The Smuggling Story of Two Firths.* Wyre Forest Press 1994 ISBN 1-897725-06-X

INDEX OF NAMES

Moore, Phil (son) 152, 215, 216, 231-235

Moore, Philip (brother) 9, 36, 59, 64, 69, 72, 73, 77, 157, 245, 246

Moore, Sally 19, 231, 237-238

Moore, Thomas 36

Morris, Hugh 161, 213

Morris, Robert 157, 161, 163

Morson, Alexander 55, 96, 97, 171, 174, 196, 203, 204-206, 210

Moure, John, 154, 273

Mowat, John 43, 71, 73, 78

Muir, James 83, 84

Muirhead, James 81

Munn, Dugald 172, 181

Munn, Duncan 155

Munn, James 152

Munn, John 150-152, 154-158, 163, 165, 169-174, 182, 202, 203, 218, 221

Munro, Ebenezer 57, 58

Murchie, Daniel 191, 192, 194

Murdoch, George 93

Murdoch, John 93

Murdoch, Peter & John 21, 22, 60, 89, 90, 94, 127, 131-135, 169, 232

Murphy 191

Murray, 243, 275

Murray, Betty 261, 263

Murray, John 258, 259

Murray, Robert 254, 261-263

Murray, Thomas 243, 261-263

Musendine, Daniel 109, 112

Mylrea, Daniel 200, 231, 250, 251, 270, 271

Mylrea, Thomas 263, 264

Nasmith, Thomas 187

Nathan, David 72

Nibloe, Pat 197, 198

Neilson, Samuel 187

Nimmo, John 190

Oliphant & Co 125, 126

Onge, John 101, 102, 225, 231, 234-237, 239, 241, 244, 247, 249, 251, 253, 254, 267, 273

Orr, James 77, 79, 80, 158

Orr, John 151, 200

Orr, Thomas 55, 127, 214

Oswald, Alexander 212

Oswald, Richard & Alexander 106

Oswald & Co, Richard 6-8, 13, 18, 31-33, 41, 44, 55, 66-68, 81, 105, 122, 123, 125, 144, 145, 196, 205, 237, 239, 243, 260, 269, 271

Paterson, Bound 80

Paterson, Duncan Forbes 185, 213, 215

Paterson, George 85

Paterson, Hugh 123

Patrick & Co, Robert 99, 101

Peacock, William 191-194

Perdon, William 97

Picken, John 86, 215, 216

Piersy, James & George 14, 52-54, 104, 129, 136, 139, 141

Pollard, William 120

Pollock, Will 191

WYRE FOREST PRESS

Wyre Forest Press was established in 1992 to publish books on smuggling history and related contemporary documents. the *Isle of Man in Smuggling History* was followed by a series on Scotland's Smuggling Story. One further title in this series - covering the Borders - will be published in 1995. A description of this aspect of Scotland's maritime history will continue with a series of Smuggling Trail booklets, covering smaller areas. Aimed at the local historian, schools and tourists, these will include maps and planes of locations where major smuggling events took place. The first booklets in this series, covering Galloway and Cowal, are planned for 1995 onwards.